W9-CGX-496

Battles of the
Dark Ages

Battles of the Dark Ages

British Battlefields AD 410 to 1065

Peter Marren

Pen & Sword
MILITARY

Pen & Sword Military
an imprint of
Pen & Sword Books Ltd
47 Church Street
Barnsley
South Yorkshire
S70 2AS

Copyright © Peter Marren 2006

ISBN: 1-84415-270-7
ISBN: 978-1-84415-270-4

The right of Peter Marren to be identified as
Author of this Work has been asserted by
him in accordance with the Copyright, Designs
and Patents Act 1988.

All rights reserved. No part of this book may be reproduced or transmitted in any
form or by any means, electronic or mechanical including photocopying, recording
or by any information storage and retrieval system, without permission from the
Publisher in writing.

Typeset in 11/13pt Ehrhardt by Concept, Huddersfield

Pen & Sword Books Ltd incorporates the Imprints of Pen & Sword Aviation, Pen &
Sword Maritime, Pen & Sword Military, Wharncliffe Local History, Pen & Sword
Select, Pen and Sword Military Classics and Leo Cooper.

Printed in the United States of America

Contents

List of Maps

Preface

The Dark Ages were, in Neville Chamberlain's notorious words, 'a far away place about which we know little'. Yet they seem to have shadowed my life, partly in my imagination but also, unexpectedly, in everyday life. As a son of an officer in the RAF I had an itinerant boyhood moving from one place to the next every two years or so. And, it seemed, wherever I went there was a local battlefield, often one so remote in time and so poorly known that it was less an actual place and more of a kind of haunting, a historical shadow where folklore reigned over fact. This gave the Dark Ages a special appeal, a distant time when the land was wild and dangerous, where wolves and eagles hovered around the places of slaughter and when the very names of people and places sounded strange and foreign. At least to my ten-year-old mind it was a magical place unbothered by the boring bits of history like laws, charters and economics.

My oldest memory is living at Riccall in Yorkshire when I think I was dimly aware of some local conflict with the Vikings that had taken place near the village a thousand years earlier (I remember being pretty amazed that a place like Riccall could be that old). Later, I was at RAF Andover at the time when archaeologists were digging up nearby Danebury Ring, the hill-fort by which an Arthurian battle was supposed to have taken place, named after a village with the splendid name of Nether Wallop. Later, when I got a job with the Nature Conservancy, I was struck by how many nature reserves had battlefields on them (a fact about which I was reminded when I was wandering over the field of Ashdown and put up a very rare stone curlew). Where I now live, in Wiltshire, you cannot walk far on the open downs before coming across ancient dykes and rings clearly designed to keep someone out. Liddington Hill, which welcomes me home whenever I return from the north or west may or may not be the real Mount Badon, Wiltshire's equivalent of Camelot. But it is certainly *my* Mount Badon, so much so that I never call this swelling green whaleback of deep history by any other name.

I first became seriously interested in ancient battlefields after reading the works of that great battlefield detective Colonel Alfred Burne. The chapters he devoted to *Ellandun, Deorham, Brunanburh* and other pre-Conquest battles were of a different kind to the rest of his books. Rather than refight these dimly remembered, though important, conflicts, he devoted his energies to finding out where they were. And that remains the essential art of the Dark Age battling – not so much refighting the battles as refinding them. Of course one can have a try at reconstructing the battles themselves – and I hope this book will be of interest to war-gamers and re-enactors refighting them – but history offers only limited help. One gamer's *Ellandun* will not be another's (and in this particular case, if war games prove anything it is that the wrong side won!).

Finding Dark Age battlefields has involved the ingenuity of historians, antiquarians and archaeologists for at least four hundred years. They needed to be found because nearly all of them had been lost. Even the greatest of all pre-Conquest battles, the battle of *Brunanburh*, is no more than a name. There is nowhere on the map by this name, and none even in the Domesday Book. As a result we do not even know whether it was fought in the east or the west (the sources say one thing, geography and commonsense quite another). Persuasive and well-argued cases have been made for *Brunanburh*s as far apart as Rotherham, Huntingdon and the Wirral. What a pity they cannot all be right! Not that I am in any position to throw stones. I regarded myself as a great expert on the battle of Nechtansmere, now known as the battle of Dunnichen. That was until I read James Fraser's new book on this subject and realized, most reluctantly, that his site was better than mine. To some extent this ambiguity is true of nearly all battles fought between 410 and 1065. For each one you seem to have at least a pair of possible battlefields (and many others have no known battlefield at all!). And that is why, with the lonely exception of the battle of Maldon, no pre-Conquest battlefield has found its way onto the registers kept by English Heritage and its Celtic sister organizations. Uncertainty hovers over nearly every one of them. Whether *Brunanburh* was fought on land that is now a golf course, or a cokeworks and railway marshalling yard, or featureless arable fields somewhere near Huntingdon we can argue about. The exact disposition of the armies we shall probably never know.

The lack of the certainty that enables us to stand in Wellington's boots at Waterloo or Chard's at Rorke's Drift may mean that pre-Conquest battles are not everyone's cup of tea. Most books on British battlefields have neglected the Dark Ages. Yet these ancient conflicts have a strange romantic appeal. In a way, the fuzzier the past, the greater is the 'tingle-factor'. Standing even in the approximate footsteps of King Alfred or other Dark Age heroes (even their *possible* footsteps) is to dip into that bran-tub of thrilling history that can lie beneath the surface of the most ordinary-looking countryside. And although the actual battlefields are elusive, the wider military strategy of ancient conflicts is still visible in the mysterious earth walls and ditches that criss-cross the landscape on the downs and moors. Dark Age battle-finding takes you to nice, hidden places tucked away in the landscape. Since the heritage industry has ignored them you are free to use your imagination and have somewhere to park the car. And, as I have repeatedly discovered, Dark Age armies liked a good view or, if not a view, then a pleasant river.

Apart from describing the best-documented battlefields in England, Scotland and Wales, my aim has been to tell a story. By profession I am a writer and journalist, and battles are one of the things I write about. I am the author of two books on the subject, *Grampian Battlefields*, which is about the Scottish north-east and has been in print for fifteen years, and *1066: The Battles of York, Stamford Bridge and Hastings*, published by Pen & Sword in 2004. I have also written articles about Dark Age and medieval battlefields, mainly for *Battlefields Review*, and conducted field research for the Battlefields Trust on the threatened battlefield of Tewkesbury.

This book describes nearly thirty battles in detail, almost all of those where some reconstruction of events is possible. I have also listed all the battles of the period – some 130 of them – which are at least dignified by a name. Along the way I have tried to find space for all the principal contenders in the Dark Age epic: British (and, as they became, the Welsh), Saxon, Irish, the Picts and Scots and the various Scandinavian factions grouped together as the Vikings. All the famous names are here: Arthur, Hengest, Oswald, Alfred, Edmund Ironside and Canute, as well as names that deserve to be better known, like Athelstan, Ecgbert, Penda and Urien. In a long introduction I have also tried to provide a sense of what it was like to be in a Dark Age battle, and your chances of surviving one (quite good, I would say, so long as you won).

I take this opportunity to thank Rupert Harding and Jane Robson for helping to bring this book to fruition and for making the task as painless as possible. I also thank my old friends in the Battlefields Trust for their help, notably Michael Rayner, Christopher Scott and Tony Spicer. I have benefited from the work of several recent historians of whom I would like to single out James Fraser and Graeme Cruickshank (Dunnichen), Professor Stephen Harding and Michael Wood (*Brunanburh*), and Alfred Smyth (King Alfred and northern history generally). I also thank Michael Rayner and Stephen Harding for permission to use copyright photographs, and Professor Guy Halsall for permission to quote from his youthful pieces, written a quarter-century ago, in *Miniature Wargames*.

A note on Anglo-Saxon names
One of the problems of Dark Age history is the plethora of unfamiliar and similar-sounding names – those notoriously 'unmemorable' 'Egg kings' of *1066 And All That*! The Saxons normally possessed only one name (though some seem to have had nicknames). Other cultures added a surname meaning 'son of', as in Bruide macBile or Olaf Tryggvason. Unlike modern Christian names, Saxon names were bestowed with great care and had a particular meaning. The 'egg' (actually Ecg-) name meant 'edge' or 'blade', which, combined with a suitable noun, gave names like 'Ecgbert' or 'sharp blade' or Ecgfrith, meaning 'edge-peace' in the sense of security.

Commoner than the 'egg' name was 'Ethel' or, more correctly, Aethel-, which means 'noble'. Hence, combined with a suitable word, we have Aethelwulf, noble wolf, Aethelgiva, noble gift, or Aethedreda, noble strength (the Saxon precursor of the Normanized 'Audrey'). Other famous Saxons names include Alfred (elf-council), Edgar (fortune-spear), Edmund (fortune-protecter) and Edward (fortune-guardian). The names were disposed individually, and were not passed from generation to generation. For example, the great king Ecgbert called his son Aethelwulf, who called his Aelfred (Alfred). However some names were more popular than others; for example, there are several Athelstans (precious stone) and Aethelreds (wise council) among Alfred's descendants.

Although the names were apparently bestowed when the child was baptized, they were definitely names to live up to. Most of the Dark Age men and women we know by name were members of the ruling class. There would be little point in calling a peasant 'noble wolf '; this was obviously a more suitable name for a warrior-prince. Someone with a name like 'Bright Blade' would be exposed to mockery if he turned out as a coward. That unlucky king Aethelred or 'Good Advice' did indeed become the object of satire, and was remembered as *Athelred Unraed*, that is 'Good Advice, Bad Advice'.

Most Saxon names are pronounced as spelt. The vowels are rolled together so that 'Aethel' sounds like ethel and Eadward as Edward. Ecg- names were pronounced as 'etch', or maybe 'edge', whilst names beginning with Ce- are pronounced as ch-, for example, Ceolwulf (ship-wolf) is Cheolwulf. The -ig in names like Tostig is silent; hence the Saxon word 'blodig' meaning 'bloody' is also pronounced that way. Names ending in -sc are pronounced -sh, so *Aescesdune*, the old name for the Berkshire downs, is Ash-dun, that is, ashdown. The Old English name Deorham is pronounced the same way as the modern village of Dyrham: that is, Dyur-ham, or, if you like, 'Durham' with a West Country burr. In this book I have used the familiar names of well-known historical characters: Arthur not Artorius, Alfred not Aelfred, Edmund not Eadmund and Canute instead of the more historically correct Knut. I have also avoided unfamiliar Saxon letters and diphthongs – which, in any case, my twenty-first-century PC seems unable to reproduce.

To Richard Seamons, Thanks Dick

Chapter 1
Introduction

The Dark Ages

When exactly were the Dark Ages? The term was apparently invented by the fourteenth-century philosopher Petrarch. Christian writers used darkness in a religious sense to describe evil and superstition, contrasted with 'the way, the truth and the light' of Christendom. But Petrarch was the first to give 'the Dark Ages' a secular meaning. His light was the cultural achievement of classical Greece and Rome, compared with the darkness that followed the Fall of Rome. Gradually the meaning of a Dark Age changed and in the British Isles began to be used to denote the period between the Roman Empire and the Norman Conquest. This was not totally 'dark' in Petrarch's sense. Indeed, the cultural achievements of the Anglo-Saxons were much respected, and pre-Conquest England came to be seen as a golden age before the oppressive feudal laws of the Norman kings. It was dark in the sense that historical records were sparse, and so much less was known about this period than the one before or the one that followed it. In more recent times, the 'Dark Ages' has sometimes been restricted to the period that is truly dark, between the Fall of Rome and the Coming of Christianity – that is, for about 200 years in which there was next to no history.

Modern historians prefer to avoid loaded categorizations like this age or that. In archaeological terms, the early centuries of Saxon England are in fact better known than the later. And some places were darker than others. Seventh-century Northern England basks in comparatively bright historical sunshine, whilst Scotland and Wales were still pretty dark as late as the eleventh century. For one important kingdom, East Anglia, there is virtually no history at all (though its best-known king's favourite helmet, purse and harp were all found at Sutton Hoo). The advantage of using a term like the Dark Ages is that it avoids offending national sentiments. The English Anglo-Saxons, settlers from northern Germany, shared their island home with people originating from modern Scotland, Ireland, France, Denmark and Norway, as well with the native 'British'. Whether well-named or not, 'Dark Ages' is a convenient term and everyone knows what it means. Besides, as someone familiar

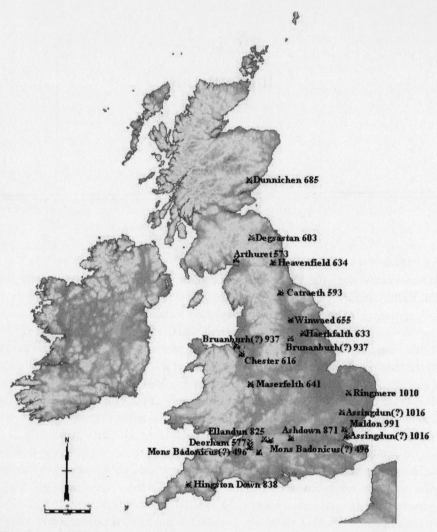

The main battlefields described in this book

with contemporary narrative documents describing the Norman Conquest and the Civil War in Scotland, I certainly came to regard it as, if not wholly dark, certainly dimly and fitfully lit. The great time-void before 1066 is a place of mist and shadow. Sometimes you see figures moving around, but you rarely see them well, and seldom know exactly what they are doing.

How Many Dark Age Battles Were There?
The Anglo-Saxon Chronicle and its Welsh and Irish equivalents are crammed with entries describing battles fought, kings, lords and warriors slain, towns besieged, and whole regions plundered and burned. But at what point did armed encounters become a battle? As it happens there is a helpful contemporary guide in the laws of King Ine

(Eye-na), who reigned from AD 688 to 725. An attack involving up to seven violent men was regarded as mere 'thievery'. Between seven and thirty-five men constituted 'a band', but any number in excess of that was classed as a *here*, which we can loosely translate as an army. Hence a conflict between two contending *heres*, composed of no more than thirty-five men – the equivalent of less than three rugby teams – on either side could by this definition be reasonably classed a battle. So, by this definition, would fights between Mods and Rockers, or rival bands of soccer supporters.

If so, there must have been a lot of Dark Age battles! It is likely that clashes of *heres* were going on all the time in some part of Britain and Ireland. In the centuries after the Roman legions departed, warfare may have been more or less permanent (though this has been disputed). The annalists probably recorded only those pitched 'battles' which were in some way significant. This is particularly true of the fifth and sixth centuries when, at least in Saxon England, a literate culture hardly existed. The records of battles of the fifth and sixth centuries were probably extracted from oral sources, such as elegies and war-songs. Their dates were retrospective, and very approximate. Indeed, they could easily be fiction.

Many of the battles recorded in pre-Conquest chronicles were small in scale. A good example is the conflict at *Merantun* in 784, which is described in unusual detail in the Anglo-Saxon Chronicle. Cynewulf, the king of Wessex, happened to be in bed with his mistress at this place (the Chronicle calls it a 'bower') when it was raided by a rival band under the leadership of one Cyneheard. Cynewulf, emerging bleary-eyed and angry with sword in hand, was set upon and killed. His small retinue chose to die fighting. This was the Battle of *Merantun*, remembered principally because it involved the killing of a famous king. Later on we are told that Cyneheard's band consisted of just eighty-four men, though, under the definition of the laws of Ine, this constituted an army. Moreover Cyneheard's eighty-four men were enough to constitute a coup – an unsuccessful one since Cyneheard and all his men were soon slain in their turn by the dead king's outraged household.

Some other famous battles recorded by the chroniclers were seemingly little more than scuffles in a field. Hengist, the mighty conqueror of Kent, was said to have invaded our shores with just three small ships. Another invader, Port, was even more short-handed: his entire army was contained in just one ship. These figures may be semi-legendary, but one of the pitched battles around the first millennium was *Aethelingadene* (probably Alton in Hampshire) where the men of Hampshire under the king's high-reeve intercepted a party of Danish raiders. After a short but fierce fight, 81 Englishmen and perhaps as many Danes lay dead, suggesting that these armies numbered in the low hundreds. Yet this was a significant event. Among the dead of *Aethelingadene* was the high-reeve himself, along with a 'bishop's officer', a bishop's son, a second royal reeve and two local thanes. In moments the battle had swept away several of Hampshire's chief fighting men.

Another small but significant fight took place on the south coast, possibly at Poole Harbour, in 897 during the reign of King Alfred. It was counted as an English victory, since they lost 62 men compared with 120 Danes. But the English losses included Lucumon, the king's reeve (king's reeves clearly led a dangerous life), along with three named leaders of their Frisian allies, and one Aethelfrith, an important official in the king's household. Again, these were high-ranking men who were hard to replace.

When, in its more detailed passages, the Anglo-Saxon Chronicle gives apparently exact figures for the combatants or casualties in various battles, they are more often than not fairly modest. In 1051, Harold, the future king, fought at Porlock and slew 'more than thirty good thanes as well as other men'. This would constitute a battle under the laws of Ine, but the Chronicle avoids calling it one, and says only that Harold put the local men to flight. Possibly the chronicler did not wish to offend the mighty sons of Godwin. A step up from this small encounter was an unnamed but clearly important battle fought in Devon in 878. The English managed to slay the Viking Ubba, a half-brother of the infamous Ivar the Boneless, along with 'eight hundred men with him and forty men of his retinue, and captured the Raven banner'. The detail about the banner is significant because no self-respecting Viking would have allowed Woden's sacred banner to be captured while there was breath left in his body. The implication is that Ubba's army was annihilated and that 840 men was more or less its sum total. Assuming that the excavated Gokstad longboat was an average ship of its time, Ubba's force would have been transported in about thirty ships, a figure comparable with the Battle of Carhampton in 836 (twenty-five ships), or Southampton in 840 (thirty-three ships).

The English, Scots and Welsh war-bands of earlier centuries may well have numbered in the hundreds rather than thousands. One early source states that in about 670 King Ecgfrith attacked the lands of the Picts with an elite mounted army (*equitatus exercitus*)[1] – yet with it he achieved all his objectives and, claims the same source, reduced the Picts to slavery. In another battle a century earlier, the Britons attacked the Roman town of Catterick with only 300 men, all of them aristocratic warriors of great renown. Evidently the preference for long-distance forays at least was for quality above quantity. Catterick was remembered not for its scale but for its heroic nature, as an example for future generations to study and follow. The same may be true of Maldon in 991, a relatively small battle, but one that was marked by self-sacrificing heroism and remembered with pride, even though, by modern standards, the English commander would have been sacked for gross incompetence.

What, then, are we to make of the apparently precise figure of 2,065 Welshmen killed at the Battle of *Beandun* in 614, or the 5,000 dead Hampshire men at *Nathanleag* in 508, or the 'thousands' of Vikings cut down after the Battle of Ashdown?[2] Perhaps only that the slaughter was great and the dead uncounted. There is good reason for supposing that the size of Alfred's victory at Ashdown, for instance, was later exaggerated for the purposes of glorifying the hero king. However, some Dark Age battles almost certainly did involve large levied armies, even coalitions. *Degsastan*, in 603 was probably one of them, fought between the highly militarized Angles of Bernicia and Deira and an alliance of northern kingdoms capable in theory of producing thousands of warriors. *Winwaed* was another battle on the grand scale, pitting Oswy, the powerful Northumbrian king, against an alliance of Welsh and Saxons from Mercia and East Anglia. *Winwaed* drew on forces from perhaps three-quarters of Britain south of the Forth. Greater still was the Battle of *Brunanburh*, which involved troops from the greater part of England, Scotland, Wales and even Ireland. *Brunanburh*, the ninth-century 'battle of nations', was a conflict of exceptional and perhaps unheard-of size, almost certainly dwarfing the Battle of Hastings. *Assingdun* and Stamford Bridge, too, may have been huge battles with troops raised from all over England. But these were the exceptions. Most Dark Age battles probably numbered hundreds rather than thousands of fighting men, and graded imperceptibly into raids, ravaging and other local mayhem.

Major kingdoms of Britain during the Dark Ages

There may be an element of chance about which battles have come down to us and which are unknown. A certain Ceolwulf, who ruled Wessex at the turn of the seventh century, was said to have 'ever made war either against the Angles, or against the Welsh, or against the Picts, or against the Scots' – high praise as contemporaries saw it – but not a single named battle in all this prodigious amount of fighting was remembered. By contrast, the *Annals of Ulster* record scores of named small battles in Ireland and Scotland. For example, a decade taken at random from between the years 490 and 500 includes the following battles:

490 or 491. Battle of *Cenn Losnada* in *Mag Fea* in which fell Aengus son of Nad-fraich, king of *Munu*: Mac Erca was victor, and the king of Caisel defeated.
493. The second Battle of *Granaivet* and the Battle of *Sruth*.
494. The Battle of *Tailtill* won over the Laigin by Cairpre, son of Niall.
495. The second Battle of *Granaivet*, in which fell Fraech, son of Finnchad: Eochu, son of Coirpre was victor.
496. The storming of *Dun Lethglaise*.
498. The Battle of *Inne Mor* in the territory of *Ui Gabla* won over the Laigin: Muirchertach MacErca was victor.
499. The Battle of *Slemain* of *Mide* won by Cairpre, son of Niall over the Laigin.
500. 'A battle'.[3]

A list of what were presumably mostly small-scale actions extracted from the Celtic annals would be a long one. For the single year 656, the year of the Battle of *Winwead* in England, the Irish annals record 'the battle of Anna', the 'battles of Cumascach, son of Ailill in which he fell', and 'the slaying of Rogallach, son of Uatu, king of Connacht'. At least five British and Irish kings were killed in battle that year. And even this was not a record; in 642 six kings died, including the blessed King Oswald, the most powerful king who had lived up to then. These were violent times!

And so to the original, impossible question: how many Dark Age battles were there? My own count from the Anglo-Saxon Chronicle is 110 field battles from 420 to 1065, not counting minor engagements or sieges. From the sparser Welsh annals, which overlap only slightly, I counted another forty specific battles among a lot more ravaging and slaying.[4] These figures suggest that one year in every four experienced a battle somewhere in England or Wales. If we added Scotland and Ireland to the list, the number of battles would be considerably more, perhaps with a battle every two years.

Dark Age Weapons and Armour
Dark Age weaponry is the subject of several books currently in print.[5] The subject has benefited from the popularity of re-enactments, which suggest how the age might have drilled and deployed its armies even when the contemporary record is silent. Facsimile weapons have shed light not only on how Dark Age weapons were used but also on how they were made. Round shields, for example, are four times more

effective at resisting missiles when bent into a concave shape. Plain wooden shields, on the other hand, are useless, splintering on the first impact. It is reasonable to suppose that no one used wooden shields without some more effective form of strengthening.

The fighting men of late Saxon times were better equipped than is sometimes implied. A law of Aethelred the Unready states that a ceorl was not the equal to a thegn, *even when* he possessed a helmet, mail shirt and a sword, unless he was also the owner of a minimum of five hides of land. In other words, even humble ceorls ruling over no more than a peasant's patch sometimes had resource to the most expensive items of military hardwear.

As for the thegn, the Saxon landowning class roughly equivalent to an eighteenth-century squire, another law specified a kind of death duty (*heriot*) on his land. In its original form this consisted of a gift to the king consisting of four horses, two of them with saddles, four shields, four spears, a helmet and a coat of mail. This seems to have been equivalent to a thegn's personal retinue of a second mounted man and a couple of foot soldiers. By implication, a thegn went to battle on a horse, attended by a small retinue. His 'death duty' to the king must have helped the latter to build up a sizeable armoury and ensure that his followers were well armed.

Shields

The shield was the universal weapon of Dark Age armies. You would not have lasted very long in a Dark Age battle without one, and probably every warrior bore one. Indeed, as even the best shields shattered after prolonged combat, they probably went into battle with a spare. According to Tacitus, writing in the first century AD, to lose your shield was considered a great disgrace. Before the kite shield came into vogue in the age of armoured knights near the end of our period, most shields were round and measured between two and three feet in diameter. They were made of wooden boards glued together with an unlikely-sounding but apparently effective rubbery mixture of cheese, vinegar and quicklime. Traditionally shields were made of limewood, but in practice any light, springy wood, such as pine, was used, on which rawhide was then stretched.

Combat shields probably bulged outwards in a lens-like shape. Experiments show that this makes them much stronger and more resistant to blows. In addition some shields were reinforced with leather or iron, fixed around the rim with short nails. Most also bore a conical metal boss attached to the middle with rivets. This protected the hand and enabled the shield to be used to parry a blow or even as an offensive weapon to smash into your opponent using the weight of your body. An opponent whose weapon had become stuck in your shield could be disarmed by a sudden twist and then forced to the ground by the weight of the shield and its projecting boss. Shields were slung around the neck by a strap and held in front of the body using a grip. The strap might have been adjustable, allowing a warrior to fight with a two-handed weapon while covering his body.

Probably most shields were brightly painted and, with the banners, formed part of the colour and spectacle of a Dark Age battlefield. Viking art often shows a cartwheel pattern of colours radiating from the centre of a shield. Those found with the Gokstad ship-burial were painted yellow and black alternatively. The shields of the Christian king Olaf's army were painted with crosses in various colours on a white background. Very likely, such colours helped identify units, or in this case a whole army, in battle. Fragments associated with shields show that some were also studded with metal objects in the shape of birds, beasts or fish. Were these good luck charms, or did they have some function of group identity?

Spears

The spear was the universal Dark Age weapon. Since slaves were forbidden arms, bearing a spear was the mark of a free man. Nearly everyone, from kings to commoners, carried a spear in battle, 'grasped in fist, lifted in hand'. In line facing the enemy you bore your shield in one hand, usually the left, and your spear with the other. The spearman had two basic choices. You could hold the weapon overarm, using it to jab at your opponent's face, and also retaining the option to hurl it. Or you could hold it underarm and, supported by the forearm, give it greater thrust-power and a longer reach. Some warriors grasped their spear with both hands for still greater force, leaving the shield to hang from its strap. Some Dark Age spears had cutting blades which must have required two hands to wield in the manner of a pole-axe.

Dark Age spears measured anything between five and nine feet long (the much longer pikes belong to a later age). The smaller, lighter ones were used for hurling as missiles. The Bayeux Tapestry shows a scene which might have been typical of an earlier age in which stacks of spears are kept in readiness for hurling. Although it isn't always possible to distinguish throwing spears from close combat weapons, the former was sometimes custom-made with a thin iron neck which bent on impact to prevent it being thrown back. Throwing spears were also often barbed for the same reason, and also, of course, to increase the injury caused. A barrage of light spears hurled from perhaps twenty to forty paces (but, in expert hands, for up to twenty paces more) would have been unpleasant to endure.

Longer spears were retained for defence. The shafts were normally made of ashwood, which grows straight and withstands hard knocks without shattering. The butt end was sometimes protected with a sleeve of iron, capable of being used as a club. There were several types of blades. The commonest were angular, with a diamond cross-section, or leaf-shaped. The former had the best chance of penetrating mail. Some spears had sharp wings which could hamstring the enemy with a sideways blow, or be used to hook down shields by the rim.

Swords

Spears were the weapon of a freeman, but a sword was the mark of high status. A pattern-welded Dark Age sword was worth at least as much as a Ferrari; in modern terms, perhaps a quarter of a million pounds. Swords had names; *Hrinting* (perhaps meaning 'roarer') was the fictional Beowulf's sword, *Quernbiter* the sword of the real

Olaf Tryggvasson, leader of the Danes at Maldon. They were heirlooms. Athelstan, son of Aethelred the Unready, considered his silver-hilted sword a kingly gift. Swords were craft-made weapons, produced by the slow art of pattern-welding in which strips of metal were repeatedly heated and hammered together. Without such work, the blades would soon break in combat. Towards the end of the period, the improving quality of iron ore meant that swords could be made more cheaply, and hence more people could afford to own one. But as late as the tenth century, nearly half of the swords found by archaeologists were produced by the old pattern-welded method. Possibly swords were more often seen in the south than the north. Some 22 per cent of Dark Age graves in Kent contained swords, compared with only 3 per cent of Anglian graves in northern England.

Dark Age swords were about a yard long, including the metal 'tang', with a double-edged blade about two inches wide. Consequently, though they were well-balanced, they were quite heavy. Dark Age warriors did not have 'sword fights'. A Viking saga reminded its listeners that the expert swordsman did not 'strike fast and furiously' but took his time to pick his strokes carefully, so that they 'were few but terrible'. The sword was a bludgeon used to hack at the parts of a warrior not covered by his shield, notably his head or forward leg. An overarm blow crashing down on an opponent's head would have been fatal. Other blows could disable your opponent and expose him to the kind of wounds sometimes found on Dark Age skeletons – repeated cuts on the bones of the head, arms and legs. Viking sagas are full of images of arms and legs being severed with a single blow – which, surprisingly, the victim often survived. Swords also had a heavy pommel, shaped like a tea-cosy, which not only acted as a counterweight to the blade but at close quarters could be used to deliver a disabling blow to the head or chin. Versatility was an asset to any weapon in sweaty, close-order fighting.

Swords were carried in wooden, leather-covered scabbards lined with oily fur or wool to keep the blade free of rust. The scabbard was often richly decorated and was another mark of high status. It was suspended either from the belt with the help of a couple of supporting straps, or from a shoulder harness or baldric.

Ninth-century sword found in Abingdon, now in the Ashmolean Museum, Oxford. The silverwork on the hilt-guards incorporates the symbols of the four Gospel writers: a fit weapon for a Christian warrior fighting a heathen foe.

Armour

Mail is perishable and rarely survives, even in burials. It was also expensive, and, like the sword, was the mark of the wealthy professional warrior. The scraps of mail surviving in the Sutton Hoo burial suggest that seventh-century mail consisted of a short-sleeved shirt that reached down to the hips. By the eleventh century, the mail shirt had become a coat covering the body down to the knees, or, in Harald Hardrada's case, the calves. Mail was made up of thousands of metal rings about a third of an inch in diameter and 'woven' in alternate rows of riveted and welded rings. A hip-length mail shirt or byrnie weighed about 25 pounds (11 kg) – no mean weight, especially considering that most of it had to be borne on the shoulders. It was fine so long as the fighting was static but mail was awkward to wear on the march, especially when going uphill. One reason why the Vikings lost the Battle of Stamford Bridge was that on a hot day they had decided to leave their armour behind with the ships. Similarly King Magnus of Norway threw away his ring-shirt during a battle in 1043. It could be more trouble than it was worth.

Mail gave the wearer a good degree of protection against cutting and glancing blows. It was less effective against arrows and spear thrusts. Some warriors probably wore a leather shirt under their mail. Kings and other wealthy men wore elaborate belt buckles and shoulder clasps. Nineteenth-century engravings of Saxon warriors often show them wearing fish-scale armour. This might have been cheaper and easier to make than mail, but not a single example has been found in this country. The most convincing example is on a stone carving of a Frankish warrior. Much cheaper than mail was leather. Padded leather 'jacks' were a surprisingly effective form of

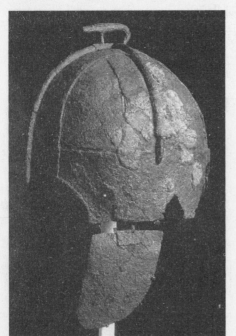

body protection, whose quilted lining absorbed glancing blows. Deer hide worn by Vikings was said to be quite as strong as mail, and infinitely lighter and more flexible.

The better class of Dark Age warrior also wore protective head gear. At the top end, this consisted of an elaborate helmet. Early helmets were made of metal bands riveted together with nasal guards, neck-guard and hinged cheek-pieces similar to the helmets of the late

Seventh-century Saxon helmet unearthed from a burial during aggregate quarrying at Wollastone, Northants, in 1997. The boar emblem on the crown indicates that its wearer was a high-status warrior, possibly a king. The remains of a sword and a bronze bowl were found nearby.

Roman Empire. The Sutton Hoo helmet also has a face-mask, complete with metal eyebrows and a moustache. Some helmets bore crests. The seventh-century Benty Grange helmet gives an idea of what the great kings of Northumbria might have worn in battle, which in this case probably bore a plume of horsehair – somewhat like the knights of Rohan in the film of *The Lord of the Rings*. By the eleventh century, helmet design seems to have become simplified and more standardized. Canute and Harold Godwinson wore the familiar conical helmet with its nasal guard, apparently without any decoration or symbols of rank.

Other weapons
Spear and shield were the main weapons of Dark Age warfare. Other weapons were perhaps a matter of personal choice. Most people carried a knife for domestic use, and it would have made a familiar and useful weapon for close-quarter fighting. A longer single-edged combat knife could be almost as long as a sword when it was known as a *seax*. A rare piece of statuary from eighth-century Mercia shows a mailed horseman carrying a *seax* suspended horizontally from his belt. A *seax* attached to a pole would become a primitive pole-axe.

Combat axes became important in the eleventh century, and the long-shafted Danish axe was the housecarl's weapon of choice. Axe action is vividly shown on the Bayeux Tapestry, and was particularly suited to defence against a mounted charge. For most of our period axes may have been used for throwing rather than swinging. Light axes were thrown in such a way that the blade struck the target with great force. Even when they missed their target, men would naturally duck if an axe came whizzing their way. Hence throwing-axes were used to disrupt the enemy line in the last vital seconds before the lines collided.

Every hunting man of the Dark Ages was familiar with the bow. The bow of choice was the longbow, up to six feet long and made of a single piece of yew, ash or elm. Yet bows and arrows are surprisingly rare finds in this period. The Bayeux Tapestry shows only a single, forlorn English archer. On the other hand, 'bows were busy' at the Battle of Maldon.[6] The bodkin arrow seems to have evolved specifically as a war-arrow designed for piercing mail. Archers were certainly used for a long-distance missile shower before throwing-spears, axes and possibly slings came into play. However they do not seem to have been deployed in a mass, as the Norman archers were at Hastings. Perhaps the bow was seen as a rather low-status form of soldiery, compared with spears, swords and axes, and so there were never enough of them.

Battle Tactics
Battle was a high-risk strategy. It brought matters to a decision and could save the country from the horrors of rampaging armies. On the other hand, if one lost a battle one risked losing everything, including, of course, one's life. No quarter was given to high-status prisoners in the Dark Ages. Even kings were summarily knocked on the head. A sensible commander therefore did everything possible to avoid battle unless he was confident of winning. Battles tended to happen when two forces were

more or less equally matched, or thought they were, or when the commander had run out of other options. The Dark Ages have plenty of examples of desperate measures taken to avoid battle with a superior force. King Oswy of Northumbria offered to buy off his enemy King Penda in 655. A few years before, his rival King Oswin of Deira had disbanded his army and sent them home rather than face Oswy in battle.

Once battle had become inevitable, Dark Age commanders would choose their ground carefully. When Penda refused to be bought off in 655, Oswy reduced the odds by deploying in a strong position on high ground, forcing Penda's forces to advance through a flooded river valley. A striking number of Dark Age battles were fought by fords in rivers. Perhaps the river not only secured at least one flank but enabled the army to be supplied by boats. At *Brunanburh* one flank of Athelstan's army was secured by a stream and the other by a wood. Finding a short line with secure flanks enabled a smaller army to negate the enemy's superior numbers and create several lines of defence. Another consideration was to have somewhere to retreat if things went badly. For example, at Dyrham in 577 the British commanders probably fought in front of their hillfort, retreating behind its stout walls as they were pressed back. Not that, in this case, it did them much good.

Dark Age battle tactics are difficult to reconstruct for want of evidence. The only detailed account of a real battle is Maldon, where tactical considerations went no further than standing firm. The commander 'bade his men make a war-hedge (*wihagen*) with their shields and hold it fast against the foe'.[7] Like a hedge, the line would be long, straight and thin, and bristling with thorns – a thicket of spears. The more usual name for Maldon's war-hedge was the shield-wall (*bordweall*). The line would stand to receive a charge behind overlapping shields with spearpoints projecting. The advancing enemy would see a line of wood and metal, eyes glinting between helmet and shield, and the only flesh on display being the lower legs. Breaking through this human wall would be akin to breaching the walls of a fort, and one source did indeed compare the Battle of Hastings with a siege.

Since everyone, whether Saxon, Briton or Viking, adopted shield-wall tactics in battle, the challenge was how to break through. If the commander had chosen his ground well, it would be impossible to outflank him. Sometimes, perhaps, the opposing shield-walls simply advanced towards one another and fought it out. However there is evidence that Roman tactics were familiar to Dark Age commanders through tracts such as that of Vegetius, written down in the early fifth century.[8] As a means of breaking through, Vegetius recommended the wedge, a tactic particularly favoured by the Vikings who compared it with a charging boar and called it *svinfylking* or 'swine-array'. Well-trained troops would mass in front of the shield-wall in wedge formation some ten lines deep. The wedge would then charge forward, keeping formation in order to penetrate the line with great force at a narrow point. Once the wall was broken more men would flood in and the enemy would be outflanked or even attacked from behind.

The correct way to prevent this, according to Vegetius, was to 'swallow the charge' by receiving it in a curved formation known as the forceps. It was easier to do this in a dense formation, but of course required training and a cool commander. Both the wedge and its countermeasures depended on firmness under fire and on fighting together as a well-drilled unit. How well drilled, in fact, were Dark Age armies? No drill manuals have come down to us. On the other hand, re-enactment experience suggests that formations can be taught basic proficiency in spear-and-shield warfare very quickly. Mastery of the basic moves – open order, forming ranks, advancing from column to line and turning about (in which the shield is passed over your head) – can be learnt in a day. In terms of basic drill, levied men could be turned into soldiers in a short time. To create a soldier who would stand firm in battle was another matter. There are many instances of a Dark Age army disintegrating under pressure. Morale depended on strong leadership and a sense of comradeship. Other require-ments were personal fitness, which was probably high among the yeoman class, and courage. Re-enactments have confirmed another contemporary aspect of fighting – that, as the shield-walls lock together, it helps to shout! As anyone who attends football matches or has marched in large, noisy demonstrations will know, you lose your individuality in a pack, especially when you yell with the rest.

How did Dark Age armies find one another? Although hard evidence is scarce, it seems that armies of the period were highly mobile. King Harold famously marched from London to York in twelve days at some seventeen miles per day. This implies two things: that at least the flying columns of the force were mounted and that the roads and bridges were kept in good repair. From the striking correlation of Dark Age battle sites with Roman roads and major ancient tracks like the Ridgeway, it is evident that Dark Age armies made good use of roads. Perhaps this explains how kings like Oswald and Ecgfrith could campaign far from home without maps or a compass. They simply followed the roads. They also used scouts and presumably enlisted local people as guides, though recorded instances are hard to find from this period.

Shire armies seem to have been mustered at traditional outdoor assemblies or moots, such as Swanborough Tump in Wiltshire during Alfred's Ashdown campaign or at Egbert's Stone somewhere on or near the border of Gloucestershire and Wiltshire at the start of Alfred's victorious campaign of 878. The shire reeves were responsible for ensuring that the men arrived on time and properly equipped. National service lasted for sixty days and, as the levies showed time and again, not a day longer. On more than one occasion, Alfred's commanders had to let the Danes escape because the shire levies insisted on their rights and went home. This alone might explain why Dark Age commanders often seemed anxious to get the fighting over and done with.

To maintain speed the army marched as light as possible. Heavy war gear was carried in the rear in carts or by packhorses. Towns were expected to supply the army with food and other necessities as it marched. Bede confirms this with his story of the man who escaped death at the Battle of the Trent by pretending to be a civilian ferrying food supplies to the army. We are in the dark about living conditions on the march, but it seems that armies did bring tents with them. In *Egil's Saga*, Athelstan used his city of tents to confuse the enemy about his battle deployment.

Major towns and roads in the Dark Ages

The saga might be fiction, but it would make no sense to its listeners had not tents been a normal part of army life.

We know little about battle formations in the Dark Ages. Large armies were evidently divided into sub-units, serving under different lords. From the ninth century, the shire levies were led in battle by their respective reeves, as at Ringmere in 1010 when the men of Cambridgeshire and East Anglia fought in separate divisions. Men of the top social class, royalty or ealdormen, fought among their hearth-troops who were expected to defend their lord to the death. Ealdorman Byrhtnoth at Maldon probably acted in the way expected of Dark Age commanders by putting himself in a prominent position in the centre of the line where his banner would be visible to the rest of his force.

Swanborough Tump was the open-air moot or meeting place of the Hundred of *Swanbeorg* in the vale of Pewsey, Wilts. The county levies assembled here in 871 to resist the Danish invasion of Wessex.

Victory or defeat in a Dark Age battle depended on moral as well as physical strength. The professional Dark Age warrior, hearth trooper or mercenary, married late, if at all. The prime of his manhood was spent in the service of his lord, and he spent his leisure in the company of men, hunting, hawking and drinking. He lived on the cusp between the fiction of the sagas and praise poetry and the hard facts of military life: the former informed him of the way he was expected to behave, the latter of how heroic ideals worked out in practice. He repaid the mead he drank and the gifts he received by absolute loyalty and devoted service. One is bound to wonder: did the Dark Age warrior fear death in battle? It has been suggested that he was a fatalist: what will be, will be, and better to die gloriously than to live dishonourably. To fall in battle was considered an honourable death. Some warriors, especially the Welsh, thought that to die in bed was a disgrace. The trouble is that we do not know these people very well except through the doubtlessly idealized form of poetry. Although they might have been expected to conform to a heroic stereotype, the Battle of Maldon shows us that there were good and bad apples in every barrel. Some did indeed live and die according to their oaths. Others, it is clear, did not.

Did Dark Age Armies Fight on Horseback?
The key uses of horses on the battlefield were for intelligence gathering, the pursuit of a fleeing enemy, and for opposing or breaking up enemy cavalry formations. We know that most, if not all, Dark Age armies employed horses as transports, and on the

march. The Vikings certainly depended on horses for mobility and speed, and they blackmailed local leaders into supplying them as the price of peace. For example, the sainted King Edmund supplied horses to Ivar's great army in 867 for his attack on York, and many of the Danish raids were for horses as well as food and removable wealth.

It has been truly said that the aristocracy did not often walk (the Bayeux Tapestry shows Harold dismounting only once, to save a soldier from drowning). They rode everywhere, and their halls would have included stable yards and smithies. A horse was part of any warrior's basic accoutrement. The Gododdin's 300 warriors rode to battle at *Catraeth*, and Ecgfrith commanded a mounted force on his expedition to the lands of the Picts. Similarly Harold is known to have used mounted forces to suppress the Welsh in the 1050s. At Maldon, ealdorman Byrhtnoth rode in front of his army, although he dismounted and joined his household men before the battle commenced.

The question is not whether the armies of the age used horses but whether horses were used on the battlefield. The evidence is thin, but it is there. Even if we disregard the saga account of Harold's cavalry charges at Stamford Bridge as anachronistic, we still have the *Brunanburh* battle poem's evidence of 'chosen mounted companies' (*eorod-cysta*) used by Athelstan to pursue the beaten enemy. There is also the scene on the Aberlemno Stone which shows mounted warriors charging at a file of foot-soldiers. If, as seems likely, this stone records episodes of the Battle of Dunnichen, it forms startling evidence that, at least in the seventh century, units of the Saxon army fought on horseback.[9]

Admittedly the impression given from most descriptive accounts is that men fought entirely on foot in a compact shield-wall. At the Battle of Hereford in 1055, the local English levies are said to have fled before a spear was thrown precisely because the local commander, who happened to be a Norman, had made them fight on horseback, contrary to custom. Perhaps the use of horses by the deeply traditional English was limited by the small size of their mounts, no larger than modern ponies. Horse warfare may have come more naturally to mercenary troops from the continent, for example, from Brittany or, later on, from Normandy. According to one account, Athelstan had Frankish and Breton troops in his army at *Brunanburh*. Were these the 'chosen mounted companies'?

Images from the Dark Ages. This seventh-century Pictish stone at Aberlemno, near the battlefield of Dunnichen, portrays a hunting party complete with cryptic double mirror and crescent symbols.

Perhaps the best conclusion we can come to is that, when the occasion warranted the use of 'men on horses with big sticks', then commanders had them and used them. The Britons seem to have used cavalry on the battlefield more often than the Saxons, for example at the famous downhill charge at Mount Badon. The Vikings and Saxons routinely used horses for harrying operations, but whether units of cavalry were retained for manoeuvre and pursuit on the battlefield is more questionable. It would have made sense to keep a mounted force in reserve to pursue the enemy or to cover a retreat. The successful pursuit of the Vikings after Ashdown, for example, is hard to account for without horses.

The Fate of Defeated Opponents

What were your chances of surviving a Dark Age battle? The chance find of probable battlefield grave-pits at Cuckney and Buttington (see below) indicates that fatalities could number in the hundreds. Some battles resulted in total annihilation. At *Anderida* in 491, for example, Aelle and his Saxons 'slew all the inhabitants; there was not even one Briton left'. A hundred years later King Aethelfrith swept through the northern counties of England 'exterminating or enslaving the inhabitants'. These were wars of conquest in which the aim was to drive out the Britons or reduce them to servitude. The Britons retaliated with equal savagery, as in 632 when Cadwallon, having disposed of his English adversary, King Edwin, 'set upon exterminating the entire English race, sparing neither women nor innocent children'. 'The general fate of those defeated in battle or taken in war', comments Matthew Strickland, 'was either death or enslavement'.[10]

A stark illustration of what must sometimes have happened is displayed on Sueno's Stone in Forres, where decapitated prisoners lie in heaps, their hands still tied behind their backs. At the siege of Durham in 1003, earl Uhtred had the severed heads of enemies slain during the siege washed and groomed by local women (for which each lady was rewarded with a cow) before being placed on spikes along the public highways. The Viking era was particularly merciless. Some of the raids were marked by rape and torture. As Alfred Smyth noted, Viking poetry 'reflects a taste for violence on the part of the Norse aristocracy which verged on the psychopathic'.[11] Because these raiders gave no quarter, they were offered none. After Ashdown, the West Saxons cut down every Viking they could lay their hands on. Even the civilized Alfred had two shipwrecked Viking sailors hanged out of hand.

The risks of battle were at least as high for the warrior elite as they were for the humbler levies. Many Dark Age kings fell in battle. Of all the kings that ruled Northumbria in its years of power, only one, Oswy, died in his bed (at the not very advanced age of 58). The rest were either killed in battle or assassinated. There is some evidence that leaders, especially kings, were deliberately targeted in battle. The Dark Ages had no rules of chivalry that spared the well-born. At *Brunanburh*, five kings and seven Viking 'jarls' lost their lives; at *Winwaed*, thirty 'famous commanders' were wiped out; at Ashdown, a king and five more jarls; at *Assingdun*, a bishop, an abbot and three ealdormen. At the Battle of Maldon, the Vikings made the greatest efforts to identify the Saxon leader, Byrhtnoth, and pick him off. There were sound reasons for this. A battle generally came to a speedy conclusion after the death of the army commander, although his household men often chose to fight to the death.

It is likely that some men recorded as being killed in battle were in fact captured and executed afterwards. Such may have been the fate of the three British kings Coinmail, Condoddin and Farinmail after the Battle of *Deorham* in 577. Unlucky enough to be captured by the Vikings after a lost battle in 870, King Edmund of East Anglia was first beaten, then tied to a tree and shot with arrows. Finally they cut his head off and carried it away to prevent the king from enjoying himself in the afterlife. In 796, a captured king called Eadbehrt Praen ('Edbert the Rich') was led bound to Mercia, where his eyes were put out and his hands cut off. The bodies of fallen kings were sometimes mutilated after death. The defeated King Edwin's head was carried off as a trophy. A few years later, the severed head of the Dal Riatan King Domnall Brec was stuck on a pole where it was gnawed by ravens. The dead King Oswald's arms, as well as his head, were hung up and exhibited on the battlefield, perhaps in a parody of the crucifixion. Battles against fanatical foes of different religions (all of which took a 'fundamentalist' line), or where there was 'bad blood' between a leader and his rival, were likely to be particularly ferocious.

Nonetheless there were rules. At Tempsford in 921, Edward the Elder slew everyone who had put up armed resistance but made prisoners of the rest. There was quarter for those not directly engaged in the battle, At Stamford Bridge in 1066, Harold spared those Norwegians who had not taken part in the battle but had stayed behind to guard the ships. Bede relates the story of a Northumbrian nobleman called Imma who, when taken prisoner after the Battle of the Trent in 679, protested that he was 'a poor married peasant who had come with others of his kind to bring provisions for the army'.[12] His life was spared and his wounds treated, not so much out of compassion as because at the slave market he would be worth more healthy than sick. Later on, when Imma's real identity became apparent, his captor told him that, had he known of it, he would have put him to death there and then in revenge for his kinsmen slain in the battle. Instead he was sold to a Frisian merchant. Fortunately Imma had friends in high places and was able to buy his way out of trouble by paying the Frisian a ransom. The Imma story suggests that the fate of prisoners taken in battle was to some extent at least at the whim of their captor. It implies that, contrary to later practice, the prisoner was *more* likely to be killed if he was a noble or a warrior. Imma was spared partly because he was taken for a low-born peasant, and therefore of little account, but also because he persuaded his captor that he had only brought provisions to the field, and had not fought in the battle.

One reason why fighting was so entrenched in Dark Age culture was revenge. Dark Age aristocrats behaved rather like Sicilian bandits or rival Godfathers. Bad blood endured for decades, and caused not only village massacres and slayings but full-scale battles between rival war-lords. The Anglo-Saxon Chronicle relates one such feud between Cynewulf, king of Wessex and a sub-king called Sigebehrt. The latter had been stripped of his lands 'for unlawful actions' and driven into Sussex where he was eventually 'stabbed to death by a herdsman' (the low status of the murderer may have made matters worse). This, the Chronicle tells us, 'avenged the ealdorman Cumbra', presumably a victim of Sigebehrt. Later on, Sigebehrt's son Cyneheard in turn avenged this blot on the family honour by killing Cynewulf himself, before being slain in his turn by Cynewulf's men.

The most famous feud in Dark Age history was skilfully reconstructed by Richard Fletcher in his book, *Bloodfeud*.[13] Starting with the assassination of Uhtred, a Northumbrian nobleman, the feud passed through three generations, culminating in the massacre of one family by the other during a winter feast. However, under certain circumstances family honour could be satisfied by a payment, known as *wer-geld*, which was carefully graded according to the status of the slain. *Wer-geld* for slain kings was likely to be ruinously expensive. In 687, Kent was ravaged by a sub-king called Mul. The men of Kent managed to turn the tables and corner him in a house, which they set fire to. Mul and twelve of his men died in the flames. Mul's brother Caedwalla swore vengeance and harried the kingdom of Kent, burning and slaying without mercy. Caedwalla's wrath was finally appeased by a payment of 'thirty thousands' as *wer-geld* for the dead Mul. It sounds rather unfair that the Kentishmen should be made to pay up after having their lands ravaged twice over, but it did at least draw a line under the affair. Similarly the king of Mercia agreed to pay *wer-geld* to King Ecgfrith of Northumbria in 679 for the loss of his popular brother Aelfwine at the Battle of the Trent – even though Mercia had won the battle! Perhaps this incipient feud was nipped in the bud because Aelfwine had apparently been slain in honest battle rather than singled out for assassination.

The pagan Saxons and, still more, the pagan Vikings tend to be represented as merciless brutes, slaughtering and pillaging with few apparent restraints. The Vikings did not hesitate to slaughter the clergy. They killed three Frankish bishops out of hand in 859, and although they sometimes kept a high-ranking prisoner alive for his ransom, death was his likely lot if the ransom was not paid – for example, the grisly fate of Archbishop Aelfhere in 1013, beaten to death with ox-bones by drunken Vikings. The wars between Saxons and Welsh were also bitter. There never was much love lost between the two. The sense of being driven out from their rightful lands by the Saxon remained strong in Welsh culture and identity. The same was probably true of the Cornish (the 'West Welsh'), who were quick to make common cause with the Vikings against the English.

Christianity did at least bring some possibility of mercy and forgiveness. Bede has a story of how two captured heathen nobles were baptized before execution, an act regarded by all, including the victims, as merciful: their bodies were punished but their souls were saved. Conflicts were, on occasion, resolved by negotiation. After the Battle of Archenfield in 917, the men of Gloucestershire and Herefordshire cornered the remnant of a Danish raiding party in an enclosure. They could presumably have chosen to kill every last man at the cost of some of their own lives, but instead agreed to let them go after the Danes made oaths to depart sealed by surrendering hostages. At Sherston in 1016, both sides seem to have ignored their leaders and decided to call it off.

Looking back, the Dark Ages were not one long period of anarchic violence. Apparently quite trivial causes were often enough to start another round of ravaging and burning; the whole community paid for the sins of its leaders. But there were also periods of peace – much of the eighth century for example – and some places, like East Anglia, were apparently free of major wars, at least until the Viking age. The most violent episodes of Dark Age history were usually short and highly localized, for example, in Kent during the dimly remembered conquests of Hengest, the later conquest of north Britain under Aethelfrith, or during Ceawlin's drive to the west coast in 577. Battles and sieges are most frequent during times of rapid social interchange, during the Saxon Conquest, the internecine wars of Northumbria and Mercia and the later Viking incursions.

So what *were* your chances of surviving a battle? Probably better than even, especially if your side won, or at least held its ground. We do not have reliable figures of the dead, wounded or missing for any Dark Age battle, but there is no reason to suppose that casualties were routinely higher than in later times. Dark Age weapons were less deadly than massed Welsh longbows or powder weapons. One way of surviving was running away. The larger part of most armies was levies, whose loyalties extended beyond their lord to their homes, families and farms. Sometimes, if they mistimed their departure, a battle could be followed by a slaughter. But the non-warrior class probably had a reasonable chance of escaping the field alive if things turned out badly.

Of course, it was better to win. Although reliable figures are lacking, there does seem to be a large disparity in casualties between winners and losers. At Ashdown for example, six named Viking princes were killed, among 'thousands' of others, but no named Saxons, or at least none that the chronicler felt able to mention. Many of the casualties of a battle were killed in the pursuit afterwards. For example, at *Brunanburh* the victorious English 'in troops pressed on in pursuit of the hostile peoples'.

Why was warfare in the Dark Ages so proverbially brutal and merciless? Matthew Strickland offers two main reasons. The first is that the wars of Briton against Saxon, pagan Saxon against Christian Saxon, and then Saxon versus Viking, were to some extent wars of religion. As in the early crusades (or, perhaps, in the ideological conflict between Nazi Germany and Soviet Russia) killing a heathen was seen as a praise-worthy act.[14] And secondly, the Saxons, at least, believed that war under certain circumstances was not only just but a duty. The eleventh-century homilist Aelfric taught the righteousness of fighting for home and country against a foreign invader. As the *Brunanburh* poet expressed it, it was natural for men of royal lineage 'to defend their land, their treasure and their homes in frequent battle against every foe'. It was kill or be killed, and, beyond that, war was seen as an honourable calling. There were very few Dark Age pacifists.

Modern monument to a Dark Age battle: Fulford, at the gates of York, in 1066.

Battlefield Archaeology

Finding evidence of ancient battlefields below ground is normally a matter of luck. For pre-Conquest battlefields finds have been few and equivocal. Unlike musket balls, arrow-heads and spear-points soon rust away. Excavation of certain hill-forts has shed some light on warfare in the early Dark Ages. For example, the evidence that Liddington Castle had been refortified after the Roman withdrawal is a point in its favour as a possible site of the elusive battlefield of Mount Badon. Excavation has also revealed the layout of the Roman frontier town of Cataractonium in North Yorkshire and of everyday life in its crowded streets. But although Cataractonium almost certainly became the Dark Age settlement of Catraeth, it casts no new light on the whereabouts of the famous battle of that name celebrated in the lines of the oldest poem in British history, *The Gododdin*.

More direct evidence of a battle are mass graves. Relatively few have been discovered in Britain, but some of those few are from the Dark Ages. One such possible battle grave was found beneath the foundations of Cuckney Church in Nottinghamshire in 1950–1. It is said to have contained at least 200 skulls, and, strikingly, all of them seemed to be those of fully grown adults. Since the present church dates from soon after the Norman Conquest, the grave was clearly of earlier date and indicates a catastrophe, such as a battle, that killed adults but not children. Given Cuckney's traditional association with King Edwin of Northumbria, this may well have been a mass grave dug after the battle of Heathfelth in 632, when Edwin's headless corpse is said to have been buried at nearby Edwinstowe. Unfortunately the bones are not available for inspection by modern forensic techniques which could certainly establish their approximate date and confirm the cause of death.

What was almost certainly another battlefield cemetery, this time from King Alfred's reign in the ninth century was uncovered at Buttington, a village by the River Severn in Gloucestershire, in 1838. Building work on the south-western perimeter of the churchyard revealed pits containing up to 400 skulls among other bones which had evidently been buried all at the same time. They were assumed, probably rightly, to be the bones of Alfred's warriors who fell in the battle of Buttington in 893, following a siege of a Viking camp by the river. The event, which is recorded in the Anglo-Saxon Chronicle, resulted in the death of one Ordheh, King Alfred's thane, 'and many other king's thanes'. The bones were almost certainly those of Christians. The Vikings they were fighting were heathens and would not have been buried in consecrated ground. Again, the whereabouts of the bones today is unknown.

More evidence of ancient strife came to the surface during the building of South Benfleet railway station by the Thames opposite Canvey Island during the nineteenth century. Human bones and charred timbers preserved in the mud made a vivid reminder of the siege of Benfleet, in 894, when Londoners stormed the fortress of the Viking leader, Haesten, and captured ships and goods, as well as the Viking women and children, who were carried off to London and Rochester. Most of the ships were broken up and burned on the spot, and it was their timbers that had lain by the river for a thousand years. Unfortunately the Viking camp, whose walls were still visible in the nineteenth century, has been lost to modern development. The graves of the English fallen are said to lie near Benfleet Church.

The only pre-Conquest battlefield graves to have been investigated by archaeologists are at York and Riccall where bones bearing the distinctive marks of battle wounds were assigned to the mid-eleventh century, possibly from the invading army of Harald Hardrada in 1066. Many more graves may lie hidden and unknown, possibly in lost churchyards like the mysterious church 'of stone and lime' that King Canute had built on the battlefield of Assandun 'for the souls of those men that had been slain there'. One day, perhaps, they will be found and an obscure conflict known only from ancient annals will suddenly become famous.

Visiting Dark Age Battlefields
The problem about visiting Dark Age battles is that we can rarely be sure exactly where they are. Even some of the best-known ones have at least two possible sites.

Pre-Conquest battles were fought too long ago for traces of local folk-memory to survive, and there have been remarkably few archaeological battle finds. This is the main reason why, of all the major battlefields in England identified and registered by English Heritage, only one, Maldon, dates from before 1066.[15] Similarly, in Scotland only Dunnichen/Nechtansmere has been proposed as an official battle site.[16] The evidence for the others is simply too thin to enable the battlefield to be located, even when the general locality is known beyond reasonable doubt, as at Dyrham or Edington. Some Dark Age battles, like *Winwaed* or *Brunanburh*, were important historical events which determined the course of history and whose sites, if known, would certainly deserve protection. But until archaeology yields some unambiguous clues their famous names refuse to be anchored to a particular place.

This does not mean that Dark Age battles cannot be looked for. By combining the available sources with a reasoned discourse about what must have happened, Alfred Burne proposed plausible sites for at least nine. He may or may not have been right in each case, but it is an exercise that anyone can undertake, especially as most of the sources are now readily available (more so than when Burne was writing in the 1940s and early 1950s). To me, the mere possibility that Liddington Hill is the site of the remote Battle of Badon adds a historical *frisson* to a walk along that windy ridge. The seeker of Dark Age battles will become a connoisseur of hill-forts, like the mighty works at Old Sarum and Badbury where Briton fought Saxon for the long-term destiny of England. We might not know exactly how Cynric overcame the great walls of *Searoburh*, but we can enjoy ourselves speculating how he might have achieved it. Dark Age battles were often fought in remote country which is still remarkably unspoiled. One can still stand on Ashingdon Hill, perhaps in the footsteps of Edmund Ironside, and see, as he did, the hill of Canewdon at the opposite end of a ridge where Canute's Danes were camped, and beyond to the broad River Crouch where his ships were beached. *Ethandun*, Ashdown, Dunnichen, Hingston Down and the approximate sites of dozens of other Dark Age battle offer some fine walking in open country of hills and valleys in which an aura of the distant past still seems to cling. Even battle sites that have, at first glance, been overtaken by suburbs, like *Ellandun* or Benfleet, repay exploration. The past lives on in places like Ashingdon and Edington where the Saxon names for battles adorn the village signs, or in the Wirral whose claim to the lost Battle of *Brunanburh* has become an issue of local pride.

Many sites connected with Dark Age battles are open to the public or accessible via the footpath network, or, recently, as open land where people can now roam. Actual monuments to Dark Age battles are few, but they are increasing. *Ethandun* received a fine memorial stone during the Millennium celebrations, and panel board displays have sprung up by roadsides and car parks for Maldon, Heavenfield, Stamford Bridge and no doubt others. The 'Alleluia Battle' of *c*.429 has a fine monument erected in the eighteenth century on what was then thought to be the battlefield. A fine eighteenth-century cross marks the place near Alnwick where King Malcolm Canmore received his death-wound in 1093. A monument to commemorate the

Battle of Dunnichen was unveiled in the village in 1985. Several Dark Age battles were commemorated by churches. Those at Ashingdon (or alternatively at Ashdon), Oswestry, Heavenfield and Benfleet are believed to lie under the foundations of the existing church. If so they must have originated as places where prayers were offered for the battle dead, and should be close to, if not actually on, the scene of battle.

Chapter 2
The Saxon Conquest of England

Four centuries of Roman rule in Britain came to an end in the year AD 410. This date has become one of the turning-points of history, the supposed hinge between Latin civilization and the Dark Ages. In retrospect, as recalled in the writings of Gildas and Bede many years later, it represented the moment when the light of civilization went out. One moment Britain seemed to be a united, sunlit land of villas, well-maintained roads and orderly towns, and the next it was plunged into the feral chaos of roving war-bands, hill-forts and whole cities in flames. The unity of Britannia is supposed to have fallen apart soon after the Roman legions departed, when civic governance was replaced by anarchy, invasion and war. To the Saxons watching from the wings, it seemed that they had only to kick the door down and the land would be theirs for the taking.

In reality it probably wasn't much like that. The departure of the Roman legions was not a sudden event (and a lot of individual legionaries probably did not depart). The rot started at least as early as 367, when Roman Britannia was brought close to collapse by 'barbarian' invasions from the north and south. In the chaos, Britain's senior general (*Dux Britanniacum*) was taken prisoner, and his deputy killed. Then, in 383, many troops departed when the new general, a Spaniard called Magnus Maximus, made a bid for the Empire and took his British legions with him to Gaul. Maximus was killed the following year, but his men did not return to Britain.

The final denouement came in 406 when, according to the Greek historian Zosimus, the army in Britain set up first one rival emperor and then another. The eventual winner was Constantine III, who, like Maximus, was obliged to denude Britain of its garrisons and standing army in order to deal with the even more serious situation in Gaul, over-run by Vandals, Burgundians and Franks from central Europe. By 410, it seems, the legions had already left. All that happened in that year was that the emperor was obliged to send a circular to the cities of Britain inviting them to take responsibility for their own defence. Rome could no longer spare the men.

In practice, Britain had already taken steps to protect itself long before the climactic date of 410. However they were being constantly frustrated by emergencies across the

Channel. In the circumstances, 'independence' from Rome need not necessarily have been a disaster, since for many years Britain had been providing troops for the Empire rather than the other way round. The real problem seems to have been the failure to establish a central authority in place of the Roman governor. Britain needed a man on the spot to take charge of the army and navy, and co-ordinate the national defence: in other words, its own emperor or dictator. But without Rome, the tribes of Britain could not agree on a successor. Britain was not a unified country but a collection of tribal territories. The tribes seem to have maintained their identity throughout the centuries of Roman domination, and no doubt also their traditional rivalries and alliances. The position in 410 was as if today's central government had disappeared, leaving only the boroughs and county councils, each with their own interests and agenda. Who was to organize and command a national army, maintain the garrisons of Hadrian's Wall and guard the great military forts of the Saxon Shore?

In the decades after 410 it seems that such a leader did emerge. Later generations called him Vortigern, the *tyrannus superbus* or 'proud tyrant'. But Vortigern's power was probably much more restricted than that of the Roman governors, who had three legions to maintain order. He was more of a tribal over-king, whose authority was strictly personal, and so limited. He would have had enough trouble maintaining his authority among the British without fighting invading Picts and Saxons as well. Britain's defences, like those of the greater Roman Empire, were based on keeping the enemy out. But the enemy was already within and Vortigern urgently needed men to fight them. And so, far from keeping the external Saxons out, he invited them in as *foederati*, that is, federal troops or, as we would call them now, mercenaries.

Who were the Saxons? They were part of the people the Roman historian had described three centuries earlier as Germans. Their homeland was in what is now northern Germany and Denmark. Tradition preserved in the later writings of Bede divides them into three tribal groups. One was the Jutes from Jutland, who are said to have settled in Kent and, later, in the Isle of Wight and parts of Hampshire (the New Forest was known in Bede's day as 'the Jutish nation'). The Saxons in the middle colonized Essex, Sussex and most of Wessex; while the third tribe, the Angles, helped themselves to the rest of East Anglia, the Midlands and the land north of the Humber, soon to be known as Northumbria.

Whether the three tribes, all from broadly the same area and speaking dialects of the same language, were really as distinct as Bede makes them out to be is debatable. There is nothing particular to distinguish them archaeologically, apart from a greater sophistication in grave-goods on the part of the Jutes – and that is more likely to be due to trade between Kent and Gaul than any actual cultural superiority. Recent DNA evidence from buried bones suggests that genetically they were one and the same people. They were all effectively the English. And, of course, being English in the fifth century meant being pagan, barn-living, slave-driving and violent.

The native lowland British, by contrast, tended to live in towns, many of which now sheltered behind high walls. The better-off had villas in the country with under-floor heating and hot baths. Most of the British were Christians. They went to church and paid for goods with coins. They had a road system better than anything that people would see again until the eighteenth century. The country was fertile and well-watered with a prosperous agriculture, numerous wood-based industries, including iron and tin-smelting, glassworks and potteries. The population was around three to four million. What they may not have had was the cultural and political unity to maintain law and order once the Empire came under severe pressure. Like everywhere else in the Empire, this was a fragile civilization depending on central authority from Rome. To someone living in the middle of the fifth century and watching it all collapse about them it must have seemed like the end of the world. Quite how Roman Britain fell apart is not clear, but it certainly happened violently. The archaeological record indicates that for a long while after the mid-fifth century there was no currency, no native glassware, no hot baths and no literate clergy to record what was happening. All we have to remember this darkest of Dark Ages are words written down in later centuries from tales remembered perhaps in song and verse. They may not be accurate or even necessarily true but they are all we have.

The Conquest of Kent

Vortigern, so the story goes, invited three ship's companies of Saxons to serve him as federal soldiers (*foederati*) in his wars against the northern tribes. Their leaders were the brothers Hengest and Horsa. They were given lands in the east, and served Vortigern with distinction in the northern wars. Nonetheless Hengest and Horsa's real interest lay in founding an independent kingdom. They sent news to their compatriots on the continental mainland that Britain was fertile and its native people cowardly. Swollen by immigrants, the Saxons became a formidable military force. When Vortigern ran out of money and rations, they mutinied. Gildas says they rampaged from coast to coast. Which coast that was is unclear. He may have meant the coast of Kent.

The archaeological record tells a different story. The traditional year of Hengest's arrival at *Ypinesfleot* (Ebbsfleet) in Kent is 449. But Germans had settled in Britain long before that. Germanic objects, including brooches, pottery and the distinctive square belt-buckles worn by Germans in Roman military service, have been found over a wide area of south-eastern Britain in the first half of fifth century, from the Channel to the Humber. Hence soldiers and settlers of Saxon origin and with Saxon customs were already living in Britain long before the arrival of Hengest's modest fleet of 'three keels' (i.e. ships). Hengest is the name around which stories later clustered, but he may be a mythical figure. His name means 'stallion' (Horsa means 'mare') and possibly has its origin in a Germanic horse-god. Or possibly it was a nickname, taken perhaps from the stallion on an unnamed war-lord's banner. The myth of founding twin brothers is also reminiscent of Romulus and Remus, the legendary founders of Rome.

But at least the circumstances of Hengest's rebellion are plausible. So are the battles associated with him and recorded, along with their supposed dates, in the Anglo-Saxon Chronicle. The first of these was fought between the armies of 'Hengest' and

Vortigern, at *Agaelesthrep* or *Aegaelesford* (Aegle's Ford) in 455. It was remembered for two reasons, first, because Horsa was killed in the battle, and secondly because, as a result of it, 'Hengest succeeded to the kingdom'. This battle is also mentioned in an independent source, the *Historia Brittonum*, a collection of ancient documents preserved by the Welsh monk Nennius in the early ninth century.[1] In this version it was fought at 'the ford called *Episford* in their language, *Rhyd yr afael* in ours, and there fell Horsa and also Vortigern's son Cateyrn (Catigern)'.

The agreement of two separate sources makes it probable that this was a real event. *Agaelesthrep* has been plausibly identified with Aylesford, just north of Maidstone, one of the few fordable points on the Medway. Horsa, according to Bede, was buried 'in east Kent where his monument still stands'[2] – though unfortunately we don't know where. Tradition places Catigern's burial in the Neolithic chambered tomb called Kit's Coty, a short way north-east of Aylesbury. This may be folklore but they do say the place is haunted.

Two years later 'Hengest', this time accompanied by his son Aesc (or Oesc, and pronounced 'ash'), fought against the Britons at *Crecganford*. This is modern Crayford, many miles west of the Medway in what are now the suburbs of London. Again there is confirmation in Nennius's chronicle, which mentions a battle fought on the Darenth, into which the River Cray flows just north of the town. Crayford happens to be crossed at this point by the Roman road called Casing Street, linking

Kit's Coty, a prehistoric tomb, is associated in legend with Catigern, leader of the British resistance to the fifth-century Saxon invaders.

Rochester and London. Perhaps the most likely scenario for this battle, therefore, is that the Britons were barring a Saxon march on London by massing at the river crossing. The battle was a disaster for Vortigern. The army of 'Hengest' and Aesc is said to have slain 4,000 men; 'and the Britons then forsook Kent and fled to London in great terror'. *Crecganford* may have sealed the fate of west Kent and so consolidated the first Saxon kingdom.

The first recorded Dark Age battles, as well as many later ones, were fought by fords in rivers. The northward-flowing rivers of Kent formed natural barriers against an enemy advance towards London, and so provided good defensive positions. In the case of Crayford, the junction of two rivers forms a particularly strong defensive feature similar to those which the Vikings later used to build fortified 'ship-camps'. The British army could be supplied and reinforced by ships from London by way of the Thames estuary and the Medway. As Caesar explained in his *Gallic Wars*, crossing the Medway was a particularly difficult operation as there was only one ford. In 55 BC, the Britons had fortified it with rows of stakes along the bank and driven into the riverbed. Caesar sent his cavalry across first, and their fighting élan swept all before them. Perhaps Hengest's men, with their war-culture and battle experience, were similarly too much for the 'softer' British. The Saxons, too, could easily have used ships to supply their advance and perhaps prevent a British withdrawal by water.

The third battle, to which the date 465 was later assigned, was at a place called *Wippedesfleot*, which means Wipped's fleet or flood. It was named in honour of a British 'thegn' killed in the battle, and was perhaps remembered from an elegy of that otherwise unknown warrior. Unfortunately the name of Wipped was never attached to a later settlement, and so we do not know where *Wippedesfleot* was. It is presumably the same place as Nennius's third battle 'fought in open country by the inscribed stone on the shore of the Gallic Sea'. This was evidently a well-known stone. There was such a stone, an inscription from the original gate of the Saxon Shore fortress of Richborough, which lay close to the tidal flats of Ebbsfleet, a harbour used by the Saxons. If so, perhaps the Battle of *Wippedesfleot* followed a bold attack on the Saxon's naval base, with the retaking of Richborough as a possible objective. The reference to the Britons as 'Welsh' (*Walas*) has led to *Wippedesfleot* being included in a list of battlefields in Wales.[3] In fact, the chronicler, writing centuries later, used the words 'British' and 'Welsh' interchangeably. At this date the 'Welsh' were not confined to Wales!

The British lost twelve 'nobles' in this battle, but Nennius claims that 'the barbarians fled', leaving Vortimer, son of Vortigern, the victor. If so, *Wippedesfleot* could be interpreted as a temporary reversal of the Kentish Saxons' further campaign of conquest. However, in a fourth battle in 473, which the Anglo-Saxon Chronicle does not name, and which is missing from Nennius's manuscript, 'Hengest' and Aesc again fought against the 'Welsh'. This time the Saxons won a decisive victory, and the Britons 'fled like fire' leaving behind 'innumerable spoils'. At some point, perhaps in this battle, Vortimer was killed, and with him the British lost their most effective commander.

The still impressive walls of the Saxon Shore castle at Richborough, Kent. The castle once contained a Roman triumphal arch, possibly the 'inscribed stone by the shores of the Gallic sea' by which Saxons and Britons fought for supremacy in the South-East.

The fourth battle marks the end of the 'Hengest' cycle. Nothing more is said about him in the Chronicle, but by 488 his son Aesc had become king of Kent. (We meet Aesc again in Chapter 3.) What is most puzzling about the formation of the kingdom of Kent is how 'Hengest' and his men were allowed to settle in such a sensitive area. By seizing eastern Kent, the Saxons had at a stroke neutralized Britain's first line of defence. The great Roman forts of the Saxon Shore, Reculver, Richborough, Dover and Lympne, all lay in the area initially occupied by Hengest and Horsa. In the later conquests of Aelle and 'Port', taking the coastal forts of Sussex and Hampshire were key objectives for the Saxons. Whether 'Hengest' took the castles by storm, or whether Vortigern's regime was no longer capable of garrisoning them, is unknown.

The Alleluia Battle

The earliest recorded battle in Dark Age Britain is this strange encounter fought somewhere in the mountainous west or north between the British forces under St Germanus and an unholy alliance of Saxons and Picts. The story was first told in a Life of the saint by Constantius of Lyons, written around 480, and repeated in Bede's *History of the English Church and People* 200 years later.[4] Germanus, bishop of Auxerre, had been sent to Britain by the Pope to suppress the Pelagian heresy. This taught that men may achieve salvation through their personal efforts rather than from divine grace. Germanus was an excellent choice for an emissary, having had military experience as well as a reputation as a miracle-worker. He visited Britain twice, once in 429, when he reported that the country still seemed peaceful and prosperous, and again in about 440 when things were going less well ('The Britons in these days by all kinds of calamities and disasters are falling into the power of the Saxons'). On one of these visits, perhaps the earlier one, the Britons sought the help of Germanus and his brother bishop Lupus against the Saxons and Picts who had joined forces and were making war.

The faith and courage of the supposedly fainthearted British was buttressed by baptisms in a makeshift church. Shortly after Easter, the British forces 'fresh from the font' advanced against the enemy in hilly terrain. The account of what happened next proceeds as follows:

> Germanus promised to direct the battle in person. He picked out the most active men and, having surveyed the surrounding country, observed a valley among the hills lying in the direction from which he expected the enemy to approach. Here he stationed the untried forces under his own orders. By now the main body of their remorseless enemies was approaching, watched by those whom he had placed in ambush. Suddenly Germanus, raising the standard, called upon them all to join him in a mighty shout. While the enemy advanced confidently, expecting to take the Britons unawares, the bishops three times shouted, 'Alleluia! Alleluia! Alleluia!' The whole army joined in this shout, until the surrounding hills echoed with the sound. The enemy column panicked, thinking that the very rocks and sky were falling on them, and were so terrified that they could not run fast enough. Throwing away their weapons in headlong flight, they were well content to escape naked, while many in their hasty flight were drowned in a river they tried to cross. So the innocent British army saw its defeats avenged ... The scattered spoils were collected, and the Christian forces rejoiced in the triumph of heaven.

Having restored peace to Britain and 'overcome its enemies both visible and invisible' Germanus and his fellow bishops returned home.

The 'Alleluia Victory' is a moral tale of the power of faith (it is reminiscent of several hymns of the Church Militant, especially the one that goes: 'Alleluia, Alleluia, Alleluia, The strife is o'er, the battle won'). If nothing else it is a reminder of the part magic and terror must have played in the wars of Christian against heathen. The 'Saxons' were overcome not only by surprise but by the realization that, on this occasion at least, their gods were not as strong as that of Germanus. The story, though obviously legendary in its details, is probably based on a real event. Place-names apparently commemorating Germanus are thicker on the ground in Powys than anywhere else, and that is also where an early tradition places the battle – though Powys would be a funny place to find a Saxon in the fifth century (the most likely invaders would be Irish Gaels). Based on place-names, the battlefield is likely to be in either the Vale of Llangollen near Correg, or near Mold in Clwyd. Just to the west of Mold is a site called Maes Garmon or the Field of Germanus (Garmon is the Welsh name for Germanus). An obelisk commemorating the battle raised there in 1736 is one of the most impressive monuments to any Dark Age battle. Like the Alleluia Victory itself, belief in it having taken place here is a matter of faith.

The Conquests of Aelle, Port and Cerdic

The next cycle of battles remembered in the Anglo-Saxon Chronicle begins in 477 with a new wave of Saxon invasions on the south coast. Like the warrior remembered as Hengest, Aelle ('Ella') crossed the Channel with very modest means – just three ships. His landing place was *Cumenesora*, identified with the Ower Banks just off Selsey Bill, which was then dry land. Aelle and his three sons, called Cymen, Wlencing and Cissa, were opposed near their beach-head, but, though few in numbers, they slew many 'Welshmen' and drove others to flight into the *Andredesleag*, the well-wooded area now known as the Weald. Evidently Aelle and sons were the spearhead of a new set of 'South Saxon' invaders which had chosen the future county of Sussex as their place of abode. Aelle is a historical figure. Bede called him the first of the *bretwaldas* (broad-rulers), implying that, for a short while at least, Aelle had authority over other Saxon kings.

The crucial battle was fought 'near the bank of *Mearcredesburna*' in *c*.485. This name means something like 'stream of the agreed frontier', but too little is known of frontiers at this time to be sure which stream it was. It might have been the Cuckmere near the border of what became Hampshire and Sussex. We are not even told who won the battle, which, since the source is the Saxon Chronicle, may mean that Aelle lost it. Six years later, however, in 491, Aelle and Cissa won a decided victory at *Andredescester*, the Saxon name for the Roman fort of Anderida, now Pevensey Castle. This was one of the forts of the Saxon Shore with high flint walls, parts of which are still standing today. The fort, now several miles from the sea, then over-looked an important harbour and a substantial settlement, whose inhabitants had doubtless taken refuge behind the castle walls. To take such a place Aelle must have commanded substantial forces, including perhaps siege equipment. The storming of Anderida probably cost him dearly. At any rate, Aelle was in no mood to take prisoners, and he 'slew all the inhabitants; there was not even one Briton left there'.

With Anderida in flames and its garrison dead or fled, the victorious Aelle became king of Sussex, the first of a line that continued until the eighth century. Archaeological and place-name evidence indicates that the population was homogeneous. The Britons were 'ethnically cleansed' and the towns abandoned. The resolutely rural Saxons preferred to live in stockaded villages of wooden huts clustered around a wooden hall. The walls, colonnades, fountains and statues of the towns were left to crumble into ruins.

Another set of Saxon raiders and settlers took the remaining Saxon Shore fort of Portchester in *c*.501. By tradition they were led by one Port, and his two sons Bieda and Maegla, who arrived in only two ships (the number of ships in these raids consistently equals the number of sons). There is doubt as to whether Port gave his name to the city of Portsmouth, or whether the city gave its name to an anonymous Saxon leader. At all events a battle took place at *Portsmutha* in which 'a young Briton, a very noble man' was killed. Welsh tradition names this young nobleman as Geraint, who later took his place in Arthurian romance. An early 'Elegy of Geraint' describes his last battle at *Llongborth* or 'ship-port' which could be Portsmouth. In vigorous, if

The walls of Pevensey Castle within the Saxon Shore castle of Anderida. Here Aelle's South
Saxons besieged and massacred the Britons *c*.491.

generalized terms, the poet recalls Geraint leading a charge on a white horse 'swooping
like milk-white eagles' and 'the clash of swords, men in terror, bloody heads'. He saw
'spurs and men who did not flinch from spears'.[5] Geraint was not a local man but a
prince of Dumnonia in present-day Devon and Dorset who had come to the aid of the
local Britons. It is possible that Port was not his enemy but his ally in the battle, and
that their common enemy was the more formidable Cerdic, the traditional founder of
Saxon Wessex.

Cerdic is a well-known if shadowy figure. In Alfred's day, the kings of Wessex
traced their ancestry back to Cerdic, who first appears in the Chronicle in 494,
immediately after the 'Aelle cycle'. But Cerdic is an odd name for a Saxon king. It is
Celtic, probably a variant of 'Caradoc'. Was Cerdic a renegade Briton? According
to one quite plausible legend, Cerdic was a British nobleman from Winchester (the
Roman *Venta*) who subsequently emigrated and spent his life among the Saxons
across the Channel. His tribe was eventually pushed westwards by the Frankish
leader Clovis, and so Cerdic decided to seek his fortune in his old homeland.
Thereupon this former Briton, now Saxon by adoption, carved out a kingdom
of his own, having overcome his former compatriots in battle. Alternatively he
could be a semi-legendary ancestral figure around whose shadowy form the names
of remembered wars and battles began to cluster.

Cerdic's battles, which were retrospectively given dates between 494 and 530, are
centred on Hampshire and the Isle of Wight. Several of them are named after Cerdic
himself. He is said to have arrived in Britain with his son Cynric and five ship's

companies. As Aelle had done, he fought his way ashore at an unknown place simply called *Cerdices ora*, or Cerdic's shore. Then, in *c*.508, Cerdic and Cynric 'slew a Welsh king, whose name was Natanleod, and five thousand men with him'. Natanleod did not necessarily come from modern Wales; more likely he was a local British ruler. The district in which the battle was fought was known afterwards as *Natanleag*, meaning 'wet wood' (the 'g' is silent, hence it is pronounced 'Natanley)'. There are two Netleys in Hampshire, one by Southampton Water between the Itchen and the Hamble, and the other near Old Basing in the north-east corner of Hampshire, where tradition records an ancient battle on the still wet and boggy Greywell Moor. There is also a lost village of Netley in the New Forest, remembered in the name of Netley Bog. According to tradition, Cerdic took Winchester after the battle and established a heathen temple there on the smoking ruins of the old church.

In 514 yet another group of 'West Saxons' under Stuf and his son Wightgar landed at *Cerdices ora* with three ships. Like Cerdic, they fought a battle there 'and put the Britons to flight'. According to the Chronicle, these two were close relations (*nafa*) of Cerdic; they may have been Jutes. The climactic encounter of the series took place at *Cerdicesford* – another battle at a river crossing – in 519, by established tradition the year the West Saxon kings began their rule (however a lost version of the Chronicle used by the tenth-century chronicler Aethelweard has him establishing a kingdom *c*.500). Again, the site of *Cerdicesford* is unknown, though Charford by the River Avon in Hampshire between Downton and Breamore has been suggested.

Cerdic's last battles were fought at an unknown *Cerdicesleag* (Cerdic's-ley or Cerdic's wood) in 527, and at a place later known as *Wihtgaraesburh* (Wightgar's fort) on the Isle of Wight in 530, where they found that most of the inhabitants had fled before their arrival. The capture of the Isle of Wight at about this time is confirmed by the Welsh annals, although the Isle's name is borrowed from Wightgar, not Cerdic. *Wihtgareaesburh* was probably on the site of Carisbrooke Castle near Newport. The medieval castle stands on the remains of a late Roman fortified building which may have been among the forts of the Saxon Shore. According to the Chronicle, Cerdic on his deathbed ceded the island to Wightgar and his Jutes. Cerdic died in *c*.534. His burial place at *Cerdicesbeorg* has been identified with Stoke, near Hurstbourne in north-west Hampshire.

The locations of Cerdic's battles suggest that he gradually enlarged his territory in south Hampshire. The area around the New Forest and the Hamble was known in Bede's time as the Jutish Nation, suggesting that it was in fact Stuf and Wightgar's tribe that settled here, not the ancestors of the later Wessex kings. Inevitably, given his dates, Cerdic has become entangled with the Arthurian legend. He arrived shortly before 496, the most probable year for 'Arthur's' climactic battle at Mount Badon (see next chapter), and Arthurian theorists have linked Cerdic's battles with some of the legendary twelve battles of Arthur listed in the *Historia Brittonum*. One of these, fought by 'the river called *Dubglas*', might have been *Natanleag*, while 'the battle on the river called *Bassas*' might be the same battle as *Cerdicesford*. 'The battle in *Guennion* fort' could be '*Wihtgarasburh*'. The evidence is based on Romano-British place-names, such as the Welsh name 'Gwyn' for the Isle of Wight, aided by a lot of speculation. Cerdic and Arthur belong to a time when legend and history are hopelessly entangled. Whether Cerdic and Arthur ever met, or even whether either of them ever existed, is something theorists will continue to argue about – perhaps without ever coming to a firm conclusion!

The Road to *Deorham*

Apart from Cerdic's adventures in Hampshire, the Anglo-Saxon Chronicle has little to say about the first half of the sixth century. The next cycle of battles and conquests begins in 547, with the building of a fortress at Bamburgh by Ida, the leader of a war-band of Angles and the traditional founder-figure of the kings of Northumbria. But it has nothing to add about Ida's subsequent career except that he ruled his little kingdom for twelve years. Instead, the Chronicle turns to the exploits of Cerdic's descendants in the south. The brief annal for 552 celebrates Cerdic's son, or possibly grandson, Cynric (as he crossed the sea with Cerdic in 494 he would have been at least in his seventies) who besieged the Britons at *Searoburh*. Four years later, he and his son Ceawlin fought the Britons at *Beranburh*, and then, after an interval in which Ceawlin fought against his fellow Saxon king Aethelbert, came what was clearly an important battle at *Deorham* in 577. The Britons were slaughtered at *Deorham*, and afterwards the cities of Cirencester, Gloucester and Bath fell to the Saxons.

The impression is of a sustained campaign of conquest which resulted in the collapse of the British kingdoms in the upper Thames and lower Severn area. This is broadly borne out by archaeology, which shows Saxon settlements spreading across central southern England at this time and the fall of key British towns. For example, Silchester, the 'capital' of tribal lands in Berkshire and the middling reaches of the Thames valley, remained a functioning walled town throughout most of the sixth century, but had evidently become a deserted ruin by its close. One sign that the Britons were losing control of central southern England was their re-use of long-abandoned Iron Age hill-forts. Excavations at the hill-fort at South Cadbury in Somerset revealed that the original earth ramparts had been refortified with a 4,000-feet long stone-dressed timber platform at this time and the entrance defended by a gate-tower. The walls enclosed a large hall and other substantial buildings, and was no doubt occupied as the headquarters of an important personage.

There is no evidence that South Cadbury was attacked, but the Chronicle's *Seoroburh* and *Beranburh* were both fortified places which can be securely identified with the elaborate hill-forts at Old Sarum near Salisbury and Barbury Castle on the Ridgeway south of Swindon. *Seoroburh* or *Saerobyrig* was later Normanized as Sarum, and became 'Old Sarum' after the inhabitants moved from the windy hilltop into the valley and built a new city at Salisbury. *Seoroburh* had been the Roman town of Sorviodunum, and lay at the conjunction of the Roman roads from Winchester, Silchester and Dorchester. It was heavily fortified with multiple rings of earthworks and had its own water supply. It was large enough to enclose the later Norman castle and cathedral as well as a bustling small town. *Seoroburh*'s capture was clearly an important milestone in the Saxon Conquest of southern England. How it fell, whether by storm or after a field battle fought outside, we are not told, and archaeological evidence has not yet provided any clues. The Chronicle states simply that 'Cynric fought against the Britons at the place called *Seoroburh*, and put the Britons to flight'.

This sudden aggressive surge by the West Saxons may be due to the emergence of a new leader, Cynric's son Ceawlin (*chey-awlin*). He is not mentioned at the capture of *Seoroburh*, but was with Cynric at *Beranburh* in 556, and succeeded him as king of the West Saxons in 560. *Beranburh* or Barbury lies just above the Ridgeway close to a strategic intersection of Roman roads. The double walls are still impressive today and it must have been a formidable obstacle in the sixth century when it had no doubt been restored and refortified. Barbury Castle encloses four hectares, room enough for a substantial military garrison, and excavations there suggest that the fort was in use from the Iron Age, through the Roman occupation and into the Dark Ages. It stands close to another hill-fort at Liddington Hill, a contender for site of *Mons Badonicus* or Mount Badon, fought half a century earlier (see Chapter 3). The Saxons probably approached from the east using the Ridgeway and so attacked from the north. The capture of Barbury would bring the Ridgeway under Saxon control and open up the further advance towards Cirencester or Bath.

The Chronicle says only that the Saxons fought the Britons there, not that the Saxons were victorious or that Barbury was taken. The natural assumption is that it was not taken, and that the attack was beaten off. Things then go quiet for a decade, and when we hear of Ceawlin again it is in the context of a war against his neighbour

The walls of Barbury Castle: scene of a great battle between Briton and Saxon in 556. The battlefield may lie between the castle and the Ridgeway, here passing below the downs 400 m to the north.

to the east, Aethelbert, king of Kent, and not against the Britons. *Beranburh* may therefore have been a British victory to rank with the Battle of Mount Badon. Against Aethelbert, Ceawlin was more successful. The two Saxon armies met at a place called *Wibbandun* in 568. From the similarity of their names, *Wibbandum* has been equated with Wimbledon in south London. Opinion today is that the battle was more likely fought near the River Wey which divides Surrey from the then kingdom of Kent. Whitmoor Common between Worplesdon and Guildford is a possible battle site. The result was that Aethelbert was driven back with the loss of two Kentish 'princes', Oslaf and Cnebba. This is the same Aethelbert who, nearly forty years later, allowed St Augustine to convert the Saxons of Kent and became the first Christian Saxon king. By now the Dark Ages are becoming a little lighter.

The 570s saw the decisive turning-point in the see-saw wars between Briton and Saxon. In 571 a West Saxon kinglet called Cuthwulf fought against the 'Brito-Welsh' (*Bretwalas*) at *Biedcanford* and captured four villages (*tuns*), identified as Limbury, Aylesbury, Benson and Eynsham. Cuthwulf died shortly afterwards, and perhaps was mortally wounded in the battle. The location of *Biedcanford* is uncertain. The obvious match is with Bedford or 'Beada's ford', but that redundant 'c' is problematical. The only way *Biedcanford* could be made Bedford is if the original scribe had made a spelling mistake that was then copied faithfully by all the other scribes. But the battle was clearly fought by a river, perhaps the Ouse. The significance of the battle is that it seems to represent the mopping up of the last British enclave in south-east England, and may therefore have opened up the Midlands to conquest. *Biedcanford* decided the fate of the area broadly covered by the Chilterns and the Vale of Aylesbury, an area known by the next century as the *Chilternsaete*, an area of 4,000 hides of land (it survives today as 'the Chiltern Hundreds'). The four seemingly insignificant places mentioned by the annalist cover a wide area: Eynsham and Benson are in central Oxfordshire, Aylesbury in Buckinghamshire and Limbury is now a suburb of Luton. They were perhaps the fortified settlements of local magnates who were now overthrown once and for all. Archaeology shows no Saxon settlement in this area much earlier than 570.

The year 577 saw the climactic Battle of *Deorham*. It was important enough to be recorded woefully in the Welsh annals as 'the battle we lost'.[6] *Deorham* was Ceawlin's finest hour, the day when he finally cracked the stubborn British hold on 'the strategic triangle' defined by the Roman roads linking Cirencester, Gloucester and Bath. The British leaders were killed in the battle, and the cities all taken. It was perhaps after *Deorham* that Ceawlin was hailed as the second *bretwalda* of the Saxons. He may not have been the most powerful king in terms of territory – Ceawlin nearly always made war with allied war-lords – but he personified qualities that the pagan Saxons respected most: courage, dash, wisdom in battle and a sense of destiny. He was a true Dark Age hero; it is a pity we do not know him better.

Fortunately we do know where *Deorham* was. It is the modern village of Dyrham a few miles north of Bath, whose name means 'deer enclosure' or 'deer park'. There has been a deer park there at least since the Middle Ages, which evidently had a Dark

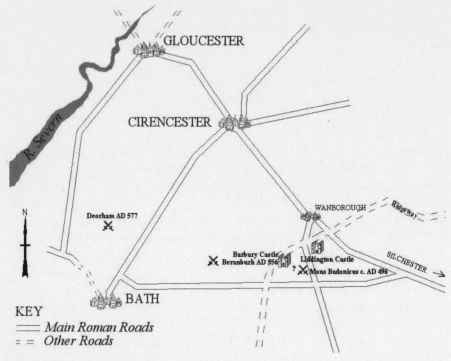

The strategic triangle, 496–577

Age precursor. We can only speculate why the battle was fought at this deeply rural spot among the Cotswold Hills. Perhaps Ceawlin, who was accompanied by his son Cuthwine, had changed his strategy from besieging hill-forts to a mobile strike into the heart of enemy territory. He seems to have chosen to march through the 'strategic triangle', avoiding the strongly defended cities and aiming to isolate the Britons of the Severn valley from those of Somerset and Devon.

The British massed to oppose him, led by three 'kings' (*kyningas* in the Chronicle, *tyranni* in British sources) named as Coinmail, Condiddan and Farinmail. It is assumed, though not explicitly stated, that they were the respective rulers of Gloucester, Cirencester and Bath. Like their compatriots at *Beranburh* and at Badon, they would have refortified the hill-forts, and it can be assumed that they rendezvoused at one of them: Hinton Hill Camp, between the villages of Dyrham and Hinton, and within a short march on mostly good roads from all three cities. They were hence in a good position to intercept Ceawlin, if, as they probably expected, his objective had been to take the city of Bath.

The landscape around the village has invited much speculation about how the battle may have been fought. Hinton Hill Camp lies on a spur of land above the Cotswold escarpment which slopes away to the west and on both flanks. It does not lie on an important road – the Fosse Way runs straight as an arrow several miles to the east – but Dyrham lies on an ancient track running westwards from Wiltshire via

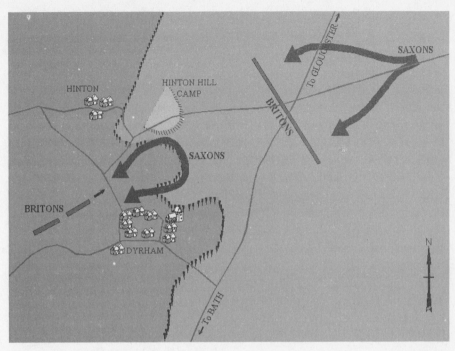

Alternative reconstructions of the Battle of Deorham by Burne (right) and Smurthwaite (left)

The battlefield of *Deorham* in Alfred Burne's interpretation as seen from Hinton Hill Camp. Ceawlin's Saxons stood on the further ridge, the Britons under their three kings on the ridge nearest the camp.

Nettleton, Stanton St Quinton and Christian Melford. Most likely Ceawlin advanced this way from the Marlborough Downs. His scouts having located the Britons massed at Hinton Hill Camp, Ceawlin decided to attack.

The best interpretation of the Battle of *Deorham* is Alfred Burne's in *More Battlefields of England*.[7] Burne found two ridges in front of the camp along Ceawlin's likely line of advance, one close to the camp, and another slightly higher one 300 yards further forward. He proposed that the British had occupied the forward line, with the other as a fall-back position. For what followed Burne seized on the one detail we know but whose significance had been overlooked: that all three British leaders were killed in the battle. Burne regarded this circumstance as unique (though it also happened at Hastings) and concluded that the British army must have been surrounded. If so, the lie of the land suggests how it might have happened. The Britons were pushed back towards the hill-fort. Then the wings of Ceawlin's army outflanked them by charging downhill and instinctively swinging inwards ('as troops do'). The Saxons joined hands in the rear of the hill-fort and cut off the Britons' line of retreat. The fort was then besieged, and, if still alive, the three kings were captured and then 'knocked on the head'.

Of course there are other possible interpretations of what might have happened. The British could have chosen to stay inside the fort with the hope of counter-attacking at the right moment, as they evidently did at Mount Badon. Or it may have been a contact battle and not involved the hill-fort at all. David Smurthwaite suggests that the Saxons attacked at dawn from the escarpment, sweeping away the Britons in the valley below before they could form up to receive the charge.[8] If so, the battle that decided the fate of Wessex could have been over in minutes. However

Caewlin's view looking towards Hinton Hill camp (marked by the trees in the distance).

Another view of the Battle of *Deorham* has Ceawlin occupying the heights above the present village and falling on the Britons as they advance. The field system shown so clearly on the scarp slope probably pre-dates the battle.

it turned out, with the annihilation of the British field army and the death of their leaders, the three cities fell to Ceawlin.

The archaeological record suggests that Cirencester and Bath both fell without a fight. It was at this point that their names changed from the British *Caer Ceri* and *Caer Baddan* to the Old English *Cirenceaster* and *Bathanceaster*. The victory marked the beginning of Saxon settlement in the Severn valley and the creation of the kingdom of the Hwicce in modern-day Worcestershire and Gloucestershire. While the Saxons could now sweep from the Cotswolds into the fertile lowlands of the Severn, the British could no longer easily penetrate the Cotswolds. Henceforth the western Britons were increasingly isolated in the far west, in Wales, and in Cornwall and Devon.

After *Deorham*, Ceawlin's triumphant career went into reverse. In 584, he and 'Cutha' (probably the same person as 'Cuthwine', and if so his son) 'fought against the Britons at a place which is called *Fethanleag*, which means "battle-wood" '. Though Cutha was slain in the battle, the Saxons may have won it since Ceawlin went on to capture 'many villages and countless booty'. However things did not go as he intended for he soon 'departed in anger to his own', that is, his own land. From place-name evidence, *Fethanleag* was first identified as Faddiley in Cheshire, but this seems an unlikely place for the battle. Sir Frank Stenton identified it much more plausibly with Stoke Lyne, near Ardley in Oxfordshire, from a medieval charter mentioning a wood then called *Fethelee*.[9] Stoke Wood, Stoke Little Wood and Stoke Bushes may be fragments of the original, much larger, 'Battle Wood'. The nearby village names include Fringford, Fritwell and Hethe, which have echoes of the lost

Old English wood. Another village, Cottisford, could possibly be named after the dead Cutha. Cutha is said to have been buried in a magnificent barrow by the road at Cutteslow, now a northern suburb of Oxford. The barrow is unfortunately long gone – it was demolished in 1261, an early victim of a road improvement scheme (the barrow was a haunt of robbers on the king's highway).

Ceawlin's last battle was fought in 592 at *Wodnesbeorh*, where 'there was much slaughter'. 'Woden's Barrow' has been plausibly identified with Adam's Grave on the Pewsey Downs. A large Neolithic long barrow surrounded by a ditch, it crowns the summit of Walkers Hill a mile from the village of Alton Priors. Adam's Grave was originally 'Woden's Grave', and the name seems also to have been borrowed by the village of Woodborough, visible beyond Alton Priors from the hill-top. *Wodensbeorh* seems to have been a civil strife in which Ceawlin was 'driven out', that is, deposed, by a younger relative called Ceol. The twelfth-century historian William of Malmesbury got hold of a story that the battle was 'the result of the Angles and the British conspiring together'. Perhaps therefore Ceol had been helped by the Britons, as King Penda was to be in the next century (though not against his own kith and kin). The battle was probably fought in the pass between the downs between Walkers Hill and Knap Hill. That this was then a boundary of some sort is indicated by the contemporary Wansdyke snaking over the downs just north of Adam's Grave. There was a second battle here in 715 when the kings of Mercia and Wessex fought on the same spot.

The site of Ceawlin's last battle: Walker's Hill, as seen from Knap Hill in the vale of Pewsey. *Wodensbeorth* or Woden's Barrow is Adam's Grave, the Neolithic long barrow that crowns Walker's Hill.

Perhaps Ceawlin tried and failed to force the passage over the downs in an attempt to retake his hard-won lands north of the Wansdyke. It is tempting to assume that the dyke played some part in the battle, but we can only speculate what might have happened, and why it was named after the barrow and not the dyke.

The Chronicle's record for 593 consists of a bare sentence: 'In this year Ceawlin and Cwichelm and Crida perished'. Perhaps Ceawlin had formed an alliance with the other two and fell attempting to retake his 'own'. The wording suggests that the three fell together in the same incident. Ceawlin's death closes the cycle of battles and campaigns of the Saxon Conquest of southern England. Ceol's successor Ceolwulf, son of Cutha, seems to have led his war-band far and wide, ever fighting 'against the Angles, or against the Welsh, or against the Picts, or against the Scots'. But the Chronicle records not a single one of his battles. Quite abruptly, the record switches to a different kind of conquest. In 601 St Augustine came to England as head of a papal mission to convert the English to Christianity. Cynegils, the son of the warlike Ceolwulf, became the first Christian king of the West Saxons. Unlike his predecessors he rests not under the turf below the wind and sky but in the sanctuary of Winchester Cathedral among bishops and saints.

Chapter 3
Mount Badon and King Arthur

What Happened at Badon?

The years around the turn of the sixth century are among the darkest in the whole of the Dark Ages. The only light in the gloom is the monk Gildas, who wrote a tract on the ruin of Britain in the mid-sixth century.[1] In his inimitable fashion, Gildas provides a generalized background to a great battle which he presents as the climactic event in the fight against the marauding Saxons, 'a race hateful to God and man'. The tract deals with the consequences of enlisting the Saxons as mercenaries and the war that followed. The Saxons said Gildas, quoting from the biblical Book of Kings, were 'like wolves unto the fold'. 'Nothing was ever so destructive to our country, nothing was ever so unlucky'. When Britain could no longer supply or pay them what they demanded, the Saxons seized the land for themselves, and 'devastating with fire the neighbouring lands and cities' they over-ran the island from coast to coast.

In a vivid passage which may owe something to Virgil's description of the fall of Troy, Gildas describes the horror of what he calls the devastation (*excidium*) of Roman Britain:

> ... all the columns were levelled to the ground by the frequent strokes of the battering-ram, all the husbandmen routed together with the bishops, priests and people, whilst the sword gleamed and the flames crackled around them on every side. Lamentable to behold, in the midst of the streets lay the tops of lofty towers tumbled to the ground, stones of high walls, holy altars, fragments of human bodies covered with livid clots of coagulated blood looking as though they had been squeezed together in a press, and with no chance of being buried save in the ruins of their houses, or in the ravening bellies of wild beasts and birds ... So entirely had the vintage, once so fine, degenerated and become bitter that, in the words of the prophet, there was hardly a grape or ear of corn to be seen where the husbandman had turned his back.

The hapless Britons fled overseas or yielded themselves as slaves. Others retreated into forests or occupied 'high hills, steep and fortified' – that is, they refortified the old hill-forts. Gildas gives no sense of a planned military campaign of conquest by the Saxon immigrants. It may have been what Michael Wood likened to 'a Dark Age gold rush', a large-scale land-grab of the fertile lands of southern and eastern England.[2] Eventually, the British were able to organize a capable resistance under the leadership of one Ambrosius Aurelianus, whose parents 'had worn the purple' 'but had been slain in these broils'. Under Ambrosius, asserts Gildas, 'our people regained their strength'. Sometimes 'our countrymen', sometimes the enemy, won the field, as if God, as with the ancient Israelites, was testing their faith. The culminating battle was the siege of Mount Badon, which he described as almost the last defeat of their foes, 'and certainly not the least'.[3]

Gildas, it may be noticed, has a nice line in invective. His choice of the word *furciferis* to describe the Saxon foes at Mount Badon has been translated as 'scoundrels', 'villains', 'hated ones' or even 'gallows-birds'. After the period of uneasy peace which followed the victory, Gildas turns to his own time, in the 530s and 540s, and uses similar words to describe the decadent successors of the noble Ambrosius. The old civic way of life, he implies, never really recovered from the Saxon onslaught. 'Neither to this day are the cities inhabited as before but, being forsaken and overthrown, still lie desolate'. This can be only partly true. While some Roman cities like Verulanium were abandoned, urban life went on in the west, and some of the ruined towns, such as Wroxeter and Silchester, were rebuilt. The larger hill-forts, like South Cadbury, were permanently garrisoned, but it is most unlikely that the entire urban population upped sticks and headed for the hills. According to Gildas, a measure of order was re-established after the war, with 'kings, public magistrates and private persons, with priests and clergymen' living ordered lives 'according to their several vocations'.

This 'wonderful' time, as Gildas remembered it, lasted about a generation, but eventually degenerated into civil strife. The new generation in the west had not experienced the same hardships and had grown wicked and fractious. The new rulers were petty tyrants, whose companions were 'bloodthirsty, vain, adulterous and enemies of God'. They were, said Gildas, a bunch of perjurers, liars and oath-breakers and their wives were whores. They despised the poor and humble and loaded the innocent with chains.

In other words they were a bad lot, sunk in infamy and not much better than the Saxons. Typical of these 'tyrants' that succeeded the great Ambrosius was Aurelius Caninus. 'What are you doing, Caninus?' shouted Gildas rhetorically.

> Are you not engulfed by the same slime, if not a more deadly one, made up of parricides, fornications, adulteries? . . . Do you not hate peace in our country as though it were a noxious snake? . . . Why are you senseless and stiff, like a leopard in your behaviour [i.e. inconstant, treacherous and probably lustful] and spotted with wickedness . . .

And so on. Caninus is described as 'the bad son of a good king'. He shares the name Aurelius: could he have been the degenerate son of Ambrosius Aurelianus (shades of Arthur and Mordred)? The nub of Gildas's complaints is that Caninus and his fellow war-lords were spending more time fighting one another rather than defending themselves from the Saxons. Britain had disintegrated into a series of warring provinces ruled by petty tyrants.

The significance of Mount Badon, therefore, was that the battle brought peace to at least part of Britain for the first decades of the sixth century, from, say, $c.500$ to 530. Both sides had evidently fought one another to a stand-still, and a period of relative peace ensued, with the Britons continuing to hold on to the west while the Saxons consolidated in the east. This pattern of events is born out by archaeology. Pagan Saxon cemeteries of fifth and early sixth century date are confined to the half of England east of a line linking Southampton and Nottingham. Judging by the scarcity of Saxon grave-goods there, the Britons also held pockets in the east, between London and Verulamium (St Albans) and around Aylesbury and Bedford.

The achievement of Britain in defeating the invaders and securing peace for a generation seems to be unique in the chaotic post-Roman Europe. So it would be interesting, to say the least, to find out exactly how the victory at Badon came about. Who led the armies to victory? Was it Ambrosius, as Gildas implies without actually saying so? Michael Wood has argued that Gildas meant to link the battle explicitly with Ambrosius, but that this fact has been obscured by subsequent editing.[4]

Meanwhile, who led the Saxons? The *Historia Brittonum* implies that Aesc, son of Hengist, was the would-be conqueror of the Britons.[5] Aesc named his own son after Eormenric, the mighty fifth-century king of the Ostrogoths who had ruled a vast empire stretching from the Baltic to the Black Sea. Aesc must have admired and perhaps wished to emulate Eormenric's achievements. However, it is assumed that his own small kingdom of Kent would be insufficient to challenge the west, and that Aesc would need allies. The obvious man was Aelle, king of Sussex (note the economic names of so many of these early kings: Aesc, Esa, Ida, Port and Stuf – Aelle, by the by, was the son of Yffe). Bede refers to Aelle as the first of the *bretwaldas* or 'broad-rulers' of England. Nowhere does he explain how or why Aelle deserved this accolade, but the implication is that he enjoyed a special status among the Saxon tribes and that others deferred to him. Perhaps, then, it was Aelle, together with Aesc, who led the Saxons at Mount Badon.

Another contender is Cerdic, the traditional founder of the kingdom of the West Saxons. In the 2004 film *Arthur* he appeared as a memorably hairy leader of Arthur's enemies. However the archaeological record suggests that Cerdic did not arrive until well into the sixth century, and if so he missed the battle. Whatever its precise composition, the Saxon army at Mount Badon was probably a powerful coalition of tribes led by men with a fresh record of military success.

Later Welsh historical tradition transfers the leadership of the Britons from Ambrosius to Arthur. Mount Badon regularly appears in Arthurian literature as the hero-king's greatest victory. Establishing whether there is a morsel of truth behind the Arthur myth is, of course, one of history's tempting grails. Everyone wants to believe in Arthur. It may well be however that his legendary exploits were grafted onto the original historical record, such as it was. Gildas does not mention him, and neither does Bede nor the Anglo-Saxon Chronicle. Was Arthur 'written out' of English history, as some have suggested, because of his victories? Or did Gildas not mention Arthur for the understandable reason that he had never heard of him?

The evidence for Arthur's leadership at Mount Badon comes from two sources compiled in the ninth century, but possibly based on older material. In the *Annales Cambriae* or Welsh Annals we find against the year 516 the famous line: 'The Battle of Badon, in which Arthur carried the cross of our Lord Jesus Christ on his shoulders for three days and nights, and the Britons were victorious.' The year is only approximate. The historical entries were transcribed from tables used to calculate the time of Easter, but those earlier than 525 are considered unreliable.

In the *Historia Britonnum* Arthur appears again as the victor of Badon Hill, 'and in it 960 men fell in one day from a single charge of Arthur's, and no one laid them low except he alone'. In this version, Arthur is described not as king, for 'there are many of more noble birth than he', but as a war-lord (*dux bellorum*). Badon was the last of twelve battles won by Arthur, all of which are named by the chronicler (see below).

The most elaborate version of the story is supplied by Geoffrey of Monmouth, writing *c*.1147. In his *History of the Kings of Britain*, Arthur emerges in more familiar form as a king-emperor, wielding a sword, Caliburn, with magical powers and with whose help he conquers not only Britain but much of Western Europe. In Geoffrey's immensely influential story, the Saxons occupy the higher ground at Mount Badon, ranked 'in wedges' on the slopes. Arthur launches assault after assault, but the Saxons stand their ground until shortly before sundown when they retreat to the hill-fort. The battle recommences the next day, with Arthur suffering heavy casualties from the Saxons counter-charging down from the heights. Eventually 'putting forth their greatest strength', the Britons gain the hill-top and close with the enemy hand-to-hand. The fighting lasts much of the day with neither side gaining the advantage until Arthur,

> waxing wroth at the stubbornness of their resistance and the slowness of his own advance, drew forth Caliburn, cried aloud the name of the Holy Mary, and thrust forward with a swift onset into the thickest press of the enemy's ranks.

This last attack broke through the Saxon's ranks, 'thousands' were slain and the rest fled, pursued by the British cavalry led by the duke of Cornwall.

Some, notably Alfred Burne, have discerned in Geoffrey of Monmouth's 'hotch-potch of myth and fable' a 'solid residue of historical matter'.[6] It is just possible that Geoffrey was using an otherwise unknown lost source, but his account of the battle reads very much like an extended gloss on the brief entries in the Welsh annals. The annals themselves have a very strong whiff of myth. The Arthur that carries the cross for three days and nights and wins the battle by single-handedly slaying 960 foemen sounds more like a heavenly avatar than a flesh-and-blood human being. (Could the suspicious figure of 960 be a characteristic Welsh literary construction: 'three three hundreds and three score'?) The inflated lines about Arthur in the normally tight-lipped annals sound like later interpolations added to a typically laconic original entry which may have said only: 'The battle of Badon in which the Britons were victorious'. Neither of the Welsh annals has anything to add beyond the obviously mythic feats of Arthur. And they still don't know who besieged who!

Dating Mount Badon

The dates of all events in the 'lost years' around the turn of the sixth century are uncertain, and that of *Mons Badonicus* is no exception. Gildas, in his usual teasing way, remarks that the battle happened forty-four years before, in the year of his birth 'less one month'.[7] Unfortunately Gildas omits to add what we need to know to make that calculation: either the year in which he was writing or the year in which he was born! For that reason, to date the battle it is important to find out roughly when Gildas was born.

A clue lies in Gildas's denunciation of King Maglocunus (Maelgwn) of Gwynedd, which implies that the king was still alive when Gildas was writing. According to the Welsh Annals, Maglocunus died in 'the yellow plague' of 547. If this is right, the latest possible date for the battle would therefore be 547 minus 44, that is, 503.

Other evidence from the lives of St David and other forefathers of the Celtic Church indicates that Gildas was a good deal older than the Welsh patron saint. He had preached before the saint's mother, St Non, in the year of St David's birth, and had later complained, in 527 or 528, that David was far too young to become an abbot. Putting it all together, this would mean that Gildas was born before 500. The Welsh annals assign his death to 570,[8] and, if so, he is not likely to have been born much before 490.

Bede seems to have worked from a differently worded manuscript of Gildas, which, being much earlier than the only manuscript to have survived, may have conveyed the author's meaning more accurately.[9] In Bede's version, Gildas dated the battle not from his year of birth but from the year in which the Saxons first arrived in Britain. By tradition, this is 447, though Bede is more cautious, implying rather than stating a date between 445 and 455. Either way, by a remarkable coincidence this brings us back to the 490s again.

Hence the evidence converges on some date between 490 and 503. Recent pain-staking work on the various manuscripts by D R Howlett[10] has left 496 as the most likely year for the Battle of Mount Badon.

Where was Mount Badon?

Finding out when a battle took place helps to pin it down within the spare chronology of the Saxon Conquest. From the circumstances of the time we can cautiously deduce who might have been available to fight the battle and what their objectives might have been. But to understand the strategic significance of *Mons Badonicus*, we need to know where it was fought. Unfortunately, locating the battlefield is much harder than establishing its date; indeed, given the scanty evidence, it may ultimately be impossible. Every scrap of evidence, the least clue, has to be examined with care. Volumes have been written on this battle without reaching a consensus.

Gildas, our main authority, offers no direct geographical information, but he does include the suggestive phrase *obsessio montis badonicus*. Much has been squeezed out of these three words. *Mons Badonicus* can be translated as Mount Badon or Badon Hill. *Obsessio* means a siege or a blockade. Gildas is clearly referring to a siege rather than a field battle, for which the appropriate word would be *bellum*. He does not say who besieged whom. But the implication is that the Saxons were besieging the Britons. Certain Iron Age hill-forts, like South Cadbury in Somerset, were refortified during the calamitous times following the Roman withdrawal. Linear defences were also being dug, like the Wansdyke in Berkshire and Wiltshire or the Devil's Dyke in East Anglia. The Saxons did not place the same reliance on fortifications. They were a free-booting army, depending on mobility and surprise. They were besiegers rather than the besieged. Hence *Mons Badonicus* was very probably a hill-fort with the Britons inside it.

Mons (genitive *montis*) is a name normally given to a separated hill with slopes on all sides. It need not necessarily be very large or high, but the hill would stand out from the surrounding scenery and be visible for miles around. It would, by implication, be a defensible site with room enough for a large settlement inside: a flat-topped hill guarding vital communications between one town and another would fit the bill. The problem with such hills is that they can be surrounded and isolated. Our *Mons* should therefore have a water supply and adequate food stores as well as strong defences of the right date.

The most helpful of the three words is of course the place-name, Badon, of which *Badonicus* is the Latinized version. There is, needless to say, no Mount Badon or Badon Hill on today's map. But, given the date and what is known of Anglo-Saxon settlement at the time, one would expect it to be somewhere to the west of the then British–Saxon frontier, roughly on a line linking Christchurch in Dorset with the Trent and the Humber. The context of Gildas and later texts indicates that the battle was fought in southern England (though there is also a northern school, of which more anon, which places it at Dumbarton Rock near the mouth of the Clyde) The two most likely candidates for Badon are the city of Bath or one of the Badburys, most likely the village of Badbury in Wiltshire, and that the battle was fought on a hill near one of them.

We do not know what the fifth-century Britons called the Roman town of Aquae Sulis, but Nennius, writing in the ninth century, refers to the marvellous baths of 'Badon'. This was probably also the name in Gildas's day, when Bath was still a British city. Various Saxon documents mention *Bathu*, *Bathum* or *Bathanceaster*, that is, the 'city of the baths'. Bath and Badon are clearly similar words; in the Domesday Book, *Bathum* was Latinized as *Bade*. (What the Saxons had done was to take the original 'd' and convert it into a 'crossed-d' or thorn, pronounced 'th' as in 'bathe'). Bath is surrounded by hills, but among them is an obvious *mons* crowned by a hill-fort of sufficient size. This is Little Solsbury Hill overlooking the Avon, two miles from the city centre. Could this be Mount Badon?

For the alternative, 'Badbury', we have to assume that the Saxons would add a '-burh' or 'byrig' to a fortified place, hence *Badenbyrig*, or as we would now say, Badbury. We must assume that *Bad* was a British word of uncertain meaning which the Saxons later co-opted (the old idea that Badbury is derived from someone called Badda has been dismissed – as J N L Myres wittily noted, 'for some unexplained reason [he] specialized in leaving his name to hill-forts').[11] There are several hill-forts called Badbury in central southern England and also further afield. The most dramatic is Badbury Ring in Dorset, but a more likely candidate is Badbury in Wiltshire, close to a hill-fort formerly known as Badbury Castle, but which has since for reasons of tenure adopted the name of the next village and become Liddington Castle.

The long and the short of it is that *Mons Badonicus* was probably either a hill near Bath or Liddington Castle near Badbury, Wiltshire, close to the M4 near Swindon. There is a good case to be made for either (and a bad case to be made for many other places which I do not propose to discuss here). Let us briefly look at each in turn.

The case for Bath
The best point in favour of Bath is the name: more certainly than anywhere else, Bath *is* Badon. Perhaps Gildas had no further need to particularize since everyone knew where it was. Bath was the original spa town and also a place of strategi importance.

The walls of Liddington Castle are still formidable.

It lay at one end of a Roman road known as Verlucio or the Sandy Lane, running westwards from the Kennet valley across the downs. In the fifth or sixth century part of this road was fortified and partly overlain by the earthwork known as the Wansdyke. This suggests that the road was part of a frontier and that the land to the south of it was strategically valuable.

Bath was also on the major north–south road known as the Fosse Way, connecting Bath with the important towns of Corinium (Cirencester) and Lindinis (Ilchester). The line of the Fosse Way and its bend westwards into Bath along the Avon valley can still be followed. In Roman times this part of Britain, broadly coinciding with the later Saxon kingdom of Wessex, was the territory of a tribe called the Atrebates. The fifth-century descendants of the Atrebates had probably reverted to their tribal homeland which was now threatened by the Saxon colonizers in the Upper Thames valley. By taking Bath, which lies only fifteen miles from the Bristol Channel, the Saxons would effectively isolate the land of the Atrebates from their British allies further north. It would also open up an invasion route into the Midlands as well as the south-west. In terms of military strategy, a move against Bath would make sense.

Little Solsbury Hill is a flat-topped isolated hill just two miles downriver of the spa city. Naturally steep-sided, it has been reinforced with impressive earthworks. Excavations have shown that the hill-fort was reoccupied in the fifth century. Bath is a valley town, protected by the river on two sides but vulnerable to attack from the north where the downs overlook the city. As a Saxon-*ceaster* it was probably a walled town. No doubt the old hill-fort was militarized as a redoubt commanding the approaches to the city from the east.

Subsequent history strengthens the case for Bath. The victory at Mount Badon put back the Saxon colonization of the West Country for generations. As we have seen, Bath eventually fell to Ceawlin after the Battle of *Deorham* in 577. Perhaps Ceawlin's strategy was based on that of his unsuccessful predecessor at Mount Badon. Long after *Deorham*, in 665, the Britons made a final attempt to snatch back the city in alliance with the Saxons of Mercia. The battle, the Welsh Annals tell us, took place on the same ground as in 496 – at *Mons Badonicus*. A second battle was fought in the same year at *Wirtgernesburh*, which has been identified with Bradford-on-Avon, a few miles east of Bath. The full evidence has been discussed in detail in a paper in the Somerset Archaeological Society by Tim and Annette Burkitt.[12]

The final straw of evidence is from Geoffrey of Monmouth's *Histories of the Kings of Britain*. Geoffrey places the battle at Bath. No one takes his legends and tall tales very seriously as history, but in placing Mount Badon at Bath Geoffrey may have taken it for granted that the battle was fought there because his unknown source said so.

The case for Liddington Castle

Liddington Castle is an oval-shaped hill-fort at the western end of a ridge of downland overlooking the villages of Liddington and Badbury. The hill dominates the skyline for miles around. The castle's bank-and-ditch is still impressive, and forms only part of what was evidently an elaborate system of earthworks along the northern and western slopes of the hill.

Like Little Solsbury, excavations at Liddington Castle in the 1970s found evidence of reoccupation and imported pottery from the time of the battle.[13] It is easy to see why the place was important. The hill-fort overlooks the conjunction of three important roads. One is the Ridgeway, 'Britain's oldest route way', which was in use throughout Roman and Saxon times and was particularly useful as a relatively dry road in winter. The others are the Roman roads from Winchester (which passes by the eastern end of the hill-fort) and from Silchester which converge at Wanborough, two miles to the north to form Ermine Street, which follows the line of the modern A419 to Cirencester. This was a crossroads of major strategic importance, and Liddington Castle was the key to it.

Liddington Hill, as an isolated and steep-sided down, is definitely a *mons*. But, as J N L Myres suggests, *Mons Badonicus* could also be translated as 'the hill-country of Badon' in which case it could apply to a larger area of downs around a place called Badon.[14] Sure enough, on the crest of the downs three miles south of Liddington Hill we find the village of Baydon. Did this Baydon exist in Dark Age times? It lies on the Roman road at its highest point – and is, in fact, the highest village in Wiltshire. But no Roman remains have been found, and no documentation of a settlement there exists before the Middle Ages. Moreover Baydon has no earthworks or defences. But the coincidence of two nearby villages called Badbury and Baydon suggested to Myres

One interpretation of the Battle of Badon has the Saxons approaching from the Ridgeway and attacking from the east. This may be the scene of the British charge that scattered their foes after a nine-day siege.

The Roman road near Baydon, Wiltshire's highest village.

that 'Badon' could well have been the name for the whole stretch of hilly country south of this part of the Ridgeway. As the most prominent as well as the best-defended of these hills, Liddington Hill is the obvious place for *Mons Badonicus*.

In his *Battlefields of England*, Alfred Burne plumps for a battlefield near Liddington Hill on the grounds of 'inherent military probability'. He assumes that the Saxons from the tribal kingdoms of Kent, Sussex and East Anglia had put aside their petty enmities and united for this decisive advance, perhaps led by the great King Aelle. Using the Roman roads they would naturally converge at this point ('What a meeting point! The roads seem almost fore-ordained for the purpose'[15]). A likely concentration point for the Britons, meanwhile, would be Cirencester, another natural communications centre for armies gathering from Wales and the Severn valley. Hence they would clash somewhere on the line of the Roman road. Following Geoffrey of Monmouth's account, Burne puts the Saxons inside the hill-fort, with the Britons, under Arthur, attacking them. Most authorities believe it was the other way round, but many agree that Liddington Castle is indeed a likely place for Gildas's *obsessio montis Badonicus*.

Summing up

The cases for Bath and Liddington Castle seem to me to be evenly matched. I incline towards Liddington Hill on the grounds that it would have been rash for the Saxons to have pushed so far west as Bath in 496, leaving the as yet unconquered hill-forts of Wiltshire threatening their communications. In the renewed war of conquest from the middle of the sixth century, Bath fell only after several decades of fighting, in which the crucial struggles were over the hill-forts at Sarum (Salisbury), *Beranburh* (Barbury Castle) and Dyrham. Barbury Castle, significantly, lies only a few miles west of Liddington Hill. It implies that Briton and Saxon were fighting over the same crucial ground in 556 as they had sixty years earlier. The key towns were taken only after the climactic battle at Dyrham had destroyed the British field army and its leaders. In 496 as in the 550s, the killing grounds seem to have been the triangle of land formed between the Roman towns of Silchester, Cirencester and Salisbury.

My other reason for preferring Liddington is a matter of the heart, not the head. I live nearby, and the long green hill with its clump of beech trees is the sight that greets me when I return home from a journey. The view from Liddington Castle towards the Thames Vale, the Ridgeway and the straight Roman road to Cirencester is full of history. When I climb the hill I experience what you might call the tingle-factor, which I did not experience on Little Solsbury Hill, impressive though it is. Michael Rayner, author of *English Battlefields*,[16] felt the same, and so did Alfred Burne ('What a place for a pageant!'). It feels right. Whether that makes the case for Liddington any stronger perhaps depends on whether the tingle-factor does it for you too.

Arthur's Twelve Victories

As we have seen, the main historical evidence for Arthur comes from the *Historia Brittonum,* compiled in the ninth century by the Welsh monk, Nennius. It consists of a list of twelve victories of Arthur which ends with the victory at Badon Hill already quoted where Arthur slays 960 men in a single charge. Arthur's twelve battles are named after obscurely named rivers, forests, mountains and cities, and it is generally agreed that the passage is based on a Welsh war-song. It reads as follows:

> Then Arthur fought against them [i.e. the Saxons] in those days with the kings of the Britons, but he himself was leader of battles (*dux bellorum*). The first battle was at the mouth of the river called *Glein*. The second, the third, the fourth and the fifth were on another river called the *Dubglas*, which is in the region of *Linnuis*. The sixth battle was on the river called *Bassas*. The seventh battle was in the Caledonian Forest, that is, the Battle (*Cat*) of *Calidon Coit*. The eighth battle was in *Guinnion* castle, and in it Arthur carried the image of the holy Mary, the everlasting Virgin, on his shoulders, and the heathen were put to flight on that day, and there was a great slaughter upon them, through the power of Jesus Christ and the power of the holy Virgin Mary, his mother. The ninth battle was in the City of the Legion. The tenth battle was on the bank of the river called *Tribruit*. The eleventh battle was on the hill (*mons*) called *Agned*. The twelfth battle was on Badon Hill and in it 960 men fell in one day from a single charge of Arthur's, and no one laid them low except he alone. And in all the battles he was the victor.[17]

Acres of print have been devoted to speculating where Arthur's battles were fought. Perhaps the first to play at this game was Geoffrey of Monmouth, more than 800 years ago, who found a site for the second battle on a River Douglas near Lincoln and another just north of that city for the seventh battle. Interestingly, some of the more plausible sites are in the north. The present-day Caledonian Forest, for example, is in the heart of the Scottish Highlands, although Welsh tradition apparently places it in the Borders. The City of the Legion could be Carlisle or Chester. Norma Lorre Goodrich, a linguist specializing in ancient French and Celtic, has suggested northern locations for all twelve, based on clues in Geoffrey of Monmouth's *Historia Regum Britanniae* and other sources. By her reckoning, the river called *Dubglas* is on the Isle of Man, the river called *Glein* in Northumberland near the Saxon fort of Yeavering Bell, and *Guinnion* castle at the Roman fort of Vinovia (Binchester) in County Durham. Even Mount Badon, which in my translation of the *Historia* is near Bath, is sited at *Kaer Alclyd*, which Goodrich translates as 'the fort of the Clyde', that is, Dumbarton Rock.[18]

It is possible that some at least of the twelve are garbled versions of battles mentioned by other sources. For example, the eleventh battle, 'the hill called *Agned*' has a second name, *Bregomion* or *Breguoin*, which has been identified with the Roman fort of Bremenium at High Rochester in the Cheviots. There was indeed a battle fought there in the late sixth century, but it involved not Arthur but Urien of Rheged, whose existence is in no doubt. Similarly there was a mighty battle between the Welsh and the Saxons at Chester, the Roman *Caer Legion*, but it took place in 613, more than a century after *Mons Badonicus*. The River Glen in Northumberland is an attractive location for Arthur's first battle, except that the Saxons did not penetrate that far until the mid-sixth century – an objection one could extend to nearly all northern locations. If one accepts the historical validity for a northern Arthur in the sixth or even seventh century, he could not have been the same man that defeated the Saxons at Mount Badon around 496. It seems much more likely that Nennius' list consists of a garbled memory of various battles to which Arthur's name was subsequently attached by the bards.

The Strife at *Camlann*

Arthur's last and most famous battle was fought at *Camlann*. Tennyson memorably described it as 'the last, dim, weird battle of the west'.[19] *Camlann* was the 'dolefulest battle', symbolized in John Boorman's film *Excalibur* by the sun sinking in orange glory to the majestic chords of Siegfried's Funeral March from Wagner's *Gotterdammerung*. It was the place where King Arthur received his death-wound at the hand of his illegitimate son Mordred, and where Sir Bedivere, after some understandable hesitation, surrendered Excalibur to the Lady of the Lake.[20]

The actual evidence for *Camlann* is a bare entry in the Welsh Annals for 537: 'The strife at *Camlann* in which Arthur and Medraut fell; and there was plague in Britain and Ireland' (*Gueith ca lann inq arthur et medraut corruer et mortililitas in brittania et in hibernia fuit*). The Latin wording is curious. The verb *corruo* means to break or fall down. In this context it certainly implies the death of Arthur and Medraut, but it also has a mythic undertone. Similarly the choice of *gueith*, usually translated as strife or struggle, instead of *bellum* or battle, is suggestive. The same word was used by the Irish annalist for what he called the 'strife of the heron-lake', better known as the Battle of *Nechtansmere*, in 685 (q.v.), fought between two kings described as brothers (*fratrueles*). Is it a hint that Arthur and Medraut were related? Were they on the same side? Or were they fighting one another? As usual, the annalist contrives to keep things nice and mysterious.

There is another passing reference to the battle in the Chronicle of *Ystrad Fflur*, recording the death in 550 of one Derfei Gadarn 'who fought at *Camlann*'.[21] Whatever could be said of Arthur, the battle seems real enough. But where was it? Without much else to go on, historians have fallen back on philology. A century ago the antiquarian O G S Crawford suggested that the name is derived from *Camboglanna*, meaning 'crooked glen' or 'crooked bank'.[22] The one known place with that name is the Roman fortress of Camboglanna on Hadrian's Wall. Crawford identified this with the fort at Birdoswald, where the River Irthing swings round in a loop to make a perfect 'crooked glen'. In their spoilsport way, archaeologists have since relocated Camboglanna further west to Castlesteads, where the river flows relatively straight. If this is *Camlann*, it is evidence for a northern Arthur, leading the fight against the enemies of the Britons on the Borders (and whoever else they might have been, they were probably not Saxons).

However there are alternative *Camlann*s. One is the River Allan in central Scotland, a winding river which has also been known as Camallan or 'crooked Allan'.[23] A battle was fought here between Aedan, king of Dalriata and the Picts of Miathi, an ancient kingdom around the Forth, in 582. The *Annals of Ulster* refer to it as the Battle of *Manann*. Adomnan, writing a century later, refers to what may be the same battle 'against the Miathi Picts'. Its interest to Arthur-seekers is in Adomnan's reference to one Artur, son of Aedan, killed in that battle. There is another reference to Artur in the Irish *Annal of Tigernach*, which records his death at the Battle of *Circinn* in 596. Was this our Arthur, and our Battle of *Camlann*? Were all these battles one and the same (despite the disparity of dates)? Promoters of this theory point out that there is 'only one battle fought between Arthur and the Britons on one side and the Picts on the other' and that this was it.[24] In this version, Arthur's rival, Medraut becomes a Pictish chieftain. A Pictish standing stone supposedly marks the site of the battle.

If so, Arthur was soon poached by Welsh poets, who remembered an Arthur in a variety of semi-legendary but decidedly Welsh settings.[25] There are even a couple of candidate *Camlann*s in Wales, a valley of Camlan and a River Gamlan. There are, for that matter, rival *Camlann*s in England. A medieval tradition followed by Malory placed 'the last dim weird battle' on the Plain near Salisbury, which Malory considered to be close to the seaside. Another candidate is the River Cam which flows past South Cadbury below the hill-fort traditionally associated with Arthur's legendary Camelot. The most celebrated of all sites for *Camlann* is the River Camel at Slaughterbridge near Camelford in Cornwall. According to Geoffrey of Monmouth, Arthur and his treacherous son Mordred came to blows at Camelford, 'may the name last forever'. Mordred had gathered a huge army of 60,000 men. Arthur's army was also very large 'although it was doomed'. This *Camlann* fits the tradition of a Cornish Arthur, born at Tintagel. The battle is celebrated there each year with bunting, a parade and a re-enactment on the battle's supposed anniversary of 6 August.[26]

To Britons living at the time, *Camlann* may have been less celebrated than another vain episode of civil strife fought in about 573, the Battle of *Arfderryd* or Arthuret. There are allusions to the battle in later bardic verses that suggest that the exploits of its heroes were being sung at the mead-bench long afterwards. The Welsh annal of *Ystrad Fflur* refers to it as 'the third futile battle of the island of Britain' (we are not told which the other two were, but, at least by implication, *Camlann* was probably one of them).[27] Arthuret was a dynastic battle between two branches of the

Arthur's Stone, a sixth-century inscribed stone in a dry streambed at Slaughterbridge, near Camelford. Nearby is a commercial 'Arthurian Centre' with tearooms and a gift shop. There are rival Arthur's Stones on Dorstone Hill, Hereford, and the Gower in south Wales, as well as Arthur's Seat in Edinburgh.

British royal family ruling in the Pennines and the Borders. Two brothers described as the 'sons of Eliffer', Peredur, king of York and a fellow king Dunaut from the Pennines, made war on one Gwendoleu, son of Ceido, who ruled in Carlisle. The armies clashed near the old Roman fort of Netherby on the Esk, ten miles north of Carlisle. The brothers won, and Gwendoleu was killed. However, losses on both sides were severe and the brothers were unable to take advantage of their victory. The winner in the dispute seems to have been another Briton, Urien of Rheged (for more on him, see Chapter 4), who became the new lord of Carlisle. Gwendoleu's bard, Merddin or Merlin, went mad with sorrow, and lived on as a hermit in the depths of 'Celidon Forest'. As for the sons of Eliffer, they fell in battle at an unknown place called *Caer Greu* in about 580 fighting the real enemy, the Angles of Bernicia led by a king called Adda. Peredur, like Urien, enjoyed posthumous fame as one of Arthur's knights. The Battle of Arthuret seems to have been a fine example of the futile civil wars of Briton against Briton which Gildas complained about so bitterly, and which became rooted in Arthurian myth.

Barring some sensational discovery, we shall probably never know which of the rival *Camlanns*, if any, is the 'real' one, just as we can never be sure which, if any, of the Arthurs on offer was the progenitor of the Round Table and the Quest for the Holy Grail. The historical basis of Arthur is so thin and slippery that enthusiasts have gone to great lengths to try to identify him on the basis that beneath all this legendary smoke there must have been a real fire. Norma Goodrich, for example, has suggested that Arthur was an adopted name of a leader of the northern Votadini tribe, and meant 'The Bear'.[28] The 2004 film, claiming to be 'the true story behind the legend', portrays Arthur as a rough, tough, half-Roman centurion. None of these theories seem to square very well with the 'traditional' Arthur, the hero-king who brought peace to Britain for a generation as portrayed in John Morris's controversial history, *The Age of Arthur*.

In fact, the early history of Britain would make more sense without Arthur. He confuses everything and sets up vain trails in all directions. None of the evidence is very convincing, and if he were not also the mighty king of medieval legend and the inspirer of great works of literature down the ages, the question would scarcely arise. The existence of a historical Arthur is surely irrelevant to the power of the Arthur myth. His legend has struck a chord in generation after generation, each of which has reinvented him after its own fashion. Whether he is 'the Once and Future King' resting in the cave with his knights, or the monarch of the Round Table dispensing Christian justice and charity in an idealized past, he has become an important part of the nation-spirit of Britain. He colours our perceptions of bygone days through stories and tales that bring history to life. King Edward III revitalized the legend of the Round Table to bolster his own conceptions of a knightly order. Tennyson created a Pre-Raphaelite version full of colour, fabrics and Wagnerian backdrops. Nearer our own time, T H White imagined a rustic, semi-comic Arthur who learned his kingly craft from watching how animals behave. That creation was in turn adapted by Walt Disney. The mythic Arthur has a resonance that seems to be perpetually beyond time and fashion.

Chapter 4
The Battles for Northern England

While the southern Britons were being driven ever further west by the steadily advancing Saxon tribes, the northern British kingdoms too were fighting for survival. In the sixth century, the land between the Forth and the Trent was divided into several Welsh-speaking Celtic lands. In south and west Yorkshire lay the ancient kingdom of Elmet, still remembered in local place-names. Further north was Rheged, which stretched from Carlisle in the west to North Yorkshire and Durham. Further north still was Gododdin, which sprawled over the Border hills from Stirling and Lothian to the Tyne. And in the far west, with its main fortified place at Dumbarton, lay the British lands of Strathclyde. The kingdoms took their names from their tribes or people. The people living in the area around Stirling, for example, were known as the Manaw Gododdin. There were probably other tribal kingdoms too, for example the lands centred on Edinburgh (*Din Eidyn*) and York. One Welsh poem speaks of no fewer than thirteen kings between the Trent and the Forth.

The ancient kingdom of Gododdin was unfathomably old. It evidently existed before the Romans came, for the Romans' name for the tribe occupying this area, the Votadini, is a Latinized form of Gododdin. The kingdom had once again become an independent entity by the sixth century, possibly with its 'capital' on the well-defended crags of Trapain Law in East Lothian. Later the settlement seems to have moved to *Din Eidyn*, that is, Edinburgh Rock, where Edinburgh Castle now stands. Gododdin, like the other northern British kingdoms excepting only Strathclyde, was destined to vanish before its history was written down. Bede, who was writing in northern England almost within living memory of the British tribal kingdoms, barely mentions Rheged, Elmet or Gododdin. Were it not for the epic poetry of *The Gododdin*, probably composed for singing at feasts towards the end of the sixth century, to which can be added the shorter poems of the bard Taliesin, they would have vanished almost without a trace. Thanks to the poetry, we at least know that the men of Gododdin and the other British kingdoms fought a long and bitter war against the incomers.

The most honoured of the Celtic war-lords of the north was Urien of Rheged, praised by Taliesin as the 'strong champion in battle' and 'the pillar of Britain'.[1] A place was later found for him in Arthurian legend. Judging from the poems, Urien indulged in the endemic civil strife of post-Roman Britain, fighting his neighbours on all sides, from the Clyde to Severn. There was even praise for a raid in which Urien and his men carried off 'eight-score cattle'. His greatest battle was at a place called *Argoed Llwyfain* in *c.*577 when he and his son Owain fought against 'a fourfold' army of Angles led by a man known only as *Fflamddwn* or 'Firebrand', and killed an important leader called Ulph. Though we know the fight was at a ford, and that it took place on a Saturday morning, its location is unknown. For a while after 577 the Britons seemed to have had the Angles on the run. 'This the English know', sang Taliesin, 'Death was theirs, burnt are their homes'.

The Anglian kingdom in the north-east had been founded by Ida, who was remembered as the founder of the royal house of Northumbria. Ida established a 'capital' at Bamburgh rock, which he fortified with a timber stockade and later with a rampart of stone and earth. Ida's successors fought against Urien and three other British kings. 'Sometimes', wrote Taliesin, 'the enemy, and sometimes our country-man were victorious'. Urien's greatest achievement was to broker a grand alliance with three British kings, Riderich of Strathclyde and two others of unknown provenance

Lindisfarne or *Metcand*, the site of a rare British victory against the Angles in the sixth century.

called Gaullauc and Morcant. Their joint forces pursued the Anglian leader, Hussa, and cornered him and his war-band on Holy Isle at Lindisfarne (*Metcaud*). Hussa was besieged for three days and nights. But just when they had him at their mercy, internal divisions resurfaced, and Urien was assassinated by one Lovan, a hireling of the 'envious' King Morcant.[2] The British resistance continued for a while under Uwain's son Owain, but when he too was killed, the path lay open for the Saxon Conquest of northern England.

The Battle at *Catraeth*

At some stage in this dimly remembered war of Briton and Angle the incident occurred that is celebrated in *The Gododdin*.[3] It became a classic tale of heroism and sacrifice, and the names of those that had taken part were sung in smoky halls in the north and west for centuries afterwards. The poem describes a battle before the walls of a place called *Catraeth*, which has been identified with the Yorkshire town of Catterick.[4] It takes the form of a lament for 300 warriors. It was composed by the bard Aneirin, who accompanied the 300 to war, and was apparently the only survivor. Two kings, Mynyddog Mwynfawr (meaning Mynddog the Rich) of *Din Eidyn* and Cynan of Gododdin, had raised a warrior army and feasted them for the space of a year; in the poem there are many backward glances to scenes of mead-drinking in torch-lit halls. Eventually the 300 set out and ride to death and glory at *Catraeth*, fighting against hopeless odds.

The Gododdin, therefore, commemorates a defeat. But in fighting to the death, true to the oaths they had taken, the '300 Gododdins' set a splendid example to their descendants at a time when the fortunes of Celtic Britain were fading rapidly. They became the very epitome of what a war-band should be: faithful, courageous and true. Cadwallon, the last great British leader, was one of those who were inspired by *The Gododdin*; his own elegy refers to 'the grief of *Catraeth*'.[5]

We can be sure that *Catraeth* was a real event for the poem was composed within living memory of the battle, when the names of the dead heroes were still familiar. Authorities differ as to exactly when the battle took place. Some assign it on historical grounds to the last decade of the sixth century, shortly after Urien's death. The reason for this is that a near-contemporary poem describes Urien as 'lord of *Catraeth*' (*Llyw Catraeth*). However, since *The Gododdin* poem fails to mention him, the implication is that Urien was killed sometime before the battle took place. One of the Welsh annals, compiled centuries later, assigns the year 593 to the battle. As usual, however, the date is problematical for a different annal records a 'great slaughter of *Catraeth*' in the year 570, when Urien was very much alive.[6] Some believe also that the language and spelling of *The Gododdin* implies a date for the battle between 550 and 570.

Catraeth is almost certainly the ancient British spelling of Catterick in North Yorkshire. The town occupies what was then a strategic position on the Roman road of Dere Street, the main north road, where it crosses the River Swale. Catterick became a first-century Roman camp, and later a thriving small Roman town,

Cataractonium, by the River Swale, just to the north of the present village. Though nothing of it remains above ground (and part of the site has been destroyed for ever by road widening), excavation has shown that ancient Catterick was a bustling place with smithies, leather workshops and even baths within the ramparts of the old camp.[7] It was still an important place during the Dark Ages. *Catraeth* was the site of Urien's *caer* or fortified hall, and a few decades later it had become an Anglian royal *vill*. According to Bede, King Edwin chose Catterick as the site of the most significant event in his reign: his baptism. A pagan Anglo–Saxon cemetery was excavated at Catterick close to the bypass and may well date from around the time of the battle.

By the late sixth century, Catterick had become a key town in the war of Britons and Angles. It lay close to both of the early Anglian kingdoms, Bernicia in the north, and Deira to the south, and was also on the boundary between the coastal lowlands and the Pennines. Clearly the place was a threat to the expansionist plans of the Angles. It seems that by the time of *The Gododdin* they had succeeded in capturing it – perhaps this event and not that of the poem was the 'great slaughter' mentioned in the annal. As Professor Alfred Smyth has pointed out, the 'control of Catterick secured the Yorkshire lowlands and consigned the Britons henceforth to an exclusively "highland" role'.[8] The battle celebrated in *The Gododdin* represented the last forlorn attempt to retake Catterick and so contain the Anglian advance.

Their names indicate that Mynyddog's warriors came from many lands. Nearly all were young men. The core of the army was Mynyddog's own bodyguard, his household men. But there were also fighting men from Gwynedd, and from south Wales, like Isag, Gwyddno's son. More famous fighters came from far and wide, including a man from 'green Uffin' and Pictish warriors from beyond the Forth, if that is meant by 'from beyond the Bannog'. The tribes spoke related Celtic languages remarkably similar to modern Welsh, and would probably have understood one another. The poem individualizes each warrior. Bradwen was so strong he could hold a wild wolf by the mane. Hyfaidd was a veteran killer who had notched up the corpses of 'five fifties' (or so he no doubt boasted). Blaen was a dandy: 'beautiful he burned in gold and purple, riding his well-fed horses'. Caradog was a Schwarzenegger-like character who was wont to 'rush into battle, a wild boar, an armed bull, killer of three kings, he fed wolves by hand'. They were led by three kings, Cynri, Cynon and Cynrhain. Mynyddog the Rich evidently preferred to remain in his hall on Edinburgh rock.

The 300 fighters were all freemen, even aristocrats. No fewer than eighty are named by the poet. Presumably men of such high status would have been attended by a retinue; at one point the poet refers to 'servants carrying their shields'. If so, the army of Gododdin would have numbered considerably more than 300. The weapons of choice for these mounted warriors were swords and broad-bladed spears, with a knife on their belt. They carried light round shields, some decorated with 'devices' or gold filigree-work. The Celtic warrior went to battle looking at his best. They wore helmets with cheek and neck-guards, and some had 'steel-blue' mail. The warrior Owain, for example, wore 'a coat of mail over his crimson undershirt', and is described elsewhere as wearing multi-coloured (painted?) armour. According to the poet, all the 300 wore golden torques around their necks: 'Men who went to *Catraeth/* famous in gold collars', he writes. Over their mail the warriors had slung colourful cloaks of red and purple. The lines at the start of *The Gododdin* convey how the young, high-born Celtic warrior would like to have been remembered:

> Man's nature, youth's years,
> is bravery in battle:
> swift thick-maned stallions
> under the thigh of bright youth,
> a broad light shield on
> a light fast horse's crupper,
> blue, shining swords and
> gold and ermine tapestry.

Did the Gododdin army fight on horseback? 'It was usual for powerful men to defend Gododdin in battle riding quick horses', says the poet, and in several places he describes how the 'great wave of our army' broke against the Saxon wall, splintering their shields with their 'dark-collared swords'. Thus Cydywal 'rushed to the attack . . . wherever he fought he left splinters of smashed shields. In battle he felled a forest of stiff spears; he shattered the front line of whole armies.'

But in other places Aneirin seems to be describing an infantry battle. 'They loved attacking with their wild shields and their spears', he writes, conjuring up a scene of close-ranked foot-soldiers advancing with spears levelled behind larger shields, one of which is described as being 'like a cattle-pen'. Elsewhere he describes a 'battle of spears', and there are passing references to the army forming up in ranks or squares and presenting a 'fortress' or a wall of shields. One hero attacked at the head of a battering-ram of shields, evidently a tried-and-tested tactic, 'crashing like thunder . . . he tore and ran through with spears above the place he rent with swords . . . Erthgi made armies howl.' The lord of Gododdin, the poet tells us, placed his best men in the front line. In defence they were a human palisade, but they were equally skilful in attack when swords were used to smash through the enemy line of shields.

In the poem the 'Saxons' appear only as an amorphous mass ('England's jumbled host'), armed mainly with shields and spears. They prevailed only because of their overwhelming numbers: 100,000 claims the poet at one point; another text of the poem says 54,000 (possibly a poetic construction from 'nine score around each one'). Evidently the Britons were outnumbered. Who led the Saxons? If the battle was fought around 590–600, the leader is likely to have been Aethelfrith of Bernicia (592–617), of whom more later. If earlier, it could have been Aethelfrith's father, Aethelric, or Adda 'Thick-knee', the Bernician leader who took York *c*.580, or even Theodoric, Urien's arch-enemy. To assemble a large enough force to defend Catterick and beat off the elite horsemen of Gododdin, the various tribes must have been united under some charismatic figure. King Aethelfrith, whose vigorous smiting of his neighbours Bede compared with King Saul, would have fitted the bill.

The Battle of *Catraeth* seems to have begun at dawn, perhaps in an attempt to take the town by surprise. Catterick was well-defended behind earth walls with the River Swale to the north. Dere Street still crosses the river by an ancient bridge which must have had a Roman predecessor since the river is unfordable. Assuming the 'Gododdins' had taken the only direct road from the north they would have encountered fierce resistance at the bridge, yet the poem mentions neither a river nor a walled settlement. Perhaps instead the battle took place north of the river on open land suitable for cavalry. Morris suggested a location at the pre-Roman earth-works of Stanwick in the angle of an ancient road fork at Scots Corner[9] – though, if so, it would suggest that the men who 'went to Catraeth' never actually got there, for Scots Corner lies ten miles further north. Or they might have used their knowledge of the Pennine hill-country to bypass the town and attack from the moors to the west, where the army garrison of Catterick lies today. Given the poem's lack of detail one could speculate endlessly about where the battlefield might have been. All we know is that the result was complete annihilation. We are led to believe that they all fought to the death, in some cases slaying seven or nine times their number before being slain in turn amid images of iron, blood and wooden splinters. With their blood, says Aneirin, they bitterly repaid the 'ensnaring mead' they had drunk:

> Though they were slain, they slew,
> none to his home returned . . .
> Short their lives,
> long the grief
> among their kin . . .
> They were slain, they never grew grey . . .
> From the army of Mynyddog, grief abounded,
> Of the three hundred, only one returned.

The enemy dead were normally left as food for crows, but, as the bodies of some warriors were returned to their homelands to be buried under 'green mounds', perhaps they were recovered by retainers under a flag of truce. The defeat was the beginning of the end for the Gododdin. *Din Eidyn* fell to the English in 638. But the final days of Gododdin echoed not to blood and thunder but wedding bells. Around 640, Urien's great-grand-daughter married Aethelfrith's son Oswy. The old kingdom of the Gododdin was carved up between Northumbrian England, British Strathclyde, the Picts of Fortriu and the Scots of Dal Riata. Aneirin had sung its swan-song.

The Battle of *Degsastan*

Aethelfrith was the first of the great kings of northern England. He was the son of Aethelric, killed in battle by the Britons of Rheged, and father of seven warrior sons, including the mighty kings Oswald and Oswy. Aethelfrith was also one of the last of the pagan English kings. He was as ruthless with priests as he was with enemy warriors. Bede describes him as a powerful and ambitious man and one who 'ravaged the Britons with more cruelty than all other English leaders'.[10] Evidently he was also cunning: Nennius refers to him as 'Aethelfrith the Artful'. During his reign of twenty-five years, Aethelfrith over-ran much of the north from the Borders to Chester and the Trent, exterminating or enslaving the inhabitants and opening the area to English settlement. It is largely thanks to him that the villages of Lancashire and Cumbria from the Solway to the Mersey have English, not Welsh names. Bede applied to Aethelfrith the chilling words of blessing that the biblical patriarch Jacob addressed to his youngest son, Benjamin: 'Benjamin shall ravin as a wolf; in the morning he shall devour the prey, and at night he shall divide the spoil'.

The advance of the English under Aethelfrith alarmed Aedan, king of the Scots of Dal Riata. Aedan mac Gabhrain was a descendant of Irish warrior-settlers who had established a kingdom in the west in what is now Argyll. He was a Christian of the Celtic Church and a friend of St Columba, the famous Irish saint and founder of the monastic settlement on Iona. He was on good terms with the neighbouring Britons of Strathclyde and, like them, must have been grieved by the debacle at *Catraeth*. Aedan had sufficient force of character and sense of direction to make him the natural leader in the fight against the English. To defeat Aethelfrith he raised in the year 603 a coalition army, uniting his own following from Dal Riata with men from what was left of the British kingdoms and Irishmen from Tara in modern Ulster.

This united Celtic army, all sources agree, was of exceptional size. We are given some impression of the size of the Dal Riatan levy in a contemporary document which shows that Aedan's homeland could levy 1,200 fighting men at any one time.[11] Adomnan's *Life of Columba* mentions a battle in which the Dal Riatan Scots suffered 303 casualties, amounting to perhaps a third of their number. However among Aedan's allies was the brother of the high-king of Ireland, Mael Umai (Maeluma), Baetan's son, who led a substantial army of his own. Hence Aedan's army might have numbered upwards of 2,000 men, which made it an exceptionally powerful force for the time.

The Anglian or English host was led by Aethelfrith's brother, Theodbald, and by Hering, son of the Hussa besieged at Lindisfarne by Urien. Both men were accompanied by their hearth-troops, and evidently fought in separate divisions. With these elite troops we might imagine some less well-armed levies, but it is likely that the English army was smaller than Aedan's. The hearth-troops were experienced in war, and rode to battle, though most of the fighting was probably on foot. Was Aethelfrith himself present? Both Bede and the Anglo-Saxon Chronicle imply that he was, but the latter also states that 'Hering, son of Hussa, led the army thither'. Perhaps Hering was a battle commander, a *dux bellorum*, much as the original non-royal Arthur was said to be.

The two armies clashed and fought at a place called *Degsastan* (or *Daegsan Stane*), 'that is, "Degsa's Stone"'. Bede described it as a famous battle, and one of the largest in the history of England up to that point. Its location is not known for certain, but

Degsastan has been plausibly identified with Dawston Rigg at the head of Lidderdale in the Scottish borders. It has been argued that the Old English *Degsastan* would have become Daystone, not Dawston, but such similar-sounding words are easily corrupted. The battle is said to have taken place in the narrow valley where the Dawston Burn joins Liddel Water at Saughtree. There are nearby place-names like 'Bloody Bush' and Cat Cairn (*Cat* is early Welsh for 'battle'), which suggest a persistent memory of ancient strife.[12]

Of the battle itself, we know only that it was very bloody and that the English won after a hard-fought struggle. Aedan's army was all but annihilated, and the Dal Riatan king fled the field with a small following. One source claims that the Irish leader Mael Umai was killed, but probably in error, since in another annal he reappears in Ireland some years later.[13] It is possible that Aedan's son Domingart was slain at *Degsastan*, since Adomnan's *Life of Columba* states that he was killed 'in a rout in battle with the Saxons'. The English losses were also heavy. Theodbald and his household men were cut off and slain to a man, suggesting that his division fought separately from Hering's. *Degsastan* was a decisive victory. 'From that day until the present [*c*.730)', wrote Bede, 'no king of the Scots in Britain has dared to do battle with the English'.

In the magazine *Miniature Wargames*,[14] Guy Halsall had a heroic try at reconstructing the Battle of *Degsastan*. In his interpretation the English occupied a strong defensive position on rising ground along the south side of the Dawston Burn, with a reserve on the flattish hill-top above. Aedan's army, consisting of units of British, Irish, Scottish and Pictish warriors fighting on foot attacked across the stream. Aedan's army is guesstimated at 5,100 to Hering's 3,200, but the game assumes that the English are better motivated and better armed. When it is played out in this way, the battle is always close-fought and either side can win. The last time Halsall played it, attempted outflanking movements by the Celtic allies were defeated while in the centre the English smashed through the weakened line giving the victory to Aethelfrith. It might have happened like that, and there again of course it might not! Dark Age alliance-armies have a poor record against presumably smaller but more tight-knit, better-led forces. A similarly 'immense' but disunited northern alliance came to grief at *Brunanburh*, 300 years later, as did the unlikely Welsh–Saxon alliance at *Winwaed* (see below), defeated by a smaller but tighter force led by Oswy, Aethelfrith's son.

Had Aedan won, the history of northern England might well have taken a different course. The English would have been contained in the lowlands and Britain could have developed as an island of roughly equal halves with Anglo-Saxon lowlands and broadly Celtic uplands. *Degsastan* was a milepost in the development of Saxon England, and paved the way for Northumbrian power over the next century.

Massacre at Chester

Despite his victory at *Degsastan*, Aethelfrith's ambitions lay in the south. He had effectively subjugated the Anglian kingdom of Deira (broadly modern Yorkshire) and his conquests brought him to the Humber and the Trent. Between 613 and 616

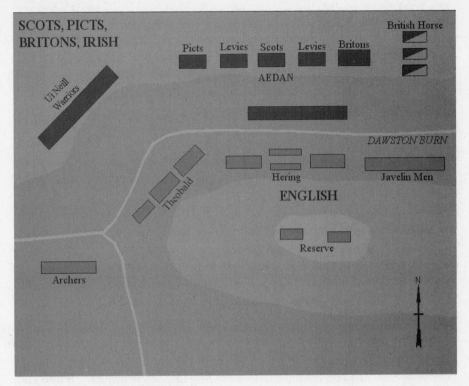

Degastan as imagined by Guy Halsall

he led an army to Chester, then known as *Carlegion*, the great Roman 'city of the legions', a still-mighty city behind its high walls on the north bank of the Dee. Chester was a British/Welsh city, whose defence was in the hands of one Solomon (Selyf) ap Cynan, son of the king of Powys (a Welsh kingdom between the Dee and the upper Severn). There are cryptic hints in early Welsh poetry that the whole power of north Wales had come to the aid of Chester.[15] Bede's reference to the conduct of the 'faithless Britons' could suggest that they had paid tribute to Aethelfrith and generally appeased him, but subsequently repudiated him. More likely Bede was referring to the Celtic Church's rejection of Roman authority (see below). To him the Celts were heretics.

However it came about, the Battle of Chester is remembered mainly for the massacre of the British priests that took place there; the Welsh annalist recalled it as 'the massacre of the saints'.[16] Evidently the British forces marched out of the city to confront Aethelfrith in the fields outside the city walls. Before battle was joined, Aethelfrith noticed a large number of monks gathered there to pray for a British victory under a military guard led by one Brocmail. The monks were from the monastery of Bangor-on-Dee near Wrexham, and they had fasted for three days in preparation. According to Bede, the 'prayer-army' of monks was divided into seven groups, each under its own head, 'and none of them contained less than three hundred monks'.[17] More plausibly, the Anglo-Saxon Chronicle says there were 200 monks, although that is still rather a lot for a single monastery. Possibly among them was Iago ap Beli, a member of the royal house of Gwynedd, who had turned monk, as royal children and even retired kings often did in the seventh century.

Told who they were, the pagan Aethelfrith retorted that 'If they are crying to their God against us, they are fighting even if they do not bear arms'. He thereupon directed his first onslaught against the monks, who were promptly deserted by Brocmail and his men. The monks were slaughtered to a man. This, Bede tells us with uncharacteristic spite, was the fulfilment of St Augustine's prophecy that 'if the Welsh will not have peace with us (i.e. the Roman church), they shall perish at the hands of the Saxons'.

There are few other details about the battle, and the battlefield probably lies under the northern suburbs of the modern city. All we know is that Aethelfrith 'destroyed the rest of the accursed army, not without heavy losses to his own forces'.[18] As a result, Chester became an English city, and Cheshire an English county. It seems to have represented the culminating point of Aethelfrith's campaign of conquest to settle the north-west England with warrior-farmers.

Good King Edwin

Just as Aethelfrith's earlier successes alarmed his northern neighbours, so his excursions into the English Midlands brought him into conflict with the Saxon king of East Anglia, Raedwald. Scarcely noticed in the Anglo-Saxon Chronicle, Raedwald was immortalized in death by the riches of his probable burial chamber at Sutton Hoo. Thanks to the Sutton Hoo treasures we can picture him in his elaborate, embellished helmet, his pattern-welded sword worn on a decorated belt with its huge, solid-gold belt-buckle, and his great cloak with its gorgeous clasps worn over a tunic of mail. He was a man of the new age, half-Christian, half-pagan, sanctified in his kingship but adhering to the old ways and surrounded by the trappings of wealth and prestige.

The immediate cause of conflict between the two English kings was the presence at Raedwald's court of Edwin (Eadwine), heir to the kingdom of Deira. Aethelfrith at first tried to bribe his fellow king to have Edwin assassinated. When that failed, he demanded that Edwin be handed over. Instead, Raedwald decided it would serve his interests better if he reinstated Edwin in his kingdom and got rid of the troublesome Aethelfrith at the same time. Secretly and speedily, Raedwald used his wide-ranging power as a *bretwalda* to gather together a large army from his extensive *imperium* in southern and eastern England. With Edwin in tow, he set out towards York in the summer or early autumn of 616.

He was in luck. Aethelfrith was left with insufficient time to summon his full strength. The Bernician king unwisely gave battle on the east bank of the River Idle, the border between the English kingdoms of Mercia and Deira. Heavily outnumbered, Aethelfrith went down fighting – but not before Raedwald's son Raegenhere had also been killed. The Battle of the River Idle reinstated Edwin on the Deiran throne and drove Aethelfrith's own brood of seven sons into exile. The battle probably took place where the Roman road from Lincoln to Doncaster forded the river at the Yorkshire village of Bawtry. Excavations in 1983 determined the exact site of the crossing a few hundred yards north of the present road bridge. The Roman road, which, given its importance, had probably been kept in good repair as far as possible, crossed the river floodplain on a causeway of oak timber piles on a layer of gravel. We can therefore imagine the battle taking place around the ford, with Raedwald's men attempting to force the crossing and break through Aethelfrith's lines on the far side.

According to Bede, Edwin became the most powerful king England had yet seen, with an ill-defined *imperium* or lordship stretching over a confederation of English kingdoms from Kent to the Scottish borders, and even at one point into Wales. His power rested on personal alliances but also, of course, on force. He consolidated English gains in the north by expelling the last British king of Elmet, made war on the Welsh in Gwynedd and Anglesey, and even took possession of the Isle of Man. But as well as making war, Edwin also upheld the peace. A century later, said Bede, the proverb still ran that in the days of good King Edwin a woman could carry her new-born babe across Britain from end to end without fear, unlikely as it may seem. On his horseback perambulations across Britain surrounded by his thegns, Edwin was preceded by a standard similar to those carried at the head of Roman legions and featuring a globe mounted on a spear.[19] As a baptized Christian, Edwin received the approval of clerical writers like Bede. Even so, he comes across not only as the first king of the English but as the first all-round 'Mr Anglo-Saxon nice guy'!

Of course some parts of Britain did not see Edwin in that light at all. To the Welsh, for example, he was 'Edwin the Deceiver'. The bitterest of his enemies was Cadwallon ap Cadfan of Gwynedd, whom Edwin had at one point driven from his kingdom to cower on the tiny island of Priestholm (Puffin Island) off the east coast of Anglesey. Cadwallon demonstrated the latent power that still remained in the British kingdoms by moving across the Pennines to strike at the English settlements while Edwin was preoccupied in Gwynedd.

In 632, in a mighty alliance with Penda, the ambitious new king of Mercia, Cadwallon's army marched on York, very probably along the same route that Raedwald had used seventeen years before. This time it was Edwin who was caught off guard. On 12 October, the two armies clashed at the Battle of *Haethfelth*, whose name in modern English is Hatfield. In the Welsh annals, where the battle is called Meigen (*Gueith Meicen*), its date is moved backwards rather improbably to the Kalends of January, that is, to New Year's Day.

Saxon *Haethfelth* was both a settlement and also the name given to a sub-province of low-lying land between the Don and the Humber. It was a desolate no-man's-land, the boundary between what Bede called 'the southern and northern English'. Like Aethelfrith before him, Edwin had probably rushed to these borderlands to defend his homeland with whatever forces he could muster. It was not enough to prevent an annihilating defeat. We can imagine Cadwallon, as his bard remembered him, 'riding in the front rank enclosed in gleaming iron'.[20] The battle was hard fought but at the end of it Edwin and his son Osfrith (the Welsh annals say two sons) both lay dead. Edwin's hearth-troops, who had shared his exile, also shared his fate, and his entire army was scattered and destroyed. Much later accounts of the battle imagined Edwin fighting over the corpse of his son with his retainers lying dead around him until at dusk he too was cut down, the westering sky turning blood-red behind him.[21] Also killed in the battle was Penda's brother, Eobba. Edwin's wife and family escaped by sea to Kent, with the aid of his bishop, Paulinus. The dead Edwin's head was cut off and carried north in triumph to York.

Where was the battle fought? *Haethfelth* covered a large area south of the upper Humber, of which the modern Hatfield Chase is but a part. Much of it is still heath and bog, though notoriously reduced to a sterile blackboard of bare peat by modern peat-cutting machines. The exact site of battle is uncertain, but it may have taken place on or near the Roman road, perhaps just east of Doncaster where the Roman road crosses the River Thorne, in an area now covered by suburbs and the M18 motorway. Local tradition, recorded in the diary of the seventeenth-century Hatfield antiquary, Abraham de la Prynne, placed it at The Lings near Hatfield, where a supposed burial mound called the Slay-Pits stood at the confluence of Lings Lane and the A18.

However it is more likely that Bede's *Haethfelth* lay well to the south near the Nottinghamshire village of Edwinstowe on the edge of Sherwood Forest. Edwinstowe is an ancient settlement recorded in the Domesday Book as *Edenstou*, and seems to

The bleak 'wastes' of Thorne Moor and Hatfield Chase may be the scene of Edwin's defeat at the hands of Penda and Cadwallon. There is a nearby panel about the battle.

be connected with King Edwin. Edwinstowe has a fine church, but there was also a chapel at nearby Cuckney, now incorporated into Cuckney church, which has stood there since at least the thirteenth century, when a hermit was given a stipend to live and pray there by King John himself.[22] Nearby farms called Hatfield Grange and High Hatfield provide another link with Bede's *Haethfelth*. Furthermore there is a defensible position for Edwin's army at Cuckney Hill which is crossed by Leeming Lane, the old Mansfield–Doncaster road. Finally, the chance discovery of some 200 adult skeletons at Cuckney Church in 1950 suggests some catastrophic event in the distant past, such as a battle. The convergence of possibilities makes Cuckney the most likely site of Edwin's last stand.[23] Could this be the expected battlefield church, where the headless body of the king was hidden from his enemies after the battle?

Old print of Edwinstowe church in Sherwood Forest, associated with the martyred King Edwin.

The Heavenly Field

After *Haethfelth*, Cadwallon and Penda devastated the defenceless lands of Edwin without mercy. One of the Irish annals mentions the 'kindling of fires in the land of Elmet' (south Yorkshire) and adds that York itself was set on fire. Archaeological excavation found that the Roman walls of York were rebuilt later in the century, suggesting that they were either in disrepair or had been demolished by Cadwallon. Spadework has shown that Edwin's royal hall at Yeavering was also burned. 'A terrible slaughter took place among the Northumbrian church and nation', wrote Bede, 'more horrible because it was carried out by two commanders, one of whom (Penda) was a pagan and the other (Cadwallon) a barbarian more savage than any pagan.' The latter was 'set upon exterminating the entire English race in Britain, and spared neither women nor innocent children'. The Welsh, for their part, praised Cadwallon as a great hero, 'a furious fiery stag' who maintained the honour of the Welsh nation and was generous to those who served him.

This was clearly a vendetta war, carried out in revenge for the ravaging of Chester and north Wales, and in the name of the ruined Celtic nations of northern England. Bede's condemnation of Cadwallon is the more severe because, as a member of the Celtic Church, the latter saw the Roman Church of Edwin and Paulinus as an alien institution, and persecuted it accordingly. The dead Aethelfrith's seven sons were invited to return from their places of exile. However they soon fell foul of Cadwallon, who had no reason to love the sons of the tyrant of Chester. One, Osric, he slew in battle during the summer of 633, and for good measure he had another, Eanfrith, assassinated. Later the names of these two kings were expunged from the record: perhaps to appease Penda, they had renounced the true faith, a crime considered worse than any war or massacre. For a year, Cadwallon, 'the last of the Britons' ruled the north, but 'not as a king but as a savage tyrant'.[24].

The eventual deliverer of the northern English was Oswald, another of the sons of Aethelfrith, who had converted to Christianity and spent several austere years as a monk on Iona. Oswald succeeded his two older brothers as king of Bernicia. In the forthcoming battle he was probably aided by his associate and possible kinsman,

Heavenfield: the Church of St Oswald stands amid trees, probably on the site of the 'Heavenly Field'. A wooden cross has been erected by the roadside to commemorate Oswald's victory over Cadwallon. There is a nearby panel about the battle.

Domnall Brecc of Dal Riata, with whom Oswald had spent part of his long exile. Michelle Zeigler has suggested that he was also accompanied by Irish war-bands, as well as the sons of Aethelfrith's hearth-troops, who had, as usual, shared their lord's exile.[25] Cadwallon, who was evidently set on exterminating the entire Bernician royal line, moved north with an 'irresistible' force. The two clashed at a place called *Hefenfelth* or Heavenfield. This was an ancient place-name even at the time of the battle, known by the Romans as *Caelestis campus*, that is, 'the heavenly field'. It lay, says Bede, 'on the northern side of the wall which the Romans built from sea to sea', that is, of course, Hadrian's Wall. Evidently a well-known pagan holy site, it was to play a resonant part in this most supernatural of battles.

Assuming that Oswald had returned to the traditional seat of Bernician kings at Bamburgh, it is likely that he had chosen the North Tyne valley around Hexham to muster men from Bernicia. Three north–south roads converge at Hexham, which is also close to the Roman road that ran along the south side of the wall from Carlisle to Jarrow (the site of Bede's monastery). Assuming that Cadwallon mustered his force at York, he probably used the helpfully straight Roman road of Dere Street to march north to deal with the emergency. He could reach Hexham from York in perhaps a dozen marches. Oswald was waiting for him and had time to choose his battlefield. It may be that superstition as much as military necessity governed the choice. Finding themselves close to the Heavenly Field, Oswald decided to take advantage of any latent powers it might retain by hastily making and erecting a tall wooden cross. And it was the king himself rather than, as one might expect, a priest, who took charge of the ceremony, as Bede relates:

> When the hole was dug in which it was to stand, the king seized the cross himself with the ardour of his faith, placed it in the hole, and held it upright with both hands until the soldiers had heaped up the earth and fixed it in position. Thereupon he raised his voice and called out to the whole army, 'Let us kneel together and pray to the almighty, ever-living and true God to defend us in His mercy from the proud and fierce enemy; for He knows we are fighting a just cause for the preservation of our whole race'.[26]

This was the story Bede and his contemporaries knew, three generations on. The battle had by then acquired strong providential overtones, but there is no reason to doubt the essential truth of the story. Oswald was appealing to both the Christians and the pagan traditionalists in his ranks by invoking the unseen powers by prayer. A wooden cross could be adapted without too much difficulty as a totemic world-tree or sacred pillar. Christianity was still new to these conservative tribes, and the English were used to seeing their king lead religious rituals. Oswald's cross-making might have been an act of piety, but it was also an effective unifying gesture.

Another Oswald legend, from Adomnan's *Life of Columba*, has the English king lying in his tent on the eve of the battle when the great Irish saint appeared before him in heavenly guise, a towering figure touching the clouds and covering the English camp with his shimmering robe. The spirit of Columba gave Oswald the same assurance that God had given Joshua: 'Be strong and unafraid, for your foes shall be put to flight and your enemy delivered into your hands.'[27] It has been suggested that the figure of Columba could just as easily have seemed to be Woden, the chief of the Germanic gods who granted victory and feasted slain warriors in Valhalla. Certainly it would be surprising if a newly converted English king, though certainly zealous in his faith, did not retain the world-view of his father and ancestors.

After all these signs and portents, the battle itself reads as an anticlimax. Oswald's army 'advanced against the enemy at the first light of dawn (and) won the victory that their faith deserved'.[28] We are led to assume that the result was preordained and that Oswald's religious fervour won the battle. That being so, the actual tactical details were neither here nor there. Perhaps Cadwallon made some blunder, or his hearth-men, weary from campaigning so far from home, were not on their best form. Bede tells us that Cadwallon was slain at a place called *Denisesburn* which he translates as Denis's Brook. *Denisesburn* has been identified with Rowley Burn, a stream that flows into the valley of Devil's Water between Hexham and Corbridge, several miles south of the wall. If so, the great Welsh king was presumably slain during a long pursuit that followed the battle.

An extra crumb of evidence has come from chance finds, in the fields by the B6318 south of the wall, of fragments of human bones and weaponry. Putting these clues together, it would seem that *Hefenfelth* was a running battle, starting somewhere near the Roman wall and ending up several miles to the south of it. If Bede is right

Hadrian's Wall, near Housesteads. Heavenfield in 634 is the only known battle to have been fought there.

Hadrian's Wall, Northumberland   Photo © Risto Hurmalainen

(and, as a wall-dweller himself, he was in a good position to know), Oswald's camp was on one side of the wall and Cadwallon's on the other. Who crossed the wall? The implication of Bede's dawn attack is that Oswald did, and that after the first clash there was a running battle with Cadwallon's force retreating southwards pursued by the enemy. The actual battle was fought south of the Heavenly Field, possibly nearer to Hexham. The Welsh annals call this battle *Cantscaul*, a name derived from the Old English name for Hexham and meaning 'enclosure of the young warrior'.[29] Perhaps the battlefield therefore lies somewhere between Hexham and the Rowley Burn.

Hefenfelth became a place of pilgrimage for the brothers of the church at Hexham. On the anniversary of Oswald's death 'they kept vigil for the welfare of his soul, recited the psalter and offered the Holy Sacrifice [i.e. said Mass] for him at dawn'. Within Bede's own lifetime, they founded a church at the place where Oswald had raised the cross. Nothing remains of the Saxon church, but it probably occupied the same space as the present Church of St Oswald's on its hill-top half-hidden in a clump of trees. A wooden cross was erected by the B6318 roadside nearby in the 1930s, and this is now accompanied by an information board about the battle. Unfortunately, nothing remains of Hadrian's Wall at this point; perhaps they plundered its stones to build the church and its settlement.

Oswald's Tree

King Oswald inherited Edwin's 'wide rule' over England and was known in his lifetime as *rex Saxonum*, king of all the Saxons. Bede goes further and claims him to be lord of all the nations and provinces of Britain, whether Anglo-Saxon, Pictish, British, Welsh or Irish. Oswald has always enjoyed a good press as the king who converted the heathen and invited his associate, Aidan, to found the monastery on Lindisfarne. Much of his power rested on personal ties of kinship and obligation between rulers. Bede presents Oswald as a kindly and generous king, a man beloved of God. Yet it is unlikely that a seventh-century 'wide ruler' could survive long on piety alone. Oswald, like his immediate predecessors, had his enemies and his wars. The Welsh remembered him as a warrior: *Lamnguin*, 'he of the bright blade'. King Oswald's personal piety and mildness of manner need not be doubted, but his saintly reputation rests on his encouragement of church missionaries and, above all, on the circumstances of his end. Like his father Aethelfrith and brother Osric, Oswald died violently in battle.

We know at least the date of the Battle of *Maserfelth*: 5 August 642. It was remembered because it became the feast-day of St Oswald in the Christian calendar. The name *Maserfelth* or Maser-field is derived from the Welsh *Maes Hir*, which, funnily enough, means Field-field. The Irish knew it as *Maes Cogwy* or *Bellum Cocboy*. Contemporary sources give no clue as to where *Maserfelth* was, but the twelfth-century *Life of St Oswald* tells us it was at Oswestry (*Osewaldstreu*) in Shropshire, where the Maser name is preserved in two villages, Maesbury and Maesbrook. Oswestry means 'Oswald's Tree', and the Welsh name, *Croesoswald* means essentially the same thing, 'Oswald's Cross'; as with Oswald's famous cross at

Heavenfield, the words 'cross' and 'tree' are interchangeable. They commemorate Oswald's martyrdom at *Maserfelth*, but it is also likely that the king repeated his cross-erecting ceremony before this new battle. It expressed the same message: 'by this sign we conquer'. But Oswald, we also learn, fought under a more conventional banner of purple and gold.[30]

The location of Oswestry indicates that Oswald was killed while on campaign against the Welsh of Powys. His adversary at *Maserfelth* was a fellow Saxon, King Penda of Mercia. Penda was a heathen, the last important Saxon king to cling to his pagan roots. Hence Oswald's defeat at Penda's hands made him Northumbria's first Christian martyr. It is doubtful in fact whether religion had much to do with the conflict. The most likely background to *Maserfelth* is that Penda had renewed his old alliance with the Welsh princes, especially Cadwallon's successor, Cadfael ap Cynfedw, with whom, according to documents preserved in Nennius's *Historia Brittonum*, he enjoyed amicable relations. Oswald, in leading an expedition into Powys, had provoked a war on two fronts, with Cadfael in the west and Penda in the east. His expeditionary army may not have been large. At all events, Oswald was cornered into giving battle. The fighting was fierce, but by the end Oswald lay dead and his company with him. The king's last words were reportedly: 'God have mercy on their souls'.

Oswald's body was mutilated. His severed head, hands and forearms were displayed on stakes. The heads of defeated Dark Age kings were commonly parted from their bodies in ceremonies that must have been full of symbolism, but the treatment of Oswald's body was particularly savage. The gruesome display may have been done in mockery of the cross erected by the king. The head and arms remained on display on 'Oswald's Tree' all winter until the following year when Oswald's younger brother and successor, Oswiu or Oswy 'came to the place with his army and removed them'. The bones, which ended up at Bardney in Lincolnshire, were enshrined as relics and reportedly worked miracles.

The battlefield was a place of pilgrimage in Bede's day. Oswald's spirit had the intercessionary power 'to heal sick men and beasts'. In a remarkable example of an early souvenir trade, soil was from the place where the king fell was bartered as a relic with such success that 'a pit was left in which a man could stand'.[31] Evidently the place was marked by a monument, and later a church was built there. This might have been at Maesbury south of Oswestry. More probably the site was on or near the present Norman church in Oswestry. Local tradition has it that a raven picked up and then dropped, one of Oswald's decaying arms. The place where it fell is marked by a natural spring near the school grounds. Local lore says the battle was fought over what are now the school playing fields. A mile north of the town is an Iron Age hill-fort, but there is no record or tradition of any connection with the battle.

An alternative site for the battle lies forty miles further north in the Makerfield district of Lancashire. The resemblance of the ancient name Makerfield, meaning 'field by the wall', with Bede's *Maserfelth* was reinforced by the excavation of a burial mound in the neighbouring village of Croft. A mass of Christian burials, numbering up to 3,000, dating from *c*.600, suggested some catastrophic event, such as a battle. Winwick Church, only a mile away, has long been associated with King Oswald, and the remains of a carved figure and a stone cross found there have been dated to the eighth century. Unfortunately the graves were destroyed during the construction of the M6 motorway. Their bones had already dissolved in the acidic soil.

Showdown at *Winwaed*

The year 642 was a memorable one. No fewer than five kings died during its course, among them Cynegils, the first Christian king of Wessex, and Oswald's associate, Domnall Brecc, killed at the Battle of Strathcarron. Oswald's fall left Penda as *rex Saxonum*, the over-king of all the Saxons in England. The thirty-year-old Oswy, last of the sons of Aethelfrith, found himself beleaguered. Bede describes Oswy as 'a man of handsome appearance and lofty stature, pleasant in speech and courteous in manner'.[32] He had the most of the necessary attributes for a seventh-century *bretwalda*, with 'regal qualities of mind and body' wedded to cunning and a ruthless will.

Penda regarded Oswy as his personal enemy. He twice invaded Bernicia and subjected it to 'savage and intolerable attacks', but Oswy was able to evade him and escape northwards. In 654, Penda, determined to make an end of the slippery northern king once and for all, made an alliance with Aethelhere, brother to the king of East Anglia, and with several Welsh princes, including Cadfael (or Catamail) of Gwynedd. He even co-opted Oswald's son Aethelwald 'to act as a guide to Penda's army against his own kin and country' (though he refused to take part in the actual fighting). Penda's large army was said by Bede to be organized into 'thirty battle-hardened legions under famous commanders (*duces regii*)'.[33] Whether by *legiones* he meant legions in the Roman sense, organized into separate ranks of veterans and spear-carriers (*hastati*), or whether they were retinues gathered around the banner of their lord is uncertain. The figure of thirty is in any case suspect since it chimes rather too neatly with Bede's other remark that Penda's host outnumbered Oswy's by an unlikely thirty to one. Clearly, though, this was a large army, perhaps one of unprecedented size. Its potential to plunder the north to the bone was awesome. Whether it would hold together in a hard fight was another matter.

Outnumbered, Oswy tried to buy off the invaders. Necessity compelled him to offer to Penda 'an incalculable quantity of regalia and presents as the price of peace'. The *Historia Brittonum* wryly notes that Oswy was in fact offering the Welsh treasures that had been stolen from them in the first place! It adds that some payment was in fact made. Oswy, besieged in a place called *Iudeu*, surrendered all the valuables of that place to Penda, who distributed them to his British allies.[34] But Penda refused to make peace with his mortal enemy, and 'declared his attention of wiping out the entire nation from the highest to the humblest in the land'.[35] Oswy then turned from appeasement to prayer, vowing to offer his one-year-old daughter Aelflaed to the service of God, together with twelve estates to build monasteries, in thanksgiving for a victory. Such a gesture would not have been a 'private' matter between Oswy and his God. It was a 'done deal' between the king and his bishops in which a significant part of the royal demesne and wealth would be handed over to the Church as the price of heavenly aid. And so, if the forthcoming battle had no other outcome, it did ensure the foundation of Whitby and eleven other abbeys, and created the circumstances for a short-lived but glorious Christian culture. Among the fruits of the battle were Bede's *History of the English Church and Peoples* and the Lindisfarne Gospels.

The great battle was fought unusually late in the season, on 15 November 655, near a river Bede calls *Winwaed*. Welsh accounts refer to it as *Maes Gai*, that is, 'the slaughter of the field of Gai'.[36] The name possibly means 'the ford across the stream'. In a rare and useful clue to its whereabouts Bede adds that the river was *in regionis Loidis*. The 'county of Leeds' had replaced the old British kingdom of Elmet (the modern city of Leeds was named after the 'county', not the other way around). Was Penda intending to restore Elmet to the British in exchange for their aid once the victory was won and the Saxons 'ethnically cleansed' from the territory? If so, it was, from his perspective, an unfortunate choice of battlefield. It had been a wet autumn and the river, swollen by heavy rain, had flooded far beyond its banks to create a formidable watery obstacle that Oswy was able to turn to his advantage.

Greatly outnumbered, the divisions of Oswy and his eldest son Alchfrith occupied the higher, drier ground above the river, forcing Penda's war-bands to struggle through the mud to reach them. Slithering and sliding about, they were forced back onto the floodland, where more of Penda's men 'were drowned while trying to escape than perished by the sword'. The battle turned into a *sauve qui peut*. All thirty of the legionary leaders, claims Bede, were killed or drowned. As was Aethelhere, of the royal house of East Anglia, and so too were most of the Welsh princes. Finally Penda himself was overtaken and killed, slain, in Churchill's phrase, 'by the sword he had drawn too often'.[37] No mercy would have been shown to the slayer of Oswald. The Irish annals record the Mercian king's comeuppance in two words: *Pantha occisio* – 'Penda dead'. The Welsh remembered the battle as 'the pool knee-deep in blood [when] twenty hundred perished in an hour'. Their leader, Cadfael escaped, into the void of Dark Age history. *Winwaed* was one of the total victories of the Dark Ages.

But where was it? There are no details of the campaign except for a statement in Geoffrey of Monmouth's dubious history that Penda's host had crossed the Humber. Battlefield detectives have looked for a site with a tendency to flood somewhere near Leeds that also has a name that sounds a bit like *Winwaed*. In 1893, a local historian, Edmund Bogg, proposed that the battle was fought on the 'high table land' of Whin Moor between the city of Leeds and the village of Barwick in Elmet.[38] His River *Winwaed* was the Cock Beck which rises on Whin Moor and runs eastwards to join the River Wharfe at Tadcaster. Prehistoric earthworks running along the north bank of the stream and thence along the boundary of the West and North Riding of Yorkshire probably formed part of the defences of ancient Elmet. There are also older earthworks by the Norman motte-and-bailey castle at nearby Barwick. This complex of defences would have formed an impressive obstacle to an attacker, especially in combination with bad weather and floods. Whin Moor is crossed by the Roman road connecting Chester and York, now marked by the A64. On the southern end of the moor is an area, now partly smothered by a housing estate, long known as Penda's Fields. Could the name be a genuine folk-memory of Penda's camp, or perhaps the place where he met his deserts?

The main problem with Whin Moor as the battle site is that the Cock Beck is a small stream not prone to extensive flooding, and there is nothing in its geography to suggest that it was any more flood-prone 1,400 years ago. The moor itself lies on poorly drained clay and contained an ancient bank and ditch running downhill towards the village of Swillington which may have contributed to the flooding effect. But it is hard to imagine a mere ditch swallowing up Penda's mighty army. To find a river of sufficient size and flood capability it is necessary to move several miles south of Whin Moor to the River Aire, which runs at this point through a flat ill-drained valley now studded with gravel-pits. Perhaps, if the battle was really fought on Whin Moor, the bulk of Penda's army was destroyed in the rout as they attempted to wade across the freezing river between Swillington and Woodlesford. The dead were said to be buried at a spot near Whin Moor called Hell's Garth.

An alternative site a dozen miles from Whin Moor was proposed by J W Walker in 1948.[39] He argued that Bede's *Winwaed* refers to the River Went which was known in the past as the Winned, the Wenct or the Wynt. It has high banks and occasionally floods, especially in late autumn. And, promisingly, it rises from a lake in Nostell Park long known as St Oswald's Pool. Walker found a plausible battlefield 'on the high ground whereon now stands the church of Wragby', which he identified with the Welsh 'Gau's Field'. Possibly Penda met his watery fate trapped in the river bend at Hessle, below Ackworth Moor Top. Oswy is said to have founded a hermitage on the battlefield. This may have been the forerunner of Nostell Priory, whose foundation charter mentions a 'wood of St Oswald'. All in all, Nostell Park and Wragby are the most likely site for the great battle.

Winwaed, like several of the more titanic battles of the Dark Ages, was not in a political sense a decisive battle. Although the ageing Penda was killed and his army destroyed, Mercia continued to be the rising power in England. For three years after *Winwaed*, Oswy ruled over Mercia, and attempted to diminish its power by dividing the kingdom in two. But the Mercians at length rebelled and proclaimed Wulfhere, son of Penda, 'whom they had kept hidden', as king. In short order they drove out Oswy's representatives and 'recovered their liberty and lands'. On the other hand, as we have seen, the battle did strengthen the Roman Church in Northumbria, and also hastened its establishment in Mercia. Not only did Oswy 'deliver his own people from the hostile attacks of the heathen', wrote Bede, 'but after cutting off their infidel head [i.e. Penda] he converted the Mercians and their neighbours to the Christian faith'.[40]

Not that Penda was a pagan fanatic. He apparently considered Christianity a good religion except that it was impossibly demanding; hardly anyone lived up to its precepts. He did not persecute Christians, and at least four missionaries, three from England and one from Ireland, were active in Mercia during his reign. Penda, one feels, was one of history's victims, the champion of a lost cause. Few mourned his passing but it is hard not to feel a sneaking sympathy for him.

Chapter 5
Dunnichen: Destiny in the North

Background

For the seventh-century kings of Northumbria, Dunnichen was a long way from home. Bede refers to it as 'a tight place of inaccessible mountains' and the Anglo-Saxon Chronicle as a remote land 'by the northern sea' (*be northan sae*). Dunnichen lay deep in the heart of a Pictish kingdom known as Fortriu (pronounced 'fortry'), which broadly coincides with today's Scottish district of Tayside. The affairs of the kings of Fortriu are recorded only at secondhand, and always very briefly, in the Irish annals. In the seventh-century melting-pot there was much interplay between the various kingdoms of northern Britain. The dominant power was the Anglian kingdom of Northumbria, which was then at the apogee of its power. To the north lay the ever-shifting tribal kingdoms of the Picts, which included Fortriu, the Scots and the Britons. The power of Northumbria at times extended over a large area beyond the present-day border at least as far as the Forth. This was particularly so during the reign of King Ecgfrith of Northumbria, who ruled from 670 to 685. Ecgfrith's southern ambitions had been checked, and he turned instead to Ireland, and to the lowlands north of the Forth. Ecgfrith (pronounced 'edge-frith', with a soft 'th' as in froth) is one of the protagonists in our battle. What took him to Dunnichen?

The answer is only hinted at in the sources but it involved his dealings with a brother king called Bridei. Shortly after he succeeded his father Oswy in 670, Ecgfrith fought a battle against the Picts at a place called the Two Rivers. The only account of it is in the *Life of St Wilfrid*, written *c.*720 by a monk called Stephan. When Ecgfrith was still attempting to establish his rule, 'while the kingdom was still weak', the Picts rebelled. 'The bestial Pictish people', writes Stephan, began to 'throw off from themselves the yoke of servitude'.[1] It seems that they overthrew Northumbria's client-king, called Drust, and refused to pay further tribute to Northumbria. Doubtless they also signalled their rejection of Northumbrian power by raiding Anglian settlements south of the Forth.

Stephan relates how the Picts prepared for war, gathering 'like a swarm of ants in summer, sweeping from their hills'. 'Being a stranger to tardy operations', King

Ecgfrith forthwith assembled a mounted force (*equitatus exercitus*), and rode north. Though outnumbered by a vast and concealed enemy, he 'slew an enormous number of the people'. Stephan repeats the legend that two rivers were filled with their corpses 'so that – wondrous to relate – the slayers, passing dry-foot over the rivers, pursued and slew a crowd of fugitives'. By these means, the Picts of that region were once again 'reduced to servitude'.

The location of the Two Rivers is unknown, though it evidently lay north of the Forth. One of the rivers was probably the Tay, the other possibly the Almond or the Earn, though this is only a guess. By means of this victory, Ecgfrith overthrew the Pictish leader, who was succeeded by the seemingly more compliant Bridei, son of Beli – also spelt Bruide or Brude in some sources, and pronounced Bridey or Broody according to taste. It seems that he and Ecgfrith were related in some way; indeed one Irish annal refers to them as brothers (*fratrueles*).[2] They cannot have been literal brothers, but they could have been cousins by marriage and may both have been grandsons of King Edwin.[3] They were also both second-generation Christians. In gratitude for helping him to the throne it was no doubt expected that Bridei would be a friendly and subservient tributary king, as his predecessors had been in the days of King Oswy.

As a king whose *imperium* or overlordship stretched well beyond his nominal kingdom in northern England, Ecgfrith spent much of his reign confronting hostile neighbours. The greatest threat, as for his predecessors, came from south of the Trent from the kingdom of Mercia. In *c*.673, Ecgfrith defeated the Mercian King Wulfhere, son of Penda, at an unknown and unnamed battlefield. But in 678 or 679 Wulfhere's successor and younger brother Aethelred turned the tables and decisively defeated Ecgfrith at 'a great battle near the River Trent'. Its location is unknown, but Elford near Lichfield, Staffordshire, has been suggested on the grounds that Elford may mean 'Aelfwine's ford' (although Elford lies on the Tame, not the Trent). Aelfwine was Ecgfrith's well-regarded younger brother, who lost his life in the battle. Ecgfrith may have been attempting to reimpose his father's policy of divide-and-rule over the large and loosely knit Midland kingdom. At any rate, the Trent seems to have been a serious and possibly decisive battle. Never again would a Northumbrian king be able to exert his will over his powerful southern neighbour, as Ecgfrith's father and uncle had.

Instead, Ecgfrith turned his attention to Ireland. In 684, the year before Dunnichen, Ecgfrith dispatched an expedition to Ireland under a deputy (*dux*) called Berct to punish an Irish kinglet for lending support to his enemies. 'In the month of June [684]', record the *Annals of Ulster*, 'the Saxons lay waste Mag Breg [i.e. the plain of Brega in County Meath], and many churches'. Berct's actions were deplored by contemporary churchmen, and not just in Ireland. In hindsight, it seemed that God was about to punish Ecgfrith for, in Bede's words, 'wretchedly wasting a harmless people that had always been friendly to the English'.[4]

Bede links these events in Ireland with Ecgfrith's expedition to Dunnichen the next year. The outraged inhabitants of Brega prayed for divine vengeance, and those responsible, claimed Bede, soon 'suffered the penalty of their guilt . . . Ecgfrith's punishment for his sin was that he would not now listen to those who sought to save him from his own destruction.' Did the Irish expedition stir up trouble in Fortriu? Or was Bridei already on a collision course with his cousin? Success for a Dark Age king was measured by the extent of his *imperium*: the more land he 'ruled', the wealthier he became, and hence his ability to reward his chief men, raise large armies and defend his frontiers was increased. Bridei was no exception. He was connected by blood and alliance to a network of Celtic and English kingdoms. One source claims that Bridei's father Beli was the king of British Dumbarton,[5] and another that the kingdom of Fortriu was the inheritance of his grandfather.[6] He may therefore have imposed his rule over an unusually large area, and been able to call on human resources considerably greater than an average tribal king.

Be that as it may, Bridei definitely had ambitions. With no possibility for the moment of extending his *imperium* southwards, he looked north and west. Around 680 he attacked the stronghold of Dunnottar, on its rock near modern Stonehaven, and a few years on took Dundurn (*Dunduirn*), a Pictish fort at the foot of Loch Earn in the Trossachs. More surprisingly, he is said to have 'annihilated' the inhabitants of Orkney,[7] which suggests a Viking-like leader at the head of a marauding fleet (the unlikeliness of an obscure king of Tayside sailing halfway round Scotland to trash the Orkneys is a reminder of how little we know about the Picts). Bridei was a 'wide ruler' on the make. Perhaps events on the Trent and in Breda encouraged him to make the momentous and perilous decision of breaking with cousin Ecgfrith and denying him his annual tribute of cattle, corn and gold. Or perhaps Ecgfrith had decided that cousin Bridei was getting too big for his boots and prepared to overthrow him as he had Bridei's predecessor. Bede, the main authority, saw the events of 685 in a different light. By ignoring sensible warnings, Ecgfrith was treading a divinely ordained path. His refusal to heed advice created its own punishment.[8]

The Name of the Battle

Scholars do not always agree about the name of a battlefield. Although the decisive battle of 1066 was known as the Battle of Hastings within a generation of the event, many authors have followed the nineteenth-century historian E A Freeman in preferring to call it the Battle of Senlac. The battle which brought the Tudors to the throne was apparently known nearer the time as the Battle of Redemore, but posterity has preferred the Battle of Bosworth or, as Shakespeare knew it, 'Bosworth Field'.

The battle in which the Northumbrian English fought the Picts in what is now Scotland in 685 has been known by several names. Until recently it was the Battle of Nechtansmere, or, in the original Old English spelling, *Nechtanesmere*. This may well have been the contemporary name of the battle in Saxon England, though its first documentary appearance is in a twelfth-century chronicle as *stagnum Nechtani*, the lake (or possibly bog) of Nechtan.[9] The earliest source refers to it only as 'Ecgfrith's Battle.[10]

The English lost the battle. What did the winners call it? The ancient Picts have left no written history, but the Irish annalists knew it as *Bellum* or *Cath Dun Nechtain*, that is, the Battle of Nechtan's *dun* or hill-fort.[11] It seems a fair bet that Nechtan's fort lay in the same area as Nechtan's lake. An alternative name recorded in the Welsh *Historia Brittonum* is *Gueith Lin Garan*, the Battle of the Heron Lake, a name which, the annalist tells us, goes back to the time of the battle.[12]

A good case has recently been made for a name-change by the battle's most zealous investigator and promoter, Graeme Cruickshank. In place of Nechtansmere, he proposes the Battle of Dunnichen.[13] Most historians accept that *Dun Nechtain*, whether it refers to a particular hill-fort or the broader lordship around it, lay in the vicinity of the modern village of Dunnichen (though its present-day inhabitants live in the valley rather than on the hill-top). The clinching evidence lies in a twelfth-century charter confirming lands on Arbroath Abbey in which the place is referred to as Dun-Nechtan. The new name is certainly a useful corrective to the usual England-centred view of history, and has been adopted in the most recent account of the battle by James E Fraser.[14] Personally I would regret the passing of *Nechtanesmere*, which, to me at least, has a mystical quality, akin to Arthur's Avalon – and with the added advantage, given the nature of Dark Age sources, that it does not anchor the battle to a particular place on the map. But to the victor go the spoils, and it seems only fair to give Dunnichen an airing. Let us hope the battle was really fought there!

The traditional site of the Battle of Dunnichen, Dunnichen Hill in the background, and a flight-pond, dug in the 1990s on the supposed site of *Nechtansmere*.

The Road to Dunnichen

Ecgfrith's expedition set out in April or May 685, once the grass had grown tall enough to feed the horses. Judging from Stephan's description of his *equitatus excercitus* at the Two Rivers, this expeditionary force may have been a surprisingly small one, perhaps more comparable to the 300 valiant warriors who fought at Catterick than a vast levied army.[15] His strategy was evidently to strike fast and hard, before the scattered enemy could muster a large enough army to oppose him. Such raids were designed to weaken the enemy more by ravaging his lands than by bringing him to battle. Two Rivers may have been less a pitched battle and more of a running series of strikes.

In his closely argued reconstruction of the battle, James Fraser proposed a tight-knit mounted army for Ecgfrith, consisting of the young unmarried men of his household seasoned with more veteran warriors. We are given none of their names, though we know the king was accompanied for at least part of the way by his bishop Trumwine. Other members of his family seem to have been with the king, for a monk of Lindisfarne referred afterwards to 'the fall of the members of the royal house by the cruel hand of a hostile sword' at Dunnichen.[16] Whether Berct, the despoiler of the Bregan churches, or Beornheth, the 'brave sub-king' who had helped his master at the Two Rivers, were with Ecgfrith we do not know. We can assume, however, that the king commanded an elite force, many of whom had previous battle experience. Nor need we doubt that they knew exactly where they were going and what they were going to do when they got there.

Ecgfrith probably mustered his men at Bamburgh rock (*Bebbanburg*), the main stronghold of his homeland of Bernicia. The road to Edinburgh (*Din Eidyn*) probably took him along the coast, on the same route as Edward I took when he invaded Scotland in 1296. Beyond Edinburgh there was a Roman road as far as Perth, and a series of old Roman marching camps stretching through Strathmore and beyond. Whether by coincidence or not, one of them, at Kirkbuddo, lies only four miles from the battlefield at Dunnichen. Until he reached Abercorn (*Abercurnig*), Trumwine's monastery on the Forth, Ecgfrith was on home turf. He could summon men to his army as he rode. Punitive operations probably began in Strathearn around the crossings of the Earn and the Tay, a fertile area, in James Campbell's words, 'well worth ravaging'. The burning of *Tula Amain*, a settlement where the Almond meets the Tay, may have been part of the 'ravaging and laying waste' remembered by the monk of Lindisfarne during the reign of Ecgfrith's successor.

Apparently meeting little resistance, Ecgfrith crossed the Tay and headed north-east through the broad valley of Strathmore, probably along the line of the present A94 from Perth and Scone to Forfar. His objective was probably Bridei's main stronghold in the area. But where was it? Fraser suggests Turin Hill, which is crowned by a large *dun* now known as Kemp's Castle. The hills and vales around Forfar are particularly rich in hill-forts and contemporary Dark Age stones, which argue that it was an important place in Pictish times, both in terms of defence and perhaps also in some spiritual way. Now drained and cultivated, it is not easy to imagine the area in the distant seventh century when long shallow lochs stretched down the valleys with small wooded or cattle-grazed hills rising through the mist. With formidable natural defences, this was truly an 'inaccessible' land, to borrow Bede's words. In certain lights and weather-moods it must have seemed an eerie place to outsiders, a mingling of land, stone and water unlike anything they had seen in northern England.

The Battle

Did Ecgfrith get lost? According to Bede, the enemy pretended to retreat, luring him into this dangerous area with its plentiful ambush possibilities.[17] But Fraser points out, reasonably enough, that Ecgfrith was an experienced warrior, would have used scouts and must have had at least a rough knowledge of the local geography. He was unlikely to have blundered on, frustrated and heedless, into an obvious trap. Yet that is exactly what F T Wainwright makes him do in a celebrated paper in the journal *Antiquity*.[18] Wainwright based his reconstruction of the battle on the depression of a vanished lake near Dunnichen which had partly filled with water in the wet winter of 1946–7. Map investigation indicated that this was the site of Dunnichen Moss, a boggy area in the valley bottom which had been partly drained and reseeded *c*.1800 (it was famous in the botanical world as the only known site of the 'cotton deer-grass').

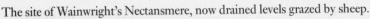

The site of Wainwright's Nectansmere, now drained levels grazed by sheep.

Bogs often grow over the sites of shallow lakes. Could Dunnichen Moss have been the site of the lost *Nechtanesmere*, the lake of herons? Wainwright thought so, and so, following him, did a whole generation of historians before 1996 (including myself, in my book *Grampian Battlefields*). The terrain suggested to Wainwright a scene in which Ecgfrith's army would have burst through the cleft in Dunnichen Hill only to fall straight into an ambush set by the Bridei. The Picts, massed inside the walls of their fort on the hill-top, must have raced down the hillside to attack the Saxons and drive them back to the boggy shores of the lake where they were cornered and cut to pieces. It is the site of Wainwright's *Nechtanesmere* that is now marked by the Ordnance Survey's crossed swords of battle, and it is by the village church, over-looking this battlefield, that a monument was raised on the 1,300th anniversary of the battle in 1985.

There is some evidence for this supposed lack of caution on Ecgfrith's part. Bede condemns his 'rashness' in being lured into remote and dangerous country by the enemy. But the problem with Wainwright's battlefield, as I discovered when I went there twenty years ago, is that the top of Dunnichen Hill is visible for miles around. Ecgfrith would have needed to be blind as well as heedless to ignore it. One overlooked clue to the battle is the use by Irish and English sources alike of the word *bellum*. As Fraser points out, for an ambush or massacre the words *interfectio* or *strages* would be more appropriate. *Bellum* is the word for an open engagement, in other words, a battle. Both language and military probability suggest a different kind of battle by a different lake in the vicinity of Dunnichen Hill.

Monument to the battle, erected close to Dunnichen church on its 1,300th anniversary in 1985.

In a timely reassessment of the battle, Leslie Alcock suggested that the fatal lake, *Nectanesmere* was not at Dunnichen Moss, after all, but at Restenneth Moss, two miles to the north-east, where another now-vanished lake once lay.[19] But would such a place, two miles as the crow flies from Dunnichen Hill, have been called *Dun Nechtain?* Possibly. One point in its favour is the presence of Restenneth Priory on what was once a promontory on the lake's southern shore. The priory is believed to have been founded in the early eighth century within living memory of the battle, and, if so, it is tempting to see a connection. If it is the same place as Naiton's church, built by English masons from Monkwearmouth on the Tyne, it might have symbolized reconciliation between the two nations after good relations had been restored by Ecgfrith's successor. Churches had certainly been built on battlefields earlier in the century, notably at *Maserfeld* and *Hefenfeld*.

However, Alcock overlooked geographical history. Analysis of peat-core samples from the valley floor indicate that Restenneth Moss was once part of a much larger lake that also took in the present-day Loch Fithie, Rescobie Loch and Balgavies Loch; in other words, that *Nechtanesmere*, if this be it, must have been a large lake around four miles long, though little over half a mile wide. Moreover it stood only a few miles to the east of another long lake, the original Loch of Forfar, leaving only a saddle of land in the vicinity of the modern town of Forfar where an army could cross the valley.

To Fraser, this Dark Age topography suggests a likely battlefield on Green Hill, a northward extension of Dunnichen Hill between Burnside Farm and Loch Fythie.[20] Here one can imagine the Picts arrayed in conventional battle order on the hillside as Ecgfrith's army crossed the tongue of land between the lochs and approached Dun Nechtan from the west. In this reconstruction the English precipitated the battle, although they were at a disadvantage with limited space to manoeuvre on the dry land between the hill and the lake.

For the battle itself, we are dependent on an unconventional and controversial source. This is not a written document but a stone, a beautifully carved upright slab about seven feet high called the Aberlemno Stone. Today it stands in Aberlemno kirkyard four miles north of Dunnichen Hill, but only two from Turin Hill, which, as Fraser suggests, may have been Bridei's 'capital' and Ecgfrith's objective. On one side is a Celtic cross, richly carved in high relief and with decorative motifs in the corners. On the other is a portrait of a battle. There are nine figures in all, arranged on three levels. At the top we see two mounted soldiers galloping from left to right. In the middle three men on foot face another mounted soldier cantering in from the right. And at the bottom two mounted soldiers face one another. To their right a figure larger than the rest is apparently sprawled on the ground where he is being pecked by a large bird. The juxtaposition of the Christian cross on one side and pagan symbols on the other suggests a date for the stone from the eighth or ninth century. The battle scene is unique in its vividness and complexity. But what battle is it, and why did it merit this exceptional monument?

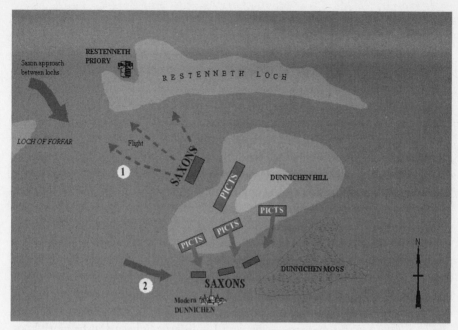

Alternative reconstructions of the Battle of Dunnichen

Past generations assumed that the Aberlemno Stone refers to some biblical event, perhaps to the fall of King Saul, or alternatively to some unidentifiable conflict between northern tribes. However, in 2000 Graeme Cruickshank made a powerful and persuasive case that the scene on this stone is none other than the Battle of Dunnichen![21] The argument turns on the proximity of the stone to the battlefield, its probable date and the details on the stone itself. To my mind the most convincing evidence is in the details of arms and armour shown on the stone. Three of the horsemen, as well as the crow-pecked figure on the ground, wear helmets with neck-guards and long nose-guards that are strikingly similar to the Coppergate Helmet excavated at York and which has been dated to *c.*750. They also wear some form of body armour, perhaps mail hauberks which are split at the hip for fighting on horseback, much like the hauberks of the Norman cavalry on the Bayeux Tapestry. They fight with shields and lances. Their horses too have quilted protection along the body. This is evidently an aristocratic army, well-equipped household warriors with war-horses and body-armour.

By contrast, their adversaries seem be less well armed, lacking helmets and wearing only light knee-length tunics. They have beards and shoulder-length hair and carry round shields with a big central spike. They fight with spears and, in one case, a short sword. With the exception of a single mounted warrior they fight on foot in a mass with swordsmen at the front covered by spearmen in the second rank, and another line of spears in reserve. There is nothing here to contradict Cruickshank's interpretation that these men are intended to be Ecgfrith's Saxons and Bridei's Picts fighting it out.

The fallen figure is probably meant to be Ecgfrith himself. The carrion-bird, probably a crow or a raven, reminds us of the war-poem of *Brunanburh* with its 'horn-beaked raven with dusky plumage' enjoying the feast of the battle-dead.

If we accept that the Aberlemno Stone as an accurate portrayal of the fighting men of Dunnichen, then it should contain clues to the battle. Its most surprising revelation is that at least some of Ecgfrith's men fought on horseback. This turns on its head the traditional view that, while the Saxons might ride to the battlefield, they always fought on foot. This tradition may however date from later times when the bulk of Saxon armies were made up of the *fyrd*, county levies who in most cases would not have been able to afford to own a war-horse. Judging from Stephan's account of the Two Rivers campaign, Ecgfrith's northern expeditions were well-mounted and presumably capable of fighting on horseback when the occasion demanded.

Was Dunnichen, then, a cavalry charge against infantry? The stone certainly gives a sense of horses galloping towards the enemy, and of the foot-soldiers braced to resist with spears or pikes, much as the men of Robert the Bruce did at Bannockburn. Bridei evidently had horsemen of his own which, to judge from the final scene on the stone, he kept back for a perhaps decisive sortie once the English efforts to break the line ran out of steam. The Battle of Dunnichen was not one of those battles that went on all day. According to the anonymous monk of Lindisfarne, it began at the ninth hour, that is, at three o'clock in the afternoon (the remarkable precision about the time suggests that our monk had heard it from an eye-witness). Perhaps Ecgfrith had staked the outcome on a glorious charge straight at the enemy. More likely, as an intelligent if impetuous king, he would have tried hit-and-run tactics that worked so well for Duke William at Hastings. Probably he was overcome by sheer force of numbers. A timely sortie from Bridei's horse might have hemmed the English in at the bottom of the hill on their exhausted mounts. Floundering in the mud by the lakeside, the king 'and a great part of his soldiers' were cut down one by one by Bridei's lightly armed militia. Ecgfrith was probably among the last to fall, his bodyguard lying dead around him, true to their oaths. Not all the English were slain. Some were captured and taken into servitude, and at least a few escaped and returned to England. St Cuthbert, then at Carlisle, heard of 'the woeful disaster' within a few days.[22]

Given the likely odds, one might wonder why Ecgfrith accepted battle, when, with his mounted *equitates*, he might easily have made a tactical retreat. In war-games, even when the forces are fairly evenly matched at three Saxons to four Picts, Ecgfrith tends to do badly. The best Guy Halsall playing Ecgfrith could manage was to extricate the English army from a hopeless position.[23] But perhaps, as Fraser suggests, the option of retreat was not really open to the Saxon king. Loss of face could have fatal consequences. Although Ecgfrith may not have been expecting to fight a pitched battle, he may have welcomed the opportunity to achieve a swift and spectacular victory. What he might have overlooked was the ability of the formidable Bridei to transform the Picts from the disunited tribes of the 670s to a united kingdom with shared goals and common purpose: something close, perhaps, to a sense of national identity.

After the Battle

We are told more about the reactions to the news of the battle than about the battle itself. According to the monk of Lindisfarne, St Cuthbert had predicted the death of King Ecgfrith twelve months before the battle.[24] At the actual moment of the battle, Cuthbert was in Carlisle admiring the city walls and 'the well built in a wonderful manner by the Romans'. Suddenly the holy bishop paused for a moment with downcast eyes, leaning on his staff. Then, raising his eyes heavenwards he cried out with a groan, 'O O O! I think that a battle is over and that judgement has been given against our people in the war.' And so of course it proved when, a few days later, 'it was announced far and wide that a wretched and mournful battle had taken place at the very day and hour in which it had been revealed to him'.[25]

Despite Ecgfrith's shortcomings, Cuthbert was obviously grieved at his death. Cuthbert's brother bishop Wilfrid, who had fallen foul of the king, was less charitable. While celebrating Mass he is said to have had a vision of a headless Ecgfrith falling, and his soul being dragged off to hell by a pair of demons, 'sighing with a terrible groan'.[26] What may have been another portent is recorded in the Anglo-Saxon 'F' Chronicle. In the year 685, it says, 'it rained blood and milk and butter was turned into blood'. Red rain is a rare but genuine phenomenon, apparently caused by tiny marine algae. Presumably it was held to foretell bloody events, though, unfortunately for that theory, this particular chronicle doesn't mention the battle at all!

There is also a reaction from the opposite perspective preserved in the Irish annals in the form of a poem, the *Inui Feras Bruide Cath*, attributed to a Riaguil of Bangor. In James Fraser's translation, the relevant lines run as follows:

> Today the son of Oswy was slain
> In battle against iron swords;
> Even though he did penance,
> It was penance too late,
> Today the son of Oswy was slain
> Who was wont to have dark drinks;
> Christ has heard our prayer
> That Bridei would avenge Brega.

Like Cuthbert, the poet attributes Ecgfrith's destruction to his predations in Brega the previous year. Evidently the king repented what had been done there, but repentance did not save him. The relevance of 'the dark drinks' is obscure, but it is clearly part of the imagery of doom.[27]

Symeon of Durham preserved a story that Ecgfrith's remains were taken across Scotland for burial at St Columba's foundation on Iona, known by the Irish annalists as the island of Hi. One possible reason for so surprising a resting place is that Ecgfrith's brother and successor as king, Aldfrith, had, like Oswald, been a monk at Iona. However, it is more likely that the royal remains would have been claimed by the Abbey of Whitby where Ecgfrith's father Oswy lay among other members of the family. Whatever the truth of the matter, the evident respect shown to the dead king can only be because both sides at Dunnichen were Christians. As we have seen, the pagan Penda mutilated and dishonoured the bodies of Kings Oswald and Edwin, as the pagan Vikings were to do to the ninth-century Saxon Kings Aelle and Edmund. Christian kings still had no compunction about killing one another, but mocking a man's soul after death was a different matter.

The news of the battle and the death of the king with most of his following was clearly a shock for the English. Kings had been killed in battle before, but never against northern tribesmen. The event was sensational enough to be recorded in the English, Scottish and Irish annals, and has even been called the best recorded episode in Pictish history.[28] Dunnichen was a famous battle, but was it a decisive one? Bede certainly thought so. From this point on, he wrote, quoting Virgil for an appropriate phrase, the hopes and strengths of the Anglian kingdom 'began to ebb and fall away'.[29] The Picts drove out or enslaved the English settlers north of the Forth, and sent Bishop Trumwine packing. The fall-out spread to the Scots of Dal Riata and the Britons of Strathclyde, who recovered the liberty they had lost under Oswy and Ecgfrith. The compiler of the *Historia Brittonum* agreed: 'the Picts with their king emerged as victors, and the Saxon thugs never grew thence to exact tribute from the Picts'.

These judgements have led some historians to regard Dunnichen as 'among the great and decisive battles of Scotland'[30] and even 'the first battle of Scottish Independence'.[31] It may be, however, that Saxon power in the area was already waning before Ecgfrith rode to his doom at Dunnichen. Bede includes the earlier seventh-century Kings Edwin, Oswald and Oswy among his *bretwaldas*, but significantly not Ecgfrith. The real turning-point, as Fraser suggests, may have been the Battle of the Trent in 679, when Ecgfrith was heavily defeated by the Mercians. While Bede's view cannot be dismissed lightly, since here he was reporting events from his own lifetime, there were at least two more clashes between Northumbrians and Picts in the Strathearn area in the opening years of the next century, in which the former devastated lands as far north as Strathtay. Dunnichen may, Fraser argues, have only seemed decisive in retrospect. The immediate effect of the battle was the succession of the childless Ecgfrith by his scholarly and more peacefully inclined brother Aldfrith. Aldfrith was in turn succeeded by his son, Osred, but within a generation Osred was assassinated and the dynasty of the house of Aethelfrith, the kings of Northumbrian greatness, brought to an inglorious end. Looking back, some may have seen Dunnichen as marking the beginning of the end.

At any rate, Dunnichen has become the most famous of all the Dark Age battles fought in the north. It helps that we know roughly where and exactly when the battle took place. The 1,300th anniversary of the battle, and, still more, the identification of the Aberlemno Stone by Graeme Cruickshank as a unique Dark Age battle monument, caught the popular imagination. Hence, alone among pre-Conquest Scottish battlefields, Dunnichen is a listed battlefield. It already features prominently in a recent novel, *Credo*, by Melvin Bragg. It can surely be only a matter of time before someone turns it into a film.

The Battlefield

The old 'Wainwright battlefield' and the new 'Fraser variant' lie within two miles of one another on opposite sides of Dunnichen Hill, a few miles ESE of Forfar (OS 1:50,000 map no. 54). The grid co-ordinates are approximately NO 515492 and 493511 respectively. A good starting-point is the churchyard in Dunnichen from where you have a view over the Wainwright battlefield and can imagine Ecgfrith's men falling back in confusion towards the lake as they are enveloped by Pictish warriors pouring down the slope of Dunnichen Hill. Although nothing now remains of the original lake, or even the bog that replaced it, a pond dug to attract wild duck in the 1990s does at least mark its approximate centre. The monument to the battle, unveiled in 1985, stands nearby, along with a cast of the Dunnichen Stone, a slab inscribed with Pictish symbols. Although the stone could be roughly contemporaneous with the battle, it has no obvious connection with it. The original is now on display at the Meffan Institute in Forfar. In 1998 a new cairn commemorating the battle was raised by the footpath between Dunnichen and the neighbouring village of Letham, closer to the centre of the Wainwright battlefield. It is dedicated to the memory of the late Scott Kidd who led the fight to save Dunnichen Hill from quarrying in the 1990s (see below).

Next the visitor should ascend Dunnichen Hill via the minor road and then the track that lead to the summit. On a clear day there is a grand view southwards over the Wainwright battlefield of crop fields and pasture, and beyond over the hills, vales and scattered woods eastwards of the Sidlaw Hills. The hill was once crowned

New monument to the battle raised on the northern shore of the lost lake where Ecgfrith and his men fought to the death.

by a stone rampart that may have formed part of the defences of the original *dun*. Unfortunately it was destroyed in the nineteenth century to provide material for stone walls. In 1947 Wainwright found a 'broken line of what seems to be a stone wall or earthwork' which he thought worthy of further investigation (but has not, so far, received any). This was probably the same grassy terrace with scattered rocks that I remember from a visit to the battlefield in 1983. Unfortunately a communications mast has since disturbed the hill-top, and in 1991 the entire hill was threatened when a company applied for planning permission to remove 4.5 million tonnes of andesite stone from its vicinity over thirty years. The application was objected to by historians from all over Scotland and beyond, on the grounds that it would 'destroy the visual explanation for Bridei's battle strategy',[32] not to mention any possible remaining archaeological evidence. The application was withdrawn, but the threat remains. On the more positive side, the Save Dunnichen Hill campaign drew attention not only to the importance of the Battle of Dunnichen but to Scottish battlefields more generally.

The Fraser battlefield is easily accessible as the A932 from Forfar passes straight over it in the vicinity of the farms of Foresterseat and Murton. From here you can see across Loch Fythie to the broach-tower of Restenneth Priory in the middle distance. Behind you lie the now wooded slopes of Dunnichen Hill, crowned by a communications mast, where Bridei's men may have stood in spear-bristling lines, with Bridei himself at a command post further up with his small corps of mounted warriors. The priory ruins on their promontory on the north-western side of

Loch Fythie by the B9113 are open to the public and are well worth visiting. Surprisingly the site seems never to have been investigated by archaeologists.

Finally, one should seek the Aberlemno Stone in the kirkyard of Aberlemno just off the B9134 from Forfar to Brechin. The side showing the scene of battle faces eastwards towards the church, which can make photography awkward without artificial lights. Early in the morning is probably the best time. The whole area around Forfar is rich in Pictish antiquities, and a visit to the battlefield could form part of a fascinating Dark Age tour in a fascinating and surprisingly little-known area.

The Aberlemno Stone shows scenes of battle which match the events of Dunnichen. Could this be a genuine Dark Age war memorial?

Chapter 6
King Ecgbert and the Vikings

King Ecgbert was founder of the dynasty that produced Alfred and all the later Saxon kings of England, and hence is the ultimate patriarch of our present royal family. His name should be pronounced 'Edge-bert', though in older histories he is 'Egbert', one of Sellers and Yateman's 'wave of egg-kings' who helped to make the Dark Ages so unmemorable. Ecgbert was Alfred the Great's grandfather. Hence his fame, such as it is, is mainly retrospective, but in his day Ecgbert was one of the great *bretwaldas* who ruled, at least for a while, large parts of England. He was the first great king of Wessex and at the height of his power his *imperium* stretched from Cornwall to Northumbria. Fortunate in war, he won most of his many battles, reigned for thirty-eight years, and died in his bed aged well over 60. Ecgbert lived up to his name which means 'bright-edge', or, more loosely translated, 'sword of destiny'.

The events of Ecgbert's reign are known to us only in outline. The Anglo-Saxon Chronicle mentions events and battles but provides no context, no causation and, needless to say, no detail. Like several other Dark Age patriarchs, Ecgbert came to the throne by means of a coup. His father Eahlmund was king of Kent, but also had some sort of claim to Wessex as well. In the days of the great Mercian King Offa, Ecgbert found it advisable to go into exile in France. After Offa's death, he returned in triumph as king of Wessex in 802. On the very day of his accession there was 'a great battle' at Kempsford in Gloucestershire between the men of Wiltshire under their ealdorman Weohstan and the men of the Mercian province of Hwicce (roughly present-day Worcestershire) under theirs.[1] Both leaders lost their lives, but Ecgbert's Wiltshire men were victorious.

Although the issue is not spelt out in the sources, it is likely that the battle was the result of Egbert's accession and his removal of Wessex from the confederation of kingdoms under Mercia's control. What the Battle of Kempsford seems to have decided was that north Wiltshire and Somerset, long-disputed between Wessex and Hwicce, would henceforth become part of Wessex. The sour relations between Ecgbert's Wessex and Mercia continued. A lost annal transcribed by the antiquarian John Leland in Henry VIII's reign records a battle between Ecgbert and the then

Mercian King Ceolwulf in about 820 at *Cherrenhul* between Abingdon and Oxford. Ceolwulf lost the battle, and, shortly afterwards, his throne. The more famous Battle of *Ellandun* in 825 may in part have been the new King Beornwulf's desire to overturn the verdict at *Cherrenhul*.

Meanwhile Ecgbert had trouble on his far western border. In the Dark Ages Cornwall was known as West Wales. Its history is largely unrecorded, but the county remained an isolated but independent enclave of ancient Britain, Celtic in language and culture. Cornwall makes a rare entry into the Anglo-Saxon Chronicle in the early ninth century. Perhaps as punishment for raids into Devon and beyond, Ecgbert made war on the Britons of West Wales. In 815 he ravaged Cornwall 'from east to west'. Ten years later, in summer 825, there was a pitched battle between the West Welsh and the Englishmen of Devon at *Gafulford* (Galford Down, near Lydford on the western boundary of Dartmoor). We do not know whether Ecgbert was present, but he was certainly in the area that summer, for he witnessed a charter at Crediton on 19 August. Alfred Burne had a theory that Ecgbert was able to make war in the far west safe in the knowledge that his northern boundary with Mercia was guarded by the linear earthwork known as the Wansdyke.[2] Since then archaeological opinion has moved its likely date backwards to the time of the Saxon Conquest. It was already known as the 'Old Dyke' (*Ealden Dic*) in Ecgbert's time. However, the most recent work on the Wansdyke assigns it to a mid-Saxon date, around the seventh century.

That Ecgbert did in fact risk attack from the north was borne out by the later events of summer 825. While he was dealing with the emergency in Devon, Ecgbert received the unwelcome news that King Beornwulf of Mercia had mobilized a large army in the Cotswolds. Beornwulf had chosen that moment to confront the expansionist tendencies of Ecgbert's Wessex and reassert the century-old pre-eminence of Mercia. Ecgbert's submission was demanded, though Beornwulf probably expected him to fight. The death in battle of Ecgbert and his son Aethelwulf would be the simplest and perhaps the most desirable solution to Wessex–Mercian relations.

But Beornwulf was no Offa. He had become king in 823 after the deposition of his predecessor. He was evidently not of the direct royal line and ten years earlier had been a mere ealdorman. Although he could call on the men of Kent, Essex and Middlesex, as well as Mercia, for support, Beornwulf may nonetheless have lacked regal authority. In other words, although he might have led an impressive looking army, some of its members were probably not wholehearted about serving Beornwulf, especially when faced by an opponent like Ecgbert. At any rate, Ecgbert's response was swift. With his mounted troops he returned east, and within weeks of witnessing the charter at Crediton he was back in Wiltshire and ready to settle scores with Beornwulf.

The Battle of *Ellandun*

Ellandun (or *Ellendun*) was one of history's showdowns. It was fought on a hot day, probably in September 825. The only detailed source is in the Winchester Annals (*Annales de Wintonia*). The battle was of special interest to Winchester Abbey because it was fought on abbey land. Though it is long on rhetoric and short on fact, the part of the chronicle devoted to the battle is best read in full. I have drawn on the translation from the original Latin by Tony Spicer:

> Beornwulf, king of the Mercians, deriding the ability of king Ecgbert, and believing that his experience was worth more than Ecgbert's, wanted to play him at the game of war. He invited and provoked the latter's army to battle in order to make him pay homage. Ecgbert consulted his noblemen, and the choice was taken to drive off shame with the sword. It was more honourable to be slain than to submit their freedom to the yoke. The battle took place in the summer season at *Ellandune*, now in the manor of the priory of Winchester (*nunc manerium Prioris Wintoniensis*). The kings came together to fight with unequal forces, both in number and quality. Against each hundred soldiers of Ecgbert, who were pale and thin, Beornwulf had a thousand, ruddy and well-fed, as behoves the soldiers of St Mary. They clashed together valiantly, each man giving of his best. The Mercians were put to the sword without mercy, but as much as they were conquered, so they excelled themselves with valour, and threw themselves back into the conflict regardless of the danger. They fell more copiously than hailstones, with more of them overcome from sweating than from battle. The ground was covered with the bodies of men and horses. Beornwulf himself, no longer king of the Mercia but the Moribunds, lest he shared the fate of his soldiers, sought flight for himself, and he would not have wished to lose his spurs for three ha'pence.[3]

The other main source, the Anglo-Saxon Chronicle, merely notes that Ecgbert and Beornwulf fought at *Ellandun*, that Ecgbert was victorious 'and a great slaughter was made'. Henry of Huntingdon's Norman chronicle adds that 'the brook (*rivus*) of *Ellandune* [sic] ran red with gore, stood dammed with battle-wreck, and grew foul with mouldering corpses',[4] which at least indicates that heavy fighting took place around a stream. All these sources have a second-hand air. If, as the Winchester annal insists, Ecgbert really had been outnumbered by ten to one, with his own troops tired and starving, he would most assuredly have lost the battle! As Alfred Burne put it, they were 'thin perhaps, but certainly fit, whereas the Mercians were probably soft and fat in comparison'.[5] It is not even clear who attacked who. Beornwulf was undoubtedly ready for war, but he seems to have hung around the border without invading the Wessex heartland.

As for the fighting, the Winchester annal makes an interesting reference to dead 'men and horses', implying that cavalry as well as the more usual shield-walls of infantry were used by both sides. The battle was evidently long and bloody, and the Mercians did not give up easily but repeatedly charged at Ecgbert's disciplined line. Where was *Ellandun*? The battlefield was obviously known to the Abbey of Winchester, but there is no reference to a memorial church, and its site was eventually forgotten. When antiquarians became interested in battlefields again 900 years later, there were two candidates: Wroughton near Swindon, which used to be called Ellingdon (or, in the Domesday Book, *Elandun*), and Allington near Amesbury. The latter location would indicate that Beornwulf had struck deep into Wessex, while the former suggests that he was massed defensively on the border. The matter was settled in 1900 by a Mrs Story Maskelyne who used medieval charters to prove that the manor of Ellingdon had been owned by Winchester Abbey, while Allington was not. *Ellandun* was undoubtedly Ellingdon and not Allington. It suggests that Ecgbert had ridden from Exeter along the Fosse Way, and thence along the road from Bath either to Chippenham or to the Kennet valley. Assuming he advanced straight to *Ellandun*, his march would have taken him over downland tracks to reach the battlefield from the south.

The size of Ecgbert's army is unknown; all we know is that it was large enough. With the king was Aethelwulf his eldest son, Ealhstan the bishop of Sherborne and the ealdormen Wulfheard and Hun of Somerset. After the battle, we are told that the first three (Hun was apparently killed in the battle) were dispatched to Kent with 'a great force' of shire levies or *fyrd*, presumably part of the force that had fought at *Ellandun*. On the assumption that Ecgbert had abandoned most of his western army in Devon but had summoned every man he could from Somerset and Wiltshire, Halsall calculated that he might have commanded up to 3,000 men, but probably not more.[6]

Beornwulf's army could have been much larger. A charter from October the previous year had been witnessed by the Mercian king and nine ealdormen, named

Battle of *Ellandun* as imagined by Guy Halsall

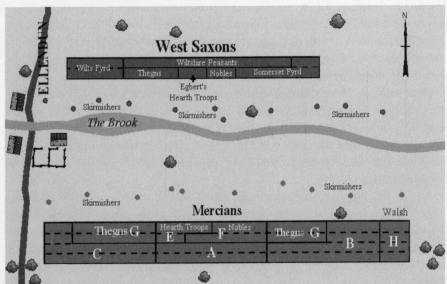

Lydiard House may stand on the Mercian position at *Ellandum*, with Egbert of Wessex forming up on the ridge 800 yards to the south. The house is an Elizabethan manor later rebuilt as a Palladian mansion. Its park was landscaped with trees, lawns and lakes in the eighteenth century.

Sigered, Eadwulf, Eadberht, Ealheard, Egberht, Beornoth, Uhtred, Mucel and Ludeca (the last named later became king in his turn). Some or all of these could have followed their king to war, as could the king's brother, Bynna. A suspect medieval source claims that Beornwulf led 'one thousand knights', which we could take to mean men of property with their own mounts.[7] Assuming that they were accompanied by their retinues, and adding a levy from the three tribal territories nearest to *Ellandun*, Halsall computes that Beornwulf could have commanded around 5,000 fighting men, although the uncertainties are very large.

There is little more one can say about the battle itself. It is presented to us as a gruelling struggle in which more died from exhaustion and suffocation than from wounds. It is tempting to suggest that the fittest side won. In war-games, assuming that the Mercians outnumber Ecgbert by 5 to 3, the outcome is unpredictable. Ecgbert wins only if his men are given a higher rating by their battle-hardiness and élan in attack. On equal terms, 'Ecgbert had better say his prayers'.[8] The battlefield might offer clues if only we could locate it. The ninth-century geography of the Wroughton area was reconstructed from charter evidence by Dr G B Grundy.[9] He showed that Saxon *Ellandun* covered a large area west of modern Swindon, including not only Wroughton but the parishes of Lydiard Millicent and Lydiard Tregoze. The battle probably took place not on the downs but on the gentler slopes of the valley of the River Ray to the north-west of Wroughton. Grundy identified ancient trackways that would have led the two armies to converge a little way west of the two Lydiards. The 'brook of Ellandune' might have been the Ray or one of two small streams that flow into it from the Lydiards.

Alfred Burne accepted Grundy's broad conclusions, but found what he considered to be a better battlefield about three-quarters of a mile to the east.[10] He placed the opposing forces on two parallel east–west ridges astride the ancient road which ran from Wroughton to Cricklade. According to his theory of 'Inherent Military Probability' the two armies would have instinctively looked for a ridge within sight of one another but out of missile range. The ridges are low with a dip in the middle, where one of the streams runs from south-west to north-east. The lie of the land, as well as its scale, reminded Burne of Waterloo.

Unfortunately Burne's battlefield has since been obscured by housing and roads. Spicer identified Beornwulf's position, to the north, as the prominent ridge occupied at the western end by the grand sixteenth-century mansion of Lydiard House and its church. A stream runs across the battlefield through broad reedbeds. Could this be Henry Huntingdon's gory *rivus of Ellandune*? The southern ridge is now completely obscured but Spicer discerned a slight rise along walkways between the houses and gardens, and at a business park at the western end. Another, more prominent ridge lies just beyond Park House Farm about 500 yards to the south.[11]

Lydiard Park and its environs are open land with public access. 'Grundy's Ellandun' is centred on a large field to the immediate west of the park run as

Old road past Park Farm: the ridge in the distance extends from the now built-up Windmill Hill where Burne placed Ecgbert's men at *Ellandun*.

A Mercian view of Ecgbert's initial position on the rise in the distance. In this scenario he advanced over the ground now occupied by Park Farm and engaged the Mercians somewhere near the stream skirting Lydiard Park.

Sketchmap of battlefield of *Ellandun* (after Spicer, 2001)

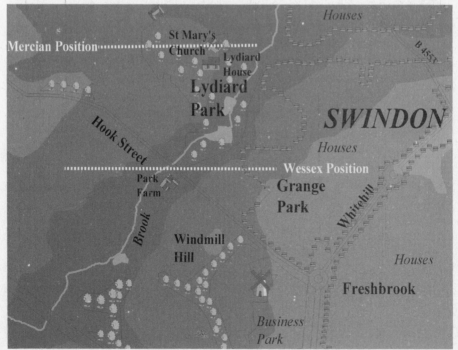

an 'Events Field'. Lydiard House and its park are now owned by the Borough of Swindon which manages it as a popular amenity (referred to in the brochures as 'a Swindon surprise'). The park itself is a creation of the eighteenth century and involved planting trees and damming the stream to form lakes. Before the peasants were evicted to make room for the park, there was an ancient settlement here which may well have existed in Saxon times. We can imagine *Ellandun* being fought over a mixture of pasture and ploughland at the height of the harvest, with half-built stooks of hay scattered about, and with a length of still-wet marsh, soon to redden with blood, running along the length of the battlefield.

There is a small exhibition, including archaeological finds, in the cafe by the car-park. But there is as yet no mention of Ecgbert or the Battle of *Ellandun*.

What makes a battle decisive is what happens afterwards. After *Ellandun*, Ecgbert sent an army under his son Aethelwulf into Kent to recover the king's patrimony there. Beornwulf's client-king, Baldred, was sent packing across the Thames. Not only Kent, but also the failing kingdoms of Sussex and Essex submitted to Ecgbert 'because they had been wrongly forced away from his kinsmen'. By the end of the year, Beornwulf had been killed by the East Anglians, who, seeing the way the tide was running, also 'turned to king Ecgbert as their protector and guardian against fear of Mercian aggression'. In 829, Ecgbert conquered Mercia itself 'and all that was south of the Humber'. He took his army as far as the River Dore near Sheffield, where the Northumbrians 'offered him submission and peace; thereupon they parted'. In the following year, Ecgbert's all-conquering army of Wessex marched into Wales, and that too 'he reduced to humble submission'.

Wind-carting in the 'activities field' west of Lydiard House. This is Grundy's battlefield, a mile west of Burne's proposed site.

Four triumphant years of war made Ecgbert one of the most powerful of all Saxon kings up to that time. However his hold on Mercia was only temporary. In 830, perhaps while Ecgbert was otherwise engaged in Wales, the deposed Mercian king, Wiglaf, 'obtained the Mercian kingdom again'. But Ecgbert was at least able to hang on to Kent and Sussex, and, on his death, hand them on to his son. The legacy of *Ellandun* was a strong, internally cohesive kingdom of Wessex which, under Ecgbert's grandson Alfred, withstood the Danes and unified England under the rule of Ecgbert's house.

The First Viking Raids

In the mean time Saxon England faced a new and terrible enemy. Ship-borne raiders had been attacking British coastal settlements and monasteries since the end of the eighth century. They were variously known as 'northmen', 'pirates' or 'strangers' (*gaill*). In England they were better known as the Vikings, which is probably based on the Norse word *vik* and meant 'fjord-dweller'. The sudden appearance of the longships has been attributed to over-population in the Scandinavian countries, obliging adventurers to try their luck in the lands beyond the sea. Equally they may have begun to raid foreign coasts simply because they could – developments in ship-building and navigation had provided the Viking with the means to cross the seas and loot the rich lands beyond. The first incursions were acts of mere piracy. The treasures of the Church were obvious 'soft' targets. As pagans, the Vikings had no compunction about pillaging the house of God. They probably despised Christianity with its doctrine of turning the other cheek. Their Odin was a war-god, who embodied the virtues of bravery, bloodthirstiness and cunning. Christian meekness was not something they respected.

The first recorded Viking raid on Saxon England was at Lindisfarne in the dead of winter in 793. The looting of the famous monastery was accompanied by scenes of rape and slaughter that shocked the Western world. Three years later they were back, raiding along the Northumbrian coast, including Bede's monastery at Jarrow. This time events did not go all the Vikings' way; 'one of their leaders was slain, and some of their ships besides were shattered by storms: and many of them were drowned there, and some came ashore alive and were at once slain at the river mouth [i.e. of the Tyne]'. This and subsequent quotations are from the Anglo-Saxon Chronicle unless otherwise stated.

For years after this setback, the Vikings confined their raids to less well-defended targets in western Scotland, including the monastery of Iona, and in Ireland. But from *c*.835, when 'the heathen devastated Sheppey', the raiders returned to England. In 836, Ecgbert's men 'fought against twenty-five ship's companies at *Carrum*' (Carhampton, on the Somerset coast between Minehead and Watchet). 'Great slaughter was made there', but the English were driven off. Carhampton was a royal estate, as we know from King Alfred's will. Evidently it was well worth looting because the Vikings returned there in 843, once again beating off the defenders before going on an orgy of 'plundering, looting [and] slaughtering everywhere', as the Frankish annals record. With a relatively small force 'they wielded power over the land at will'.

Two years later, the war in Cornwall was renewed. The West Welsh united with 'a great pirate host', probably on the basis that 'my enemy's enemy is my friend'. The ageing Ecgbert 'made an expedition against them'. The resulting battle was fought at *Hengestesdune* ('Stallion's Down', now Hingston Down, just west of the Tamar near Callington). Hingston Down is a bowl-shaped granite hill and local landmark, bearing many intriguing tumuli and earthworks. It lies six miles from the nearest tidal river, suggesting that the Vikings were already well-established in West Wales, and not merely passing through.

The hill forms a strong defensive position dominating the lowest crossing of the Tamar between Tavistock and the settlement of *Callwic*, modern Callington. Its location suggests that the West Welsh and their Viking allies occupied the hill to resist Ecgbert's invasion. There are numerous ancient earthworks there which might have been enlisted as entrenchments. Unfortunately there is no detailed account of the battle. The forces involved may not have been large; the Viking bands were from a fleet of thirty ships, implying a crew muster of perhaps 1,000 men or less. All we know is that in his last battle Ecgbert 'put to flight' both Britons and Vikings. Hingston Down was a decisive battle which ensured that West Wales or Cornwall would henceforth be part of England, not Wales or a Viking Irish Sea dominion. The native Cornish were in large measure dispossessed, much of the county becoming part of the king's estate or being given to the Church. In the following year, the founder of Alfred's line died, having reigned with conspicuous success for thirty-seven years and seven months. He was buried in the old church at Winchester where his bones still remain, in a wooden box high above the choir of the Cathedral.

The Vikings, however, did not go away.

The Viking Onslaught

The first raiders were a rootless mixture of Norwegian adventurers and settlers. The raid on Lindisfarne in 793 was probably made by a splinter group from a larger fleet that was already settling the Northern Isles and the Hebrides. Judging by the predominantly Norse names there today, the native population must have been displaced, driven out or enslaved. The very name of Orkney changed from *Inse Orc* or 'Boar Isle' to the Norse *Orkneyjar*. By the early 800s, Vikings were looting the defenceless Irish monasteries from firm bases in the isles and later in Ireland itself. In 841 a permanent Viking war-camp and trading settlement was established at Dublin that was henceforth to dominate the Irish Sea. They had also sent expeditions into the territory of the Picts and Scots, slaying 'men without number' at an unknown battlefield in 839.[12]

The Norse Vikings seem to have sought out places similar to home in the islands and along the mountainous Irish coast. What strikes a different note is the devastation of Sheppey in 835, which was only the start of intensified raids on the south English coast from Kent to Cornwall. Who were they? While the Anglo-Saxon Chronicle refers to all the earlier raiders as 'pirates' or 'shipmen', these later foes it usually calls 'Danes'. These shipmen were equally adept seamen and no less savage, but they came from modern Denmark, a lowland country of fertile farmland. A westward wind across the North Sea would take them straight towards East Anglia, the Thames estuary and the English Channel. There they would find not only portable wealth but settled farmland as good as anything at home. A Dane could feel very much at home in Norfolk.

The Irish annals distinguish the 'fair-haired' Vikings, or 'gentiles' from the 'dark' sort. The fair ones were the early Norse pirates and settlers, whilst the 'dark gentiles' were Danes. For example, in 851 'the dark heathen came to *Ath Cliath* and made a great slaughter of the fair-haired foreigners, and plundered the encampment, both people and property'.[13] *Ath Cliath* was the old name for Dublin, whose harbour the fair-haired Norse had fortified as a trading post. Now they in turn were war-prey. The climactic naval battle between the Norse and the Danes took place on Strangford Lough and was said to have lasted three days and nights. But 'the dark foreigners got the upper hand and the [fair-haired ones] abandoned their ships to them'.[14]

The names of the Danish leaders were long remembered: Ragnar Lodbrok ('Long-breeches') and his reputed son, Ivar the Boneless. Viking nicknames were usually candid. 'Boneless' is still used in Norway to describe a crafty, sly character – 'No bones – you can't hear him coming'. Theories that Ivar was a cripple and had to be carried about in a litter are the result of English literalism. The result of the Viking war in Ireland was that Ivar and another leader called Olaf the White were made co-kings of Dublin and the effective rulers of the new Viking empire in Ireland and the Isles. But this was to be only the start of their adventures.

In the south, the raids increased. Twelve separate raids are recorded by the Anglo-Saxon Chronicle between 835 and 860, and these may be only the larger ones. In 840, ealdorman Wulfheard won a victory against thirty-three ship's companies at *Hamwic* (Southampton), but in the same year his fellow ealdorman Aethelhelm of Dorset was killed fighting 'the Danes' at Portland. Three years later there was another battle at *Carrum* or Carhampton in Somerset, and, as before, the Vikings were victorious, beating King Aethelwulf, who was apparently there in person. More battles followed: at the mouth of the River Parrett in Somerset in 845, and at *Wiceganbeorg*, possibly Wigborough, also in Somerset, in 850.

In the same year, King Aethelwulf's brother or son, Athelstan, assisted by ealdorman Ealhhere, destroyed 'a great host' at *Sandwic* (Sandwich, then a coastal town). One account says that Athelstan and Ealhhere 'fought in their ships', which implies that they took a leaf out of the Vikings' own book and fought the first reported naval battle in English history against them. They 'captured nine ships and drove off the rest'. This may have been the main Viking fleet beached close to the place at Ebbsfleet where Hengist and Horsa had landed in 449. Alfred's biographer, Bishop Asser, dates this successful attack to the following year, and, if so, it could have followed the defeat of the Viking land army at the Battle of *Acleah*.[15] However it seems safer to follow the Anglo-Saxon Chronicle's order of events.

Unfortunately the fleet was not driven very far. Ominously, that year the Danes established a winter-camp on Thanet, indicating that a major invasion was imminent. In 851, the Danish Vikings mustered what was said to be a fleet of 350 ships. This figure takes some swallowing. Assuming the excavated Gokstad and Oseburg ships to be average-sized longboats, with fifteen or sixteen pairs of oars, a fleet this large could in theory carry up to 10,000 men – greater than the likely population of London. If the force was anything like this large, it must have represented a full-scale invasion, perhaps led by Ragnar and Ivar in person. This was an army capable of operating in the countryside far from its base, and of storming the largest towns. It marked a new phase in Viking activity in which the warriors left their ships in fortified bases and swept across country on horse or foot, pillaging as they went.

From its base in Thanet, the great army stormed the walled city of Canterbury, with its church treasures and wealthy halls. Then, entering the mouth of the Thames, the fleet rowed upriver and assailed London. The army of Burgred, king of Mercia, 'who had come to do battle against them' was ignominiously put to flight. Left undefended, London, already England's largest city, capitulated. From London the host turned southwards into Surrey. Somewhere, at a place called *Acleah* (or *Aclea*), the showdown battle between Englishmen and Danish Vikings was fought. The former were led by the doughty Aethelwulf of Wessex and his eldest son, Aethelbald, the ruler of Kent. News that Aethelwulf was on the way may have dictated the Vikings' move into Surrey. Perhaps after the feeble performance of the Mercians, they were expecting an easy victory.

However, Aethelwulf was made of sterner stuff. The best description of the Battle of *Acleah* is Bishop Asser's, written some forty years later, although it may only be a gloss on the Anglo-Saxon Chronicle's single sentence.

> Aethelwulf and Aethelbald with the whole army fought for a very long time at the place called Aclea (that is, 'oak field'), and there, when battle had been waged fiercely and vigorously on both sides for a long time, a great part of the Viking horde was utterly destroyed and killed, so much so that we have never heard of a greater slaughter of them, in any region, on any day, before or since; the Christians honourably gained the victory and were masters of the battlefield.[16]

The last sonorous phrase was borrowed almost word for word from the Chronicle. The composition of Aethelwulf's army is unknown, but we can be sure it was a large one, and probably included levies from Kent, Hampshire and Berkshire, as well as Surrey, all fighting under the banners of their respective ealdormen.

The Battle of *Acleah* saved southern England from conquest much as *Ethandun* did twenty-five years later. The main reason so important a battle is so little-known is that we do not know where *Acleah* was. The Chronicle specifically mentions Surrey, and the only place in the county with a similar name is the village of Ockley, a few miles south-west of Dorking. Ockley lies on the arrow-straight Roman road of Stane Street, which linked Chichester with London and existed in Saxon times, so it is a plausible place for the battle. We can imagine Aethelwulf rendezvousing with his son Aethelbald at the head of the Kentish levy and then heading towards the capital by the fastest way. Local tradition places the battle on Ockley's village green, the largest in the county, though historians have preferred the slopes of Leith Hill to the north of the village.

The trouble is that the early name for Ockley was not *Acleah* but *Okele* or *Okalee*, and meant not 'oak field' but 'Ock's' or 'Occa's field'. The appropriate modern name for *Acleah* is not Ockley but Oakley. There are several Oakleys in Hampshire, Oxfordshire and beyond, but none, unfortunately, in Surrey. The nearest Oakleys are East Oakley, now a dormitory town west of Basingstoke, and Oakley Green near the Thames between Windsor and Bray. For either we have to assume that the Vikings continued to march through Surrey and then turned east into Hampshire. There is also an Oakleigh on the Thames marshes near Higham in Kent, a few miles east of Gravesend. If Oakleigh was the place, the battle suggests a successful counter-offensive by Aethelwulf, driving the Vikings back to their ships. Without more evidence, *Acleah* will remain an elusive battlefield (and how helpful it would have been had the chronicler told us a bit more about it instead of wandering off into Aethelwulf's mythical ancestry from Adam, via various Eoppas, Baldegs, Finns and Wigs!).

Despite their defeat at *Acleah*, two years later the Vikings were back at their usual staging-post on Thanet in 853. The stout-hearted ealdorman Eahlhere of Kent, joined by ealdorman Huda with the men of Surrey, attacked them at their base in Pegwell Bay, and another battle ensued along the shore where the ships were beached. With the advantage of surprise, the English had at first the upper hand, but 'the battle there lasted a long time and many men on both sides fell or were drowned in the water'. Both Eahlhere and Huda were killed, and, reading between the lines, it is likely that their deaths resulted in the flight of the county levies, as was to happen in similar circumstances many years later at the Battle of Maldon.

Nevertheless, the desperate defensive struggle of 850–3 brought Wessex a breathing space. Old King Aethelwulf went off to Rome with his youngest son Alfred. Burgred of Mercia found he had the leisure to ravage Wales again, while England enjoyed one of the first royal scandals in English history when the new King Aethelbald carried off and married his father's teen-bride, Judith. But the lull did not last. In 860 'a great pirate host' landed at Southampton and marched on Winchester. Despite its stout walls, the city was successfully stormed. The men of Berkshire and Hampshire under ealdormen Aethelwulf and Osric marched to the relief of the town and a battle was fought outside the walls. After a bitter struggle the Viking host was put to flight. This was probably the same Viking force that was active on the Seine in the following year, under a leader called Weland.[17] According to Frankish sources, they had assembled a fleet of 200 ships on the River Somme, later joined by eighty more. The Battle of Winchester in 860 could have been a victory to rank with *Acleah*. At any rate, the Chronicle describes the next five years as a time of 'good peace and great tranquillity' – though, if so, it was the last such time for many years to come.

The Great Army

It was in 865 that the trouble really started. A 'heathen host' landed once more at Thanet, and this time the Kentishmen bought peace with money. Not that it did them much good, because 'under cover of the peace, the host went secretly inland by night and devastated all the eastern part of Kent'. But this army, though formidable enough to overawe the men of Kent, was only the forerunner of what became known as 'the Great Army' (*micel here*). A huge fleet led by Ivar the Boneless sailed from the north and descended on the fertile plains of East Anglia. They established a winter-camp and came to an understanding with the East Anglian king, Edmund, who, in return for relative restraint on their part, provided the host with what they needed, including horses. Ivar had not come just to raid. This was a conquest army in search of territory and farmland. It probably drew ship's companies from France as well as Ireland, and Ivar may well have commanded between three and four hundred ships and a land army of up to 5,000 men.[18]

Their preparations made, the land army rode north towards York, while the longboats sailed along the Lincolnshire coast and into the Humber. The plan must have been to take York in a pincer movement between land and water. According to a *Life of St Edmund* written a century later, Ivar (known as 'Hinguar' in the source) chose to lead the fleet, and he took the city by surprise.[19] The host occupied York on All Saints Day, 1 November 866. It is said that the city walls had been allowed to fall into disrepair; if so, this was culpable negligence amounting to a death wish.

Ivar had timed his invasion well. Northumbria was in a state of civil war between rival kings, Osberht and Aelle (Ella), the former rejected by the people, the latter 'not of royal birth'. According to a legend eagerly pounced on by the makers of the 1958 film, *The Vikings*, this Aelle was a cruel and capricious tyrant who murdered Ivar's father Ragnar Lodbrok by throwing him into a pit of snakes. The real Aelle was new to the throne when the Vikings attacked, and commanded only a faction of his countrymen. It took several months for Aelle and Osberht to patch up their differences, but in March the following year the rival kings gathered 'great levies' and besieged the city. Some of their men forced their way into the streets of York and there was a bloody conflict inside and outside the walls. But the English were no match for Ivar's force. Both kings perished in the fighting, along with no fewer than eight of their ealdormen. Later accounts claim that the unfortunate Aelle was captured and then sacrificed to Odin in a gruesome ritual known as the blood-eagle in which the victim's lungs were torn out and spread like wings on his back. The earliest written source is a lament for Canute composed *c*.1035, in which 'Ivarr'

> who ruled at Jorvik
> Cut an eagle
> on the back of Aella.[20]

Aelle's unpleasant fate was evidently a well-known story, and is not at all unlikely.

The Viking's capture of York, the city of Edwin, effectively brought the curtain down on the northern Anglo-Saxon kingdom. Henceforth the old kingdom of Deira became the Viking kingdom of Yorvik, while an isolated and diminished Bernicia continued a notional independence north of the Tyne. In the fertile vale of York there was a wholesale redistribution of land in favour of the Viking settlers; the leaders 'shared out the land of the Northumbrians and they proceeded to plough and support themselves', as the Chronicle puts it.

By 868, Ivar could move on to the next phase of his plan: the invasion of Mercia. Following the same tactic as in 866, the Great Army seized a defensible site, this time the town of Nottingham (*Snotingaham*) clustered around its high rock by the River Trent. They established winter-quarters there while the leaders raided the surrounding countryside, robbing churches, seizing horses, cattle and stored food, and collecting protection money. Once again, Burgred, king of Mercia, appealed for aid to his brother-in-law Aethelred, king of Wessex. Since the great raid of 851, Wessex and Mercia had become allies in the face of the common threat. The two kingdoms had acted in unison in 851, and two years later Aethelwulf lent troops to Burgred against the Welsh, after which Burgred received Aethelwulf's daughter in marriage. The army of Wessex marched north, led by the young king himself, accompanied by his brother Alfred in the latter's first military campaign. There was a stand-off at Nottingham. The Vikings, safe inside their impregnable position on Nottingham Rock, declined to risk a general engagement. In the end 'peace was made' between them. This probably means that the Great Army was bought off. If treaties made with Viking armies across the Channel are any guide, this would have been a huge sum – chests of gold and silver as well as corn and livestock. After that, the Great Army returned to York and Alfred and Aethelred went home.

The End of the Kingdom of East Anglia

Mercia's reprieve was East Anglia's downfall. In 869 Ivar descended for the second time on East Anglia, establishing his winter-quarters at Thetford. This important town in the centre of East Anglia controlled the main roads, and was then much closer to the sea-lanes of the Wash than today. Whoever controlled Thetford effectively controlled East Anglia. This time, King Edmund chose to fight. Probably outnumbered, Edmund was killed in a fierce battle on 20 November 869 and his kingdom over-run. The traditional site of the battle is at Hoxne, near Diss in Suffolk, about twenty miles east of Thetford. However, according to Abbo of Fleury, who wrote a life of the sainted king a century later, the king was killed near a wood at *Haegelisdun*, which Dr Stanley West has identified with an old field name, Hellesdun, at Sutton Hall near Bradfield St Clare, six miles south-east of Bury St Edmunds.[21] The site is close to a Roman road and also to the place where the king was buried. Nearby place-names such as Kingshall Farm and Kingshall Green indicate a folk-memory of a king who could well be Edmund. Putting it all together, Bradfield St Clare seems a more likely site for the battle.

A different and seemingly incompatible tradition claims that Edmund did not fight at all, but died meekly as befits a Christian martyr. The monk Abbo, who wrote the *Vita Sanctis Edmundi* at the request of the monks of Ramsey Abbey, claimed to have received some of the details from Archbishop Dunstan, who in turn had heard them from Edmund's own armour-bearer (this is just about possible). Abbo claimed that 'Hinguar' (Ivar) had come from the north by sea, and came secretly to 'a city', presumably Thetford, which the Vikings surprised and then burnt, slaughtering the inhabitants. Ivar sent word to Edmund that he would allow him 'to reign in future under him' so long as Edmund agreed to share his 'ancient treasures' and royal estates with the conquerors. No English king could honourably accept such conditions, but Abbo has Edmund doing just that but on one condition: that Ivar should accept baptism and become a Christian. However, Ivar was not interested in becoming a Christian. The king was seized in his own hall and taken before the terrible Viking leader. Then he was beaten, tied to a tree and shot with arrows 'until he bristled with them like a hedgehog or thistle'. Finally they chopped off his head and threw it into a bramble thicket.[22] The king's body and head were recovered, and buried locally in a small chapel built for the purpose. Around the year 906, his remains were exhumed and buried at Bedricesworth, soon to become known as Bury St Edmund.

Another version of the tale was preserved by the well-informed twelfth-century Lincolnshire historian Geoffrey Gaimar. According to him, King Edmund did indeed fight the Vikings, and afterwards escaped to a 'castle'. He was taken prisoner, and revealed his identity in a riddle. When asked who he was, he replied: 'When I was in flight, Edmund was there and I with him; when I turned to flee he turned too.' He was held until 'Ywar' and 'Ube' (Ivar's brother, Ubba) came. Then he was martyred in much the same way.[23]

That Edmund was in fact captured and ritually sacrificed to Odin in some horrible way is all too likely. Coins struck to commemorate the martyred king were being circulated within a generation of his death, and his cult was firmly established by the ninth century. Perhaps, as Smyth suggests, the Anglo-Saxon Chronicle did not want to make too much of this in case it detracted from its hero-king Alfred.[24] King Edmund's death marked the passing of the old kingdom of East Anglia. The Vikings looted and destroyed the rich East Anglian abbeys, Crowland, Huntingdon, Ely and, above all, the great abbey at *Medeshamstede* (Peterborough), whose monks and abbot were all slaughtered. King Alfred himself recollected a few years later how 'churches throughout England stood filled with treasure and books – before everything was ransacked and burned'.[25] By burning the abbeys, the Vikings managed to wipe out independent East Anglia's entire history, literature and culture. Thus did East Anglia become a Viking province, the new Denmark.

The map was also being redrawn in the far north. Danish, Irish and Norwegian Vikings contended for control of the isles. In 866, Olaf the White, 'the greatest warrior-king of the western seas' sailed from Dublin with a formidable fleet. He led a campaign into the central lowlands of Scotland and 'plundered all the territories of the Picts and took their hostages'. In 870, he was joined by Ivar, fresh from his rape of East Anglia, to beseige *Alt Cluith*, the stronghold of the Britons of Strathclyde on Dumbarton Rock which controlled access to the Clyde. The fortress surrendered when the well ran dry after a siege of four months. It was comprehensively plundered and then destroyed. Ivar and Olaf returned to Dublin with a fleet of 200 ships, 'bringing away with them into captivity in Ireland a great prey of Angles and Britons and Picts', among them Artgal, king of Strathclyde.[26] 'A great prey' – the misery of the survivors, packed into the freezing, reeking hulls of the longships, with no future beyond a lifetime of slavery and abuse, is hard to imagine. King Artgal was executed by Ivar in Dublin at the request of Constantine, king of the Scots. The campaigns of Olaf and Ivar in the north effectively eliminated the independent British and Pictish kingdoms and set the stage for a unified Scottish kingdom to emerge. Meanwhile the erstwhile Viking warriors and pirates became farmers, landlords and fishermen, and, in some areas at least, even began to speak Gaelic.

As for the fearful 'Hinguar', otherwise known as Ivar the Boneless, 'king of the Norsemen of all Ireland and Britain', he died, apparently in his bed, in 873. The whereabouts of whatever bones he possessed are unknown.

Chapter 7

The Battles of King Alfred

So far the Viking conquest of England had gone more or less to timetable. One by one the old Saxon kingdoms had fallen or been neutralized: Kent, Northumbria, East Anglia, Mercia. By the winter of 870–1, it was the turn of Wessex, ruled by the young King Aethelred, elder brother of the future King Alfred. With Alfred we get a rare eye-witness view on the conduct of the wars by the king himself. Commenting on the looting of church treasures in England, he believed that 'we lost wealth as well as wisdom because we did not wish to set our minds to the track'.[1] Rulers in East Anglia and the north had lost everything through a policy of vain hope and appeasement. The only way to deal with the Vikings was to resist them, at any price.

Judging from their actions in 870–1, the Vikings expected Wessex to follow the pattern of East Anglia – half-hearted resistance and one big battle followed by collapse, paving the way for Viking settlement as the new masters. Instead of harnessing the whole might of the Great Army for the effort, Ivar went to settle Northumbria and pursue his ambitions further north. The conquest of Wessex was left to his brother Halfdan, with reduced forces. As ever, the numbers involved in the campaign of 870–1 are unknown, but are likely to be large by Dark Age reckoning. As we have seen, Ivar's host may have numbered 5,000 armed men. Even assuming that Ivar took half that number north with him, Halfdan could still have disposed of 2,000–3,000 fighting men.

The Viking strategy for the conquest of Wessex followed the precedent set in France and northern Britain. They would build a fortified winter-camp where their ships could be safely beached and which could be supplied by river. From this base they could plunder and raid over a large area. They could terrify the wretched inhabitants into paying them geld and supplying the necessities of life, which in France a few years earlier had included livestock, wine, cider and flour – evidently the Vikings had their own baking ovens. In the summer sailing season, Halfdan's war-band would be reinforced and, if their earlier successes were any guide, they would then seek out and try to eliminate the king of Wessex, as they had done so summarily to his counterparts in Northumbria and East Anglia.

In the dark days of December 870, Halfdan led 'this heathen army of hateful memory'[2] from East Anglia towards the Thames, almost certainly using the straight, and perhaps still paved, Roman road from Thetford to the river bridge at Wallingford – a strategically important crossing which Alfred later fortified as a *burh*. Being mounted, Halfdan's army could have made the journey in less than a week. Meanwhile Halfdan's ships made their way up the Thames from their fortified base on the Thames estuary near London. It was a repeat of their successful strategy at York – to co-ordinate actions by land and sea, and establish a defensible base that could be supplied by water as well as by land.

For their base of operations they chose Reading, then a small settlement on the confluence of the Thames and the Kennet. Why Reading? To begin

Statue of Alfred the Great in the market place at Wantage. Reputedly the figure's features were based on those of the artist's patron, Lloyd-Lindsay. It portrays Alfred in the role of warrior and law-giver, axe in one hand, charter in the other.

with, the place could be defended quickly and easily. Halfdan's defences at Reading were probably on King's Meadow just east of the present-day railway station. The river and an associated dyke called Plummery Ditch formed a loop around the site leaving a front of only half a mile (730 m) to be strengthened with walls. Establishing what they called a ship-fortress close to a navigable river was a tried-and-tested Viking tactic. They had already done so in France on the Loire and the Seine, and in Ireland on the Shannon. In the course of Alfred's wars they would do so again in Dorset between the Frome and the Tarrant, and at Buttington in Shropshire inside a meander of the River Severn. Contemporary accounts describe earthen ramparts linking the rivers, probably topped by a wooden palisade with a fortified gate and watch-towers. Alfred's later system of fortified *burhs* seems to have been inspired by Viking fortifications, and followed a similar pattern.

Another consideration was that Reading was a royal estate. Again and again in Alfred's wars, the Vikings tended to target the king's own property, perhaps in order to draw out the king himself, but also no doubt because that was where the richest pickings were likely to be.

Prelude at Englefield

In immediate need of fuel, timber and meat, Viking foraging parties fanned out in the mid-winter countryside around Reading. On New Year's Eve, only three days after their arrival, the Vikings met an unexpected reverse. Ealdorman Aethelwulf with the men of Berkshire pounced on a large party of mounted raiders led by two jarls at Englefield, a few miles west of Reading. There was a hard-fought battle in the course of which one of the jarls was killed. One source names the dead leader as Sidroc, although another claims that Sidroc the Old, along with his son Sidroc the Young, died at the Battle of Ashdown, a week later. The rest of the party took to their heels and Aethelwulf was left master of the field.

The traditional site of the Battle of Englefield is Englefield Park near Theale, six miles west of the centre of Reading. The battle is remembered locally in Dead Man's Lane, said to be named after the battle. Aethelwulf's own household and estate lay at Pangbourne, only three miles away. As the nearest ealdorman to Reading, he would have alerted the king and, keeping watch on the enemy's movements, no doubt seized the opportunity to attack a detached portion of his army. The victory at Englefield, minor in itself, put heart into the men of Wessex. It was the first reverse the Vikings had suffered since being driven out of York three years earlier. It showed that, with watchfulness and courage, the Vikings could be beaten.

This Aethelwulf is one of the unsung heroes of old England. He was a leader of the army that had saved Winchester in 860, and he went down in glory fighting the Vikings at Reading only a few days after his success at Englefield. Technically he was a Mercian, and his body was taken for burial amongst his ancestors in Derby. But since the death of the last Mercian king, Mercia had accepted the overlordship of Alfred who had married a Mercian princess in 868. In addition, Aethelwulf's Berkshire had been drawn for reasons of self-preservation into the ambit of Wessex. The men of the Thames valley, at a time of great peril, may have begun to regard themselves not so much as Mercians nor of Wessex but as English.

Aethelwulf's bold stroke at Englefield was probably made in the knowledge that the royal brothers Aethelred and Alfred were on their way at the head of 'a great levy'. Four days after Englefield, and without further ado, Aethelred and Alfred's army stormed up to the half-built gates of the Viking fortress, 'hacking and cutting down all the Vikings they found outside'. But the Vikings fought back 'like wolves', bursting out of the camp and, after a struggle, beating back the attackers in disorder. Ealdorman Aethelred was among the fallen. The defeat at Reading was a hard lesson for Aethelred and Alfred. It looks as though, taken unawares by Halfdan's winter offensive, they had hoped to surprise the enemy in turn by the speed and fury of their response. But with ninth-century military technology, which evidently did not include siege engines, armies fortified behind walls with sufficient food and water were virtually impregnable to attack.

The Battle of Ashdown

Despite this reverse, Aethelred's army remained intact. Only four days later, on 8 January 871, he was able to take on the Viking host again at the famous Battle of Ashdown. Where was Ashdown? Unfortunately for battlefield seekers, Ashdown, or *Aescesdun* in Old English, is not a specific place but the old name for the Berkshire Downs, the range of chalk hills that stretches from Reading to Marlborough. The battle clearly took place somewhere along its length, but where? It almost certainly took place on or near the Ridgeway, the ancient track running across the northern part of the downs. Given that Aethelred was given only four days to reform his battered force, the battle must have been near the Reading end (of which more below). This is all the more likely if credence is given to the chronicler Geoffrey Gaimar, writing many years later, that the Saxons were driven *eastwards* from Reading before doubling back over the River Loddon at Twyford.[3]

Battle of Ashdown 871 (conjectural)

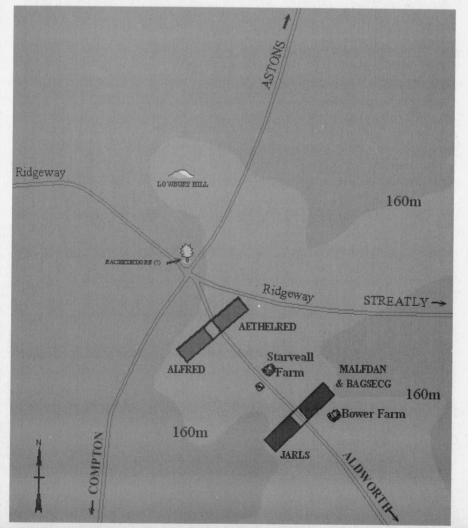

The Berkshire Downs are a cold bleak place in early January. Surprisingly none of the sources mention the weather that day, but for an army camping out of doors in the dead of winter the chance to bring the campaign to an early conclusion was perhaps something to be leapt at. For the battle itself we are given an unusual amount of detail, an indication of its importance in the career of the young Alfred. The army of Aethelred and Alfred, we are told, aroused by the grief and shame of their defeat, were 'in a determined frame of mind'. The size of their army is unknowable, but even after the setback at Reading it was clearly large enough to offer a serious threat to Halfdan. Quite why the latter decided to risk battle in the open when he was secure enough inside his ship-camp is unclear. It was contrary to his usual practice of enticing the enemy to attack him from a strongly defended position. Perhaps Ashdown marked the beginning of his intended push westwards into Wiltshire. Or may be Halfdan was over-confident, thought he had the Saxons on the run and came out to finish them off.

Both armies formed into two divisions, 'shield-walls of equal size'. On the Viking side, one host was led by Halfdan himself and his fellow king Bagsecg. The other host was led by an unspecified number of subsidiary leaders described as 'jarls'. The division of the army probably reflected different Viking groups. The Saxons, too, naturally formed into two divisions, clustered around the separate households of Aethelred and Alfred. It seems that the brothers had agreed in advance that King Aethelred's division would fight Halfdan, and Alfred's the jarls. We are not told on which side of the field the divisions were, but it is usually assumed that Aethelred was on the left and Alfred on the right.

Alfred reached the field first and in better order than his brother. Aethelred, so the story goes, delayed in his tent to hear Mass and offer lengthy and interminable prayers for victory over the heathen foe. We are invited to believe that Aethelred placed more hope in prayer than in his men. Asser, our source for this tale, claims to have heard it from eye-witnesses who were no doubt imploring the pious king to get a move on.[4] Even so, it should be taken with a large pinch of salt. Asser's praise of his hero, King Alfred, tended to be at the expense of Alfred's older siblings. In the Anglo-Saxon Chronicle, the brothers are given equal credit for the victory at Ashdown; if anything, since the king is mentioned before Alfred, it was Aethelred's battle. But in Asser's version of events, Aethelred never does anything except in concert with his younger brother. As Professor Smyth points out in his detailed analysis of the sources, this has the hallmarks of later editing of the facts.[5]

While Aethelred dallied in his tent, the Vikings arrived on the field with disconcerting speed and formed up into shield-walls on a ridge of higher ground some distance to the east. Alfred, says Asser, was left with the choice of retreating or attacking before his brother's arrival. He chose to attack, commanding his men to close ranks to form a shield-wall and advance without delay at the army of the jarls. Strengthened by divine counsel, Alfred 'acted courageously, like a wild boar'.

Like a wild boar: the phrase has echoed down the centuries, but what does it mean exactly? Many men of Alfred's day hunted boars, and knew all about the desperate courage of the cornered beast and the way it would charge directly at its tormentors.

It has been suggested that the words the Welsh-born Asser chose to express Alfred's bravery were influenced by his knowledge of Celtic poetry in which the word *twrch* (boar) was used to describe a brave warrior.

But another more meaningful explanation is possible. Asser could have been alluding to a battle formation known as a *caput porcinum* or boar's head. When a mass of infantry moved forward to the attack a group of picked men formed up into a wedge, rather like a rugger scrum, with a couple of men in the front row, three or four in the second rank, and so on, creating a human spearhead that would, if all went well, smash through the enemy ranks at a fixed point. The human wedge was a battle tactic known to the Romans, and was also employed by the Vikings who believed that the secret had been divulged to them by Odin himself. In large formations there might be more than one boar's head, so that the line would move forward in a zigzag with wedge-shaped clumps of infantry advanced ahead of the main line. The correct thing to do when faced with bristling boar's heads advancing rapidly towards you under a hail of missiles was to form up into an arc or V-shape, known by the Romans as the *forceps*. Then, if the charge went off at half-cock, the defending side had a good chance of enveloping the wedge in a pincer movement.[6] Other things being equal, the laurels would go to the side with the greatest courage and discipline. Being at the sharp end of a boar's-head charge is, battle enactors assure me, an exciting experience. Apparently one is carried along on the cusp of the charge and forcibly propelled into the enemy ranks. The front runners of the wedge would fly over the shield-wall.

Perhaps Alfred, then, took a leaf out of the Vikings' own military manual and charged straight at the banners of the jarls with his best men out in front in wedge-formation. Since both sides favoured the boar's-head tactic, in which momentum was all-important, the Vikings probably advanced in their turn. The two armies clashed together, writes Asser, 'with loud shouting from all, one side acting wrongfully and the other side set to fight for life, loved ones and country'. The fighting went 'to and fro, resolutely and exceedingly ferociously' for some time, during which (though Asser doesn't bother to mention it) Aethelred's men eventually arrived on the field and launched themselves into the fray.

With armies of the shield-wall, the most dangerous moment comes when you decide to call the whole thing off and retreat. For the Vikings at Ashdown that moment came after an hour or two of bitter fighting on the cold windy down. It might have been after the death of Bagsecg, who was certainly killed in the battle or its subsequent rout. But with the vengeful Saxons pressing on, perhaps calling up their mounted reserves, the Vikings were prevented from withdrawing in good order. It became a matter of *sauve qui peut*, and the fleeing Vikings were cut down without mercy. According to the Chronicle the dead, scattered over the down for miles, numbered in their thousands. Apart from King Bagsecg, they included no fewer than five of the jarls, whose names were Osbern, Fraena, Harold and the two Sidrocs. No mention is made of Saxon casualties. The slaughter ended only at nightfall – just before five o'clock in early January – but the following day any Vikings still at large were rounded up and slaughtered.

Ashdown was hailed as a great victory for Wessex. Thanks to its importance in the story of Alfred the Great it has become one of the best-known battles of pre-Conquest Britain. But why the Saxons won it isn't made clear. Ashdown was only the start of Alfred's 'year of battles' with the Vikings. He fought eight other battles and, apart from Ashdown, lost all of them. The significance of this lone victory with its claimed thousands of Viking dead was probably exaggerated, since the Vikings were able to field another army and beat Alfred and Aethelred with it only two weeks later. The implication, given the similarity of arms and military tactics on either side, is that at Ashdown the Vikings were outnumbered. But the reason why Alfred fared so poorly in subsequent encounters with Halfdan's Vikings may have been that he lost so many of his best men at Ashdown and the fighting at Reading. We could speculate that there was something of a backs-to-the-wall spirit about Ashdown, a knowledge that Englishmen's wives and children, home and hearth were sheltering behind their locked shields. The merciless slaughter of the defeated Vikings suggests the release of a mighty catharsis of revenge.

Where did the battle take place? Asser tells us he had himself seen the field and the famous leafless thorn-bush (*nachededorn*, 'the naked thorn') around which Alfred's men traded blows with the jarls.[7] However, his description of the field with the Vikings on a ridge of ground higher than that of the West Saxons is too vague to pinpoint. For Ashdown, like most Dark Age battles, one has to rely on the balance of probability. There is no warrant for the assumption some have made that the Saxons had been falling back throughout the four days that separate the assault at Reading from the Battle of Ashdown. On the contrary, the sources imply that it was the Saxons and not the Vikings that had taken the initiative. They were seeking a decisive battle, not evading one. The most likely place, given all the particulars, is on the downs up to a day's march from Reading.

The Blowing Stone at Kingstone Lisle is said to have been the assembly place for the men of Wessex before the Battle of Ashdown.

Its distance from Reading is one of the problems of the traditional site for the battle, at Uffington Castle on White Horse Hill. It lies close to the Ridgeway but at some thirty miles west of Reading is at least two days' march away in mid-winter conditions. The tradition was partly based on the belief, now known to be incorrect, that King Alfred had had the White Horse carved in the chalky turf as a memorial to the battle. Local place-names provide supporting evidence. In Saxon times the land around Uffington was within the Hundred of *Nachededorne* – an echo of the naked thorn? – while the nearby village of Ashbury was referred to as *Aescesbyrig* in one of Alfred's charters.[8] Surely these names could not be a coincidence?

On a more fanciful level, folk-tales have used the story of Ashdown to provide an explanation for various monuments and artifacts. Alfred is supposed to have summoned his men by sounding a mighty blast on a perforated sarsen stone, known as the Blowing Stone, which still stands in the corner of a cottage garden near Kingston Lisle, two miles east of Uffington. The army supposedly gathered at Alfred's Castle, an Iron Age enclosure on Swinley Down three miles south of Uffington, while Aethelred's men assembled at Hardwell Camp, a similarly sized area a mile away in the parish of Compton Beauchamp. By the same set of traditions, the body of King Bagsecg was taken to Wayland Smithy, the chambered tomb by the Ridgeway, for burial, while the dead jarls were interred at Seven Barrows near Lambourne. The rank and file was buried in the valley below Kingstone Hill, where sarsen stones mark their last resting places. Ashdown House, the seventeenth-century mansion now in the care of the National Trust, took its name from the proximity of Alfred's Castle. Needless to say there is no foundation in history for any of these tales.

The case for Uffington was effectively blown out of the water by Alfred Burne.[9] Burne agreed that winter conditions would have obliged any large force to use the relatively dry Ridgeway, and that the battle must have taken place somewhere on the high downs west of Reading. But, he argued, Uffington was too far to the west,

Ashdown: Lowbury Hill, a green whaleback in a sea of rape. In Alfred's day these were equally bare sheep-grazed downs.

and would have left the royal manors of Wantage and Lambourn at the mercy of the invaders. Moreover, the wording of Asser and the Chronicle does not suggest an army in hot-footed retreat, and implies that the defeated Vikings, stragglers and all, made it back to their Reading fortress on the same day as the battle.

Burne's favoured site was on the downs just below Lowbury Hill, the tallest of the billows of downland, and commanding a prominent position near the Ridgeway about twelve miles from Reading and three from Goring with fine views on all sides. Moreover, the hill stands above an ancient crossroads, claimed by Burne to be the site of a traditional moot or meeting place for the villages of the Hundred. Perhaps Asser's 'naked thorn' marked the site in a way reminiscent of the 'hoar apple tree' at Senlac in 1066. In Burne's interpretation, the West Saxons were expecting support from their Mercian allies, and so would have chosen such a place, visible for miles around, for a rendez-vous. He also found a place to match Asser's description in two ridges separated by a shallow valley. The clinching evidence seemed to be the mass of thorn bushes by the crossroads, exactly where he expected Asser's 'naked thorn' to be. In this interpretation, Aethelred and Alfred formed up on either side of the Ridgeway below Lowbury Hill, while the Vikings deployed to face them on Louse Hill near Starveall Farm a few hundred yards further down the track to the south-east. Both armies advanced and clashed in the valley 'known by the gypsies as "Awful Bottom"'.

From my own walk around 'Burne's Ashdown' I would be inclined to move the battlefield a few hundred yards to the east. If the crossroads was indeed the mustering place for the Saxon army it would surely have lain not in the centre but on the western end of the battlefield. The Saxons might therefore have formed up on the ridge between the thorn bush and the hollow where Starveall Farm stands today. The Vikings would then have occupied the corresponding ridge where Bower's Farm now stands, with the heaviest fighting taking place on the slopes and in the hollow in between. Burne found it a fine setting for a battle, 'the wide sweep of the downs, the wildness and solitude – the natural arena for a conflict'. Since the war almost the whole of this part of the downs

Nachededorn: bushes at an ancient crossroads, possibly marking Alfred's start-point at the Battle of Ashdown.

The distant ridge now occupied by Bower Farm was probably the Danish line at Ashdown. The two armies clashed in the valley in between (below) where Starveall Farm now sits.

has been put to the plough, and it is now far from wild in an ecological sense. The chalky tracks on which the warriors reached their day of destiny at Ashdown run between ribbons of hedges. Burne's site of the Naked Thorn lies in a waterlogged hollow from which banks of blackthorn and hawthorn scrub radiate like a starfish. The area is popular with cyclists and off-road vehicles using the Ridgeway, but, disappointingly, there is no memorial or information about the battle anywhere. An alternative site of the battle is close to the A417 with Aethelred and Alfred occupying Kingstanding Hill near Moulsford and the Vikings advancing along the Thames valley from Reading. However, this valley would have been boggy and perhaps impassable in January. Wherever possible, the Vikings used higher ground.

Stalemate after Ashdown

Despite their losses at Ashdown, the Vikings were able to launch a new campaign within a fortnight. For the next five months, both armies were in the field and fought a series of encounters south of the Thames in Hampshire and Wiltshire. We can imagine the beacons of Hampshire blazing their warning, from Beacon Hill near Highclere to Farley Mount overlooking Winchester and on to the Solent and the Isle of Wight. At a day's march from Reading the Vikings occupied Basing (*Basingas*), by the Loddon three miles west of the modern town of Basingstoke. This placed them within a day's march of Winchester. Aethelred and Alfred followed with their combined force, but this time things went badly. In what was probably a repeat of the battle at Reading, 'they clashed violently on all fronts, but after a long struggle the Vikings gained the victory'.

Two months later, the two armies clashed again at a place variously called *Meretun* or *Maeredun*. As at Ashdown both sides formed up in two divisions. At first the Saxons were successful and put the Vikings to flight. But later the same day the latter somehow turned the tables on their attackers 'and there was a great slaughter on either side, but the Vikings had possession of the field'. Among the English losses were Bishop Heahmund of Sherborne 'and many important men'. Where was *Meretun*? As usual its location depends on finding such a place in the Domesday Book or a Saxon charter that is also in the right area, which in this case could be in Hampshire, Wiltshire or even Dorset. Merton in Oxfordshire is too far north, Merten in Devon too far west, Merton in south London too far east. Marten, athwart a Roman road at the base of the downs, eight miles south-west of Hungerford is one possibility. Another is Martin on the boundary of Hampshire and Dorset, whose Old English name was *Mertone* and whose location might explain the presence of the bishop of Sherborne on the battlefield. It could be the same *Meretun* where King Ceolwulf was memorably assassinated in his bower a century before.

Disasters rarely come singly. Shortly after *Meretun*, and perhaps attracted by news of successes and rich pickings in the southlands of England, the Vikings were reinforced by a 'great summer host', apparently from overseas. And after Easter, King Aethelred died after a troublesome reign of only five years. Contemporaries simply reported the fact and the king's subsequent burial at Wimborne. Later tradition, also recorded on Aethelred's memorial plate in Wimborne Minster, claims that the king died from wounds received in battle, perhaps at *Meretun*. But so Nelsonian an end would surely not have gone unrecorded, especially in the epic year 871. Asser simply reports that Aethelred went the way of all flesh. Probably he died of something contracted while on campaign during those bitter winter marches and battles. Alfred's brothers all died young, and Alfred himself was in poor health for much of his life, if Asser is to be believed. And if the rigours of campaigning claimed the king himself, how many others, one wonders, died of disease or wounds during those desperate days.

Alfred was acclaimed king. The rights of Aethelred's children were set aside; they were infants and Wessex needed a war-leader. Alfred was on his throne only a month before fighting the Vikings again at Wilton, on the confluence of the Nadder and the Wylye a few miles west of Salisbury. Very probably the Vikings were heading for Wimborne, bent on killing or capturing Alfred. By one account, Alfred was attending his dead brother's funeral in Wimborne on the day the Vikings struck. Alfred summoned all the men he could and rode out to Wilton to take on the much larger Viking army gathered on a hill south of the river where Wilton Park stands today. Despite his lack of numbers, Alfred drove the Vikings back, but, once again, he advanced too far. Seeing how few their pursuers were, the Vikings rallied and drove Alfred from the field.

In six months Saxon and Viking seem to have fought one another to a standstill. The Anglo-Saxon Chronicle pauses at this point to review the campaign. There had been nine general engagements (though only six are named) 'besides those innumerable forays which Alfred and ealdormen and king's thanes rode on, which were never counted'. The Viking dead included nine jarls and one king. As for the Saxons, writes Asser, they were virtually annihilated.[10] The result was a truce. Despite beating Alfred's forces time and time again, the Vikings had taken casualties that they could ill afford, whilst Alfred could draw on the homelands of Wessex and, on occasion, Mercia and the south-east too. Even so, Alfred desperately needed to buy time to strengthen the defences of his kingdom and reorganize his armies. And so, continues Asser, with what sounds like pursed lips, 'the Saxons made peace with the Vikings on condition they would leave them, and this the Vikings did'.

They did, but they took their time about it. Though Asser could not bring himself to say as much, Alfred almost certainly bought the Vikings withdrawal with a large geld cobbled together from the royal treasure, Church wealth and taxes. Halfdan withdrew to London, having stripped the eastern counties of Wessex of corn, salted meat and herds of livestock to feed his vast horde. From Wessex he turned to Mercia, the large but decadent Midland kingdom, which could be looted much more cheaply. Alfred had gained a breathing space, but few could have doubted that the Vikings would soon be back.

And so they were. Halfdan departed north, to Repton in northern Mercia and later to the Tyne where his supporters settled to plough the vacant fields of Northumbria and, as a sideline, raid their new neighbours to the north. Halfdan fought his last battle in 877 at Strangford Lough in Ireland. But not all of the Vikings turned north. A new army, perhaps part of the summer host that joined Halfdan after *Meretun in* 871, established itself at Cambridge in 875, led by three kings, Oscytel, Anund and Guthrum. It seems that, while Halfdan was taking the lands north of the Humber for his own kingdom, the new boys had ambitions in the south. Guthrum, especially, was staking out his claim to Alfred's Wessex.

From Disaster to Triumph: The Road to *Ethandun*

The record of the first five years of Alfred's reign is disappointingly meagre. He must have used the time created by the peace of 871 to make preparations for the war which would inevitably be renewed in the near future. He began to fortify coastal and riverside defences and to build up a more effective English fleet. The opening move of the second Viking war seems to have been Alfred's. In what was perhaps a pre-emptive strike, his ships intercepted seven Viking longboats at sea, captured one and put the others to flight. However, this time the Vikings changed their tactics. Instead of establishing a base on the Thames at the borders of Wessex, Guthrum aimed to strike at the heart of Alfred's kingdom from a supply base on the south coast. Moreover, he assembled a mounted force, able to move swiftly over large distances and outpace the enemy. The Vikings were comparatively secure within fortified places capable of being supplied by river or sea. Using mobile forces in combination with secure bases, Guthrum could ransack the country for geld and livestock and, when the opportunity arose, strike the killer blow against the king. Alfred could expect the same gory fate as Edmund of East Anglia and Aelle of Northumbria. This would be a fight to the finish.

Guthrum's land army evaded Alfred's levies and made its way to the Dorset town of Wareham where supply ships awaited them. Alfred caught up with him there, but Guthrum managed to give him the slip at night and moved on by a series of fast marches to Exeter. Guthrum's fleet was not so lucky. Caught in a great storm off Swanage, 120 ships were lost. The result was a stalemate: Guthrum's men secure behind the fortifications of Exeter with Alfred's army camped outside but unable to break into the town. Negotiations followed, and another dubious 'firm peace' was sealed by an exchange of hostages and many solemn oaths, after which the Vikings were allowed to depart. Guthrum retreated to Mercia by way of Gloucestershire. The two forces shadowed one another along the borderlands in the Cotswolds and upper Thames as winter approached.

Guthrum had no intention of keeping his side of the bargain. He evidently had agents in Alfred's camp, and knew that the king intended to celebrate Christmas at Chippenham. To Chippenham came the Vikings shortly after Twelfth Night 878, when Alfred's household was doubtless nursing a communal hangover. There they attacked, and drove out or killed the only Saxon army in the field. Alfred escaped with a small company, but now all Wessex stood at Guthrum's mercy. Over the next four months Guthrum's men fanned out over Hampshire and Dorset, driving the thegns and ealdormen into the sea and, in the Chronicle's words, 'conquered (*geridan*, literally rode-over) and occupied the land of the West Saxons and drove a great part of the people across the sea'. Alfred himself took refuge with a small force 'along the woods and in the fen-fastnesses' of the Somerset Levels. There, with the help of his faithful ealdorman Aethelnoth, he fortified an emergency base on the hill of Athelney, which rose, Ely-like, from the marshes.

This was the time for what Winston Churchill called 'the toys of history', a rustic interlude in the grim struggle. One day, while sheltering incognito inside a peasant's cottage, Alfred burned the cakes and was reproved for it by the outraged housewife. The moral of the tale is of course the turning of the tables: in adversity, the great king had been transformed into a menial, obliged to take a scolding from the wife of a swineherd. In another tale, Alfred, disguised as a minstrel, sang to the Vikings while they supped at some stolen table. This yarn may reflect a military reality. Somehow

Alfred was kept abreast of events, in touch with the leaders in the counties and informed of Guthrum's whereabouts. While he abstractedly allowed the cakes to burn, Alfred was planning the counter-attack.

With disconcerting suddenness, the Chronicle informs us that in the seventh week after Easter, that is, between 7 and 11 May 878, Alfred mustered his army at 'Ecgbert's Stone'. There he was joined by 'all the men of Somerset and Wiltshire, and that part of Hampshire which was on this side of the sea'. 'When they saw the king, they were glad of him.' Asser added that the king was received 'as one restored to life after such great tribulations [and] they were filled with immense joy'.[11] The analogy with Easter and Christ's suffering on the cross followed by his joyful resurrection was not lost on Asser, or the men of the west. The march to *Ethandun* is presented to us as deliverance. From the eighth-century document known as the Burghal Hidage, it is possible that the two-and-a-bit counties could have fielded an army of 4,000 men at full strength. In the same year the men of Devon alone slew 840 Vikings in battle, including Halfdan's brother, Ubba.

The exact location of Ecgbert's Stone is uncertain. The Chronicle merely says it lay 'to the east of Selwood', and within a day's march of the next camp at Iley. One possibility is that it stood by the River Stour at Bourton where the counties of Somerset, Dorset and Wiltshire converge. A stone standing in a glade (ST 773312) nearby has been identified with Ecgbert's Stone. Another traditional site is Kingsettle Hill, three miles to the north, where in 1772 the banker Henry Hoare built a brick folly called Alfred's Tower at the place where, local tradition had it, he had raised his standard. A third possible site lies further east at Kingston Deverill. Local opinion claims that Ecgbert's Stone could be one of three sarsen stones collected from Court Hill overlooking the village and propped up in an enclosure by the church. Ecgbert is said, though without historical authority, to have held court on the hill. In his still-useful paper on ancient trackways, Dr G B Grundy pointed out that tracks converge here from all

Alfred's Tower. This famous folly crowns a hilltop in Stourhead Gardens. It was built by Henry Flitcroft for the wealthy banker Henry Hoare and completed in 1772. It is said to stand on the site where King Alfred raised his standard against the Danes in 877.

Egbert's Stone? These sarsen stones at Kingston Deverill, Somerset, are known locally as 'Egbert's Stones' or 'King's Stones'. They were brought down from the nearby Court Hill in the nineteenth century and propped up in an enclosure near the church.

directions, making it a natural rendezvous. Moreover, Court Hill is visible from miles around.[12] The site stretches the Chronicle's description 'east of Selwood' a long way but, as Burne points out, we don't know how far Selwood went in Alfred's day.

A day's march from Ecgbert's Stone, Alfred camped at a place called *Iglea* which can be identified as Iley Oak. This place marked the meeting place of the Hundreds of Warminster and Heytesbury, at what is now Eastleigh Wood, two miles south of Warminster on the edge of Salisbury Plain. Iley Oak is nearly twenty miles from Penselwood, suggesting that Alfred's army was mounted. Their line of march suggests that Alfred's objective was Chippenham, Guthrum's presumed base of operations since the rout of Twelfth Night five months before. At the Iley Oak camp, if not earlier, Alfred received news from his scouts that a large force of Vikings was blocking his march at *Ethandun*, a day's march away. Like Reading and Wilton, *Ethandun* was a royal estate, identifiable with the village of Edington (see below). Alfred probably knew it well, for it was one of the places he listed in his will. He marched. He might even have marched through the night, for Asser claims he attacked the Vikings at dawn.

Ethandun is one of the decisive battles of English history, marking the turning-point in the wars against the Vikings and paving the way for the later glories of Alfred's house. In its account of the campaign, with its unusually precise information about where Alfred camped and who was in his army, the Chronicle prepares us for a truly epic encounter, along the lines of its account of the Battle of Ashdown. Yet when it comes, all we get is a single sentence: one of the shaggy-dog stories of history. Here it is:

And one day later he went from those camps to Iley Oak, and one day later to *Ethandun*; and there he fought against the entire host, and put it to flight ...[13]

Asser adds only a little:

> When the next day dawned Alfred moved his forces and came to a
> place called *Ethandun*, and fighting fiercely in close order against the
> entire Viking army, he persevered resolutely for a long time; at length he
> gained the victory by God's will. He destroyed the Vikings with great
> slaughter . . . [14]

For the defining battle of the hero-king, Alfred's chroniclers have been oddly
reticent. Evidently, as Professor Smyth discusses in his biography of Alfred, they
told us what they wanted us to know, neither more nor less.[15] One possibility is that
Ethandun was not a battle on the grand scale like Ashdown but a lucky encounter from
which the Saxons were able to seize the initiative and bring Guthrum to his knees. In
support of this theory is the interesting fact that no casualties are named on either side.
Or maybe the chronicler wanted to draw attention to Alfred's vision and magnanimity
after winning the war, and so regarded the actual battle as a distraction.

The accounts imply that this time Alfred's men fought in a single unit, as a compact
shield-wall. Given his conduct at Ashdown, charging 'like a wild boar' at the enemy,
and his pursuit of the enemy at *Meretun* and Wilton, it seems likely that Alfred was the
attacker and that he attacked at once. The battlefield would provide a valuable
clue to what happened – if only we knew
where it was. The match of *Ethandun*
with Edington, near Westbury, is generally
accepted. There are other Edingtons, but
they are either in the wrong place or wrong
on etymological grounds. Our Edington was
the Norman *Edendone* which is consistent
with the Saxon *Ethandun* (the Saxon 'th'
was commonly 'Normanized' as a 'd') and
was, we know, a ninth-century royal estate.
The problem is to pin down where, in all
the expanse of escarpment, valley and chalk
plateau near Edington, the battle was fought.

The favourite site is Bratton Camp, on the
top of the downland scarp between Edington
and Westbury, where the White Horse
carved in the nearby scarp since at least the
eighteenth century is traditionally associated
with Alfred's victory. Bratton Camp is an

The battle stone of *Ethandun* by Bratton Camp.
The exact site of the battle is unknown.

The Westbury White Horse carved in the chalk below Bratton Camp. Though associated by tradition with Alfred's victory, its placing is probably a coincidence.

Iron Age hill-fort with a double wall and ditch which was probably even more formidable in Alfred's day. Guthrum's men may have lined in front of the camp's south wall with a secure position to fall back to. Wherever possible, the Vikings liked to fight close to a fortified base. Another possible site, which has the merit of being closer to Edington and in direct line to a course towards Chippenham, is Edington Hill, on the tumulus-studded downs above the village. At its southward end the hill forms a neck of land with a steep slope guarding its western flank and making a strong defensible position.

Burne plumps for a third alternative on the plain three miles to the south where an ancient ditch crosses the down along Alfred's probable approach route from Warminster. In his interpretation, the battle was fought at this point, after which the Vikings retreated along the ridge road towards Bratton Camp, and possibly also on another track towards the defile between Edington Hill and Tinhead Hill. Burne's site is close to the suggestively named Battlebury Hill which lies between Warminster and the ditch. On the other hand it is a long way from Edington and unlikely to have been part of that estate. Even Burne, normally so confident in his judgements, admits that in this case 'the whole battle is a matter of pure conjecture'.[16]

Alternatively, the battle may not have been fought on the downs at all but in and around the village itself, perhaps in the neighbourhood of the present-day church. In this scenario, perhaps Alfred caught the Vikings by surprise in a reversal of his own experience at Chippenham. Given the lack of topographic details in the sources only archaeology can provide an answer.

Why did Alfred win at *Ethandun*? In battles of the shield-wall, courage and determination were the main qualities needed. Military training was less important. In his Channel 4 series on medieval weaponry, Mike Loades showed that a band of untrained volunteers could be taught to master the basics of fighting with shield and spear in a day.[17] The vital thing was to stand tight and together, and perform simple manoeuvres as a unit. Alfred's men needed to know how to turn about face, and how to advance in a line. Alfred's men were tough and fit enough to endure long marches and the English climate. The necessary brutality probably came naturally too. Many of these men had family and friends to avenge. The fighting of Alfred's wars was close, upfront and personal.

What made the Battle of *Ethandun* so decisive was that Alfred was able to crown his victory by pursuing the Vikings back to their stronghold and then laying siege to it. The Viking stragglers were cut down without mercy. Alfred then 'boldly made camp in front of the gates of the Viking stronghold'. He had already captured the Viking cattle herds and horses. Now, after a fortnight, 'the Vikings, thoroughly terrified by hunger, cold and fear and in the end by despair, sought peace'. It was victory against all odds for Alfred and the men of Wessex and checkmate for Guthrum. But where did this siege take place? The Chronicle mentions only 'the fort' but in a context that suggests it has been named before. The implication is that the fort was none other than the Vikings' base at Chippenham. This seems to be confirmed in a later passage in which 'the [Viking] host went to Cirencester from Chippenham and remained there one year'. Bratton Camp and other waterless hill-forts in the area would not have been able to withstand a fortnight's siege.

The outcome is in all the history books. Alfred took hostages from the Vikings but gave none – 'never before had they made peace with anyone on such terms', comments Asser. The Vikings swore 'great oaths' to leave Alfred's kingdom immediately. And Guthrum promised to become a Christian and accept baptism at Alfred's own hands. The ceremony took place at Aller, near Athelney, three weeks later, when Guthrum became Alfred's spiritual son and acquired a Christian name, Athelstan. The peace treaty was solemnized at Wedmore, where 'Alfred freely bestowed many excellent treasures (*aedificia*) on him and his men'.

The baptism of Guthrum and his chief men was an act of enormous significance. It made Guthrum's surrender complete. The Viking leader could not have taken such a step without consulting his men. And becoming Christians themselves meant that in future they were obliged to refrain from attacking Christian society and its holy places. At a deeper level, it marked a renunciation of the failed old gods with their sacrifices of blood and an acceptance of a new way of looking at the world. Not only had Alfred won but his God had also triumphed over theirs. Surprisingly, perhaps, the treaty held. Guthrum did refrain from attacking Wessex again and henceforth issued coins under his Christian name. In the end, Alfred's achievement and his claim to greatness rest on that spiritual and diplomatic victory at least as much as his military success: 'Whether a great battle or just a fortunate skirmish, Edington was indeed Alfred's great victory'.[18]

Edington Today

Edington is proud of its association with Alfred, as can be seen from its road signs which share the modern name of the village with the West Saxon *Ethandun*. Unfortunately nothing of Alfred's *vill* survives above ground. The large and splendid priory church was founded in 1361, with a now vanished Augustinian monastery close by. Possibly it stood on or near the site of Alfred's hall, which would certainly have had a chapel. The best-known reminder of the battle is the Westbury White Horse, cut into the scarp just west of Bratton, and most easily admired from the viewpoint near Bratton Camp. Unfortunately, it was not carved in Alfred's day but nearer our own

Alfred in triumph on the road signs at Edington.

time, probably in the eighteenth century during a vogue for chalk carving. A rather stiff-looking beast whose legs are too long, its green eye faces towards Edington. Whoever cut the turf might have been thinking of Alfred and the ancient White Horse at Uffington, then thought to commemorate Alfred's victory at Ashdown. If Ashdown had one, so should they.

Edington church, built in the fourteenth century, on or near the site of Alfred's manor below a great rampart of down and close to the old road from Salisbury to Bath.

A monument to the battle was raised on 5 November 2000 close to the car-park at Bratton Camp and to Burne's 'Site B'. It is a sarsen stone from near Kingston Deverill where, according to tradition, Alfred rallied his levies before the Battle of Ashdown. A plaque inset at the base of the stone claims that Alfred's victory at Ethandun 'gave birth to English nationhood'. Although the route of Alfred's march from Iley Oak to Edington, including the ditch at Burne's site 'A' is a MoD range normally closed to the public, there is open access to Bratton Camp, and the Edington area is well-served with paths; a leaflet available in the church describes some thirty of them.[19]

Chapter 8
Brunanburh: The Greatest Battle

Background

The battle, known by the English as *Brunanburh* and by the Welsh and Irish annalists as *bellum Brune*, is one of the most famous in Dark Age history. It is also well known as the battlefield that has been 'lost': finding *Brunanburh* is the battlefield detective's ultimate challenge. *Brunanburh* was fought in the year 937, probably in August or September. Remembered as the greatest battle since the Saxons first set foot in Britain five centuries before, it was a classic confrontation between north and south, with a confederation of Vikings, Scots and Celts pitted against the English Saxons, now more or less united under the rule of Alfred's grandson, King Athelstan.

The northern half of Britain was by now a patchwork of Viking, British and Gaelic-speaking kingdoms. There were Norse rulers in York, Dublin and the Hebrides. Strathclyde, the old British kingdom in south-west Scotland and Cumbria was a melting-pot of peoples of Irish, British and Norse ancestry. 'Scotia', the old name for the kingdom of Scotland, was a rather vaguely defined area covering the central lowlands and much of the old Pictish kingdoms in the east. Its king, Constantine II of the house of McAlpin, was to play an important part in creating the alliance to confront Alfred's grandson, Athelstan.

Athelstan's ambition was to unite the island of Britain under the rule of the house of Alfred, and to at least contain if not defeat the menace of the Vikings. His power-play involved evicting the Viking king of York, and isolating the king of Dublin by wooing the 'native' kings of Scotland and Strathclyde under pledges of friendship. When Constantine of Scotland proved an unreliable friend, Athelstan enforced his will, rather as King Henry VIII did 600 years later, by invading Scotland by land and sea. He received the submission of the princes of Wales and made them pay him an annual tribute. The proud *Rex Totius Britanniae* emblazoned on his silver pennies said it all.

The Celtic and Scandinavian kings of the north and west were naturally unhappy at this turn of events. Constantine of Scotland sealed an alliance with Olaf Gothfrithsson, the Viking king of Dublin, by marriage to his daughter, a union condemned by

The tomb of Athelstan in Malmesbury Abbey.

English writers as idolatrous since Olaf was a pagan.[1] Athelstan showed his displeasure by burning and pillaging in the north, and taking Constantine's son as hostage back to England. But by exploiting widespread resentment of the power of the southern Saxons, and promising rich pickings once Athelstan was overthrown, Olaf and Constantine brokered an impressive northern alliance. It included another Olaf, the son of the ousted king of York, as well as Constantine's nephew, Owen of Strathclyde, and the wild Gall-Gaels of the Western Isles, renegade Christians who had come to 'out-Viking' the Vikings. The whole ambitious enterprise was probably stage-managed by Constantine, although Olaf of Dublin seems to have been the military leader. The plan, it seems, was to turn Athelstan out of the north and the Danelaw (as the Danish-settled Midlands were now called), and if possible to dethrone or kill him. In a royal grant made shortly afterwards, Athelstan referred to Olaf's attempt 'to deprive me of both life and realm'. For the rank and file, and no doubt some of the leaders too, the promise of plunder may have been a greater motivation.

Attracted to the cause were many great men with large followings, including at least five Irish kinglets of Viking descent. The men who served the grand alliance of 937 must have numbered in their thousands, although of course the exact size of Olaf's nd Constantine's army at *Brunanburh* is unknowable. Led by many kings, some of whom had been bitter enemies in the past, the force was potentially unwieldy. It seems that the various war-bands fought in separate units; one source refers to the 'conflict of banners' floating above the great northern army.[2] Whether everyone involved made it to the climactic battle is also uncertain. Much depends on where the battlefield was. On this, as in much else in the *Brunanburh* campaign, the sources are contradictory and none are wholly to be trusted.

Against this horde, Athelstan summoned what was effectively a national English army. With the king was his half-brother Edmund, who later succeeded him, and two royal cousins, Aelfwine and Aethelwine. The clergy were well represented, with at least three bishops, including Waerstan of Sherborne and Theodred of London. According to a later narrative called *Egil's Saga*, Athelstan was also served by a force of Vikings under Egil and his brother Thorolf.[3] With all England south of the Trent to draw on, Athelstan's army could perhaps have numbered as many as 7,000 or 8,000 armed men. The chronicler, William of Malmesbury, writing 200 years later, claims that Athelstan led 100,000 men into battle, which does at least mean that William considered it to be a very large force indeed.[4]

The convergence of the coalition northern army at *Brunanburh* is one of the most remarkable feats of arms in the Dark Ages. Had Athelstan been defeated northern Britain might have become a federation of English, Norse, Welsh and Celtic kingdoms. Perhaps Yorkshire would have become part of an enlarged northern Celtic state, or even a separate entity. Birmingham might have been a border town. As it was, the fruits of Athelstan's victory lasted only as long as Athelstan himself. When he died, two years later, aged only about 40, Olaf took the opportunity to launch another, more successful, if less ambitious, large-scale raid that took him far into the English Midlands.

The Sources
Unfortunately, the reign of Athelstan was poorly recorded by contemporaries and we are forced back onto later documents of doubtful value, notably a thirteenth-century Icelandic saga and the twelfth-century chronicle of William of Malmesbury. The one truly contemporary source is a famous Old English war-poem included in full in the Anglo-Saxon Chronicle.[5] It has been translated by, among others, Alfred Tennyson, who loved its 'rush of alliterative verse' and war-song spirit. It is indeed a fine piece of rhythmic Old English, but for the battlefield-seeker it has the disadvantages of being a poem, long on martial energy and short on information. The following is a prose summary of what it tells us.

In the year 937, King Athelstan and his half-brother Edmund fought a coalition of Scots and Vikings ('the host from the ships') at *Brunanburh*. It was 'instinctive' in the royal leaders, the poem reminds us, 'to defend their land, their treasure and their homes in frequent battle against the enemy'. The great battle began at dawn and lasted until sunset, by which time the field was dark with the blood of men 'where standards clashed and spear met spear'. By its close, many a northern invader lay in their gore, 'torn by spears, shot over his shield'. The victorious West Saxons pursued the enemy 'in troops', cutting down the fugitives 'cruelly, with blades whetted on grindstones'. Their Mercian allies, too, fought hard against the ship-borne warriors of 'Anlaf' (Anlaf is the Irish form of Olaf, that is, Olaf Gothfrithson, king of Dublin) who 'invaded our land across the tossing waters'. Among the heaps of slain lay five kings and seven earls.

Olaf himself fled back to his ships with what was left of his following. Likewise his ally, the aged Constantine, king of Scots, that 'hoary-headed traitor', abandoned the field, leaving his son among the dead, 'mangled by wounds'. Many martial deeds were done that day. The Norsemen returned to Dublin in their ships upon *Dinges mere*, 'ashamed and shameless back to Ireland'. Triumphant in war, Athelstan and Edmund returned to Wessex, leaving the dead as carrion for wolves, ravens and eagles. 'Never before in this island', the poem concludes, 'was an army put to greater slaughter by the sword since the time when the Angles and Saxons landed and won for themselves a kingdom.'

The battle poem confirms the importance of the battle as a deliverance from an unprecedented 'Celtic alliance' of Vikings, Britons and Scots. It shows the men of Wessex and Mercia fighting side by side in what was probably a key moment in the emergence of an English nation-state. Its rugged verse and gloating tone take one about as close as any document can to the spirit of the time. But the document is, after all, a poem. It celebrates the valour of the men of England but it is not the purpose of the poet to go into the whys and wherefores, nor to fix the battle in time and space. Perhaps everyone at the time knew where *Brunanburh* was, or maybe the exact site was neither here nor there.

From the Irish perspective, the *Annals of Ulster* confirm that the struggle was 'immense, lamentable and horrible, and desperately fought'. 'Several thousands of Norsemen, who are uncounted, fell', but 'a large number of Saxons fell on the other side'. Even so, Athelstan 'enjoyed a great victory'. Another Irish source, the *Annals of Clonmacnoise*, tell us that the dead of *Brunanburh* included Cellach, son of King Constantine, Gebeachan, the Norse king of the Western Isles, Owen, the king of Strathclyde and two sons of Sihtric, the erstwhile king of York. But Athelstan also suffered heavy casualties, including the two royal cousins, Aelfwine and Aethelwine, two bishops, including Waerstan of Sherborne, two unnamed ealdormen and 'a multitude of lesser men'. William of Malmesbury refers to the 'pitiable slaughter polluting the air with a foul stench'. A German cleric based at Canterbury compared Athelstan with Joshua, as the 'leader of God's earthly armies so that the king, mighty in war, might conquer other fierce kings and crush their proud necks'.[6] The same antagonism between Celt and Saxon is reflected in a contemporary note by a Welsh poet: 'Now we will pay them back for the 404 years . . . We will drive them out at *Aber Santwic*' (i.e. Sandwich in Kent).[7]

For more information about the battle one is obliged to fall back on the most detailed but at the same time most controversial source, the account of the Battle of Vinheath in *Egil's Saga*. This is an Icelandic text which tells of the wandering life of the Viking hero and warrior-poet Egil Skallagrimsson. First written down 300 years after the events it describes, it is clearly a romanticized tale of a hero whose exploits had doubtless grown in the telling. Its account of the battle assumed to be *Brunanburh* is garbled, but some scholars believe, or at least hope, that it contains a kernel of fact. The problem lies in telling fact from fiction or, as Alfred Burne put it, in sifting the good grain from the chaff. The following is a summary of the battle as told in the saga.

A Scottish king by the name of Olafr Rauthi (Olaf the Red) had invaded England with a large force of Vikings, Briton and Scots, and defeated two northern English earls whose names he gives in Norse form as Alfgeir and Gothrekr (in English, Alfgar and Godric). Hearing of this, two Welsh earls also bearing the Norse-sounding names of Hring and Adils (or Athils) deserted Athelstan and defected to Olaf with their men. Athelstan (spelt 'Athelsteinn' in the saga), faced by overwhelming enemy force and desertions in his own ranks, was advised to wait for reinforcements before fighting Olaf. Fortunately, and unlikely as it may seem, the Viking Egil and his brother Thorolf joined Athelstan with their own following of 300 warriors.

On Egil's advice, Athelstan sent a messenger to Olaf proposing to fight him at 'Vinheath' in one week's time. As was the custom, the battlefield, large enough to hold both armies, would be marked and enclosed with hazel rods ('enhazeled'), and Olaf would in the mean time be honour-bound to desist from raiding until the issue was decided by battle. 'Heath' (*heathr*) in this context means open ground, but not necessarily moorland.

The chosen battlefield was a level plain with 'a great wood' ('Vin-wood') on one side and a river on the other. To the north and south lay *borgs* or well-fortified settlements. Olaf's men pitched their tents on a hillside by the northern *borg*, which some have taken to be *Brunanburh* itself. Meanwhile Athelstan deployed his army at the southern end where the gap between the forest and the river was narrowest. The English king cunningly disguised his lack of numbers by pitching empty tents ('no man in every third tent and few in any one'). Moreover, the tents were 'so high that no one could see over them to find out whether they were many or a few rows deep'. This implies that the line of tents was situated on the crest of a southward slope.

To play for time, Athelstan made Olaf a generous, indeed impossible, offer. He promised to pay him geld of one silver shilling for every plough of land in his kingdom. When Olaf held out for even more, a three-day truce was held while, out of sight, reinforcements quietly arrived to Athelstan's camp by day and by night. At the close of the truce the English king repeated his offer of peace and friendship, but on the third and final parley he sent Olaf a different answer: Olaf should agree to become Athelstan's vassal, repay all the loot he had stolen and then double back to where he came from. 'Go back now', he told his messenger, 'and tell him this is the way things are'.

Realizing he had been tricked, Olaf prepared for battle. At the suggestion of the treacherous Welsh earl Adils, Olaf agreed that a mounted company led by Adils and his fellow earl Hring should attempt to take the Saxons by surprise by attacking at daybreak. This ruse was initially successful. Pressed by Adils's division, Alfgeir gave ground and fled the field. Next the Welsh earls turned on the division led by Egil and his brother. The two Vikings, needless to say, proved a much more formidable foe. Using the forest as cover, Thorolf cleared a path to Hring's standard. He thrust his spear through the earl's coat of mail and, thus transfixing his body, 'lifted him up on it above his own head and thrust the end into the ground'. With his men falling around him, Adils threw down his own standard and fled to the safety of the forest.

By now night seems to have fallen, and Egil rejoined Athelstan's main force which had now arrived on the field. Athelstan put his best fighters in the front rank under his own, and Egil's, command. A second body under Thorolf was detached to take on the Scots, who 'tend to break ranks, run back and forth and appear in different places'. 'They often prove dangerous if you do not keep on the alert', counselled the king, 'but will retreat if you confront them'. Athelstan's and Egil's division fought on the side nearest the river, with Thorolf's men to their left on the forest side. Olaf, too, formed his army into two columns, the Scots facing Thorolf and the Norsemen Egil and Athelstan. 'Both armies were so big that it was impossible to tell which was the larger'.

The armies crashed together and a great battle ensued. Thorolf's men advanced towards the Scots holding their shields in front of them. But Thorolf himself, advancing too far, was ambushed by Adils's men hidden in the forest and fell pierced by many spears. Seeing his brother's standard being withdrawn, Egil ran over and rallied Thorolf's men, then drove through the enemy 'chopping either side' with his sword, Adder. He eventually caught up with earl Adils and, after exchanging a few blows, killed him. They pursued the fleeing Scots, cutting them down as they ran, 'for it was pointless for anyone to ask for his life to be spared'.

Both English divisions now turned on the Vikings who were holding firm on the side nearest the river. After a great struggle, the now outnumbered and out-flanked Vikings began to crumble and Olaf was killed. There, too, no mercy was shown. Athelstan, with Egil's help, won a great victory. Thorolf was buried with battle honours nearby, while the king took off one of his arm rings and presented it to Egil, who was additionally rewarded with two chests of silver. Thus was the Battle of Vinheath concluded, according to *Egil's Saga*.

There are aspects of this tale that are plausible and which may be more or less historical. It is likely that both sides fought in two divisions. It is quite possible that the Scots broke first, and that the experienced Viking warriors put up the hardest resistance. But the saga story, like other sagas, is obviously garbled and fictionalized, as well as containing statements that are demonstrably wrong. It conflates the historical Olaf and Constantine, who both survived the battle, into one character, Olaf the Red. The four named earls are otherwise unknown to history, and although 'Adils' could be a corruption of Idwal, a contemporary prince of Gwynedd, there is no evidence that the latter was present at the battle. While hazelling was used, at least in the sagas, to surround the site of a duel rather like a boxing ring, it is most unlikely that whole armies would agree to meet on a certain date at a neatly enclosed ground to slug it out. And, needless to say, Athelstan is not likely to have entrusted command to an unknown Viking, though he may well have had Viking mercenaries in his ranks.

There are other suspicious signs. In the saga things tend to come in threes – Athelstan's threefold offer of peace, the three-day truce and the three-day rides of the messengers, to say nothing of Egil's 300 men. There is the suspicious match of the two 'good' earls and the two 'bad' ones, and the likewise chessboard symmetry of the battlefield. Ian McDougal has pointed out that Athelstan's *ruse de guerre* in hoodwinking Olaf is a stock story based on classical models.[8] Another saga, possibly by the same bard, has Harald Hardrada firing an impregnable fortress in Sicily by tying flaming brands to the backs of birds. It is not even absolutely certain that the saga's Vinheath *is Brunanburh*. In the saga the battle takes place near the beginning of Athelstan's reign, not near its end. The latest editors of the saga regard them as separate events, dating Vinheath or 'Wen Heath' to the year 925, twelve years before *Brunanburh*.[9]

Despite its limitations as a source, *Egil's Saga* has been taken seriously by those attempting to locate the battle. Maybe it is a matter of clutching at straws. There is some corroboration of the saga's description of the field in William of Malmesbury's brief mention of the 'evenness of the green plain' on which the battle was fought.[10] Likewise the chronicle of Symeon of Durham mentions a fort he calls *Brunanwerk* to the north of the battlefield standing on a hill called *Wendun*, evidently confirming at least one of the saga's *borgs*, assuming that his is an independent account.[11]

William claims he drew his information from a now lost poem praising the deeds of Athelstan. In this version, the king was criticized for his 'long leisure hours' of delay while the enemy ravaged his countrymen's lands. The Norsemen and their Scots allies had descended on Northumbria with barbarian savagery, 'driving out the people, setting fire to the fields . . . The green corn withered in the fields, the blighted cornfield mocked the husbandman's prayers.'[12] Scholarly opinion has on the whole rejected this lost poem of Athelstan's deeds on the grounds that its language sounds more like William's own time than that of the tenth century. However, the historian Michael Wood has made what I find a compelling case for reopening the issue.[13] William was an honest chronicler who had a special interest in Athelstan. His monastery at Malmesbury had even been chosen by Athelstan as his burial place (an empty tomb-chest in the surviving nave of the abbey is said to be his, though its effigy seems to have been 'borrowed' from another grave). It was also the burial place of the king's cousins Aelfwine and Aethelwine slain in the battle. Perhaps William discovered his 'ancient book' in the monastic library at Malmesbury. And, if so, could this lost book, with its bad Latin and 'excessive and bombastic style', have been a genuine document from the time of the great king? Wood argued that a forger would have been unlikely to include criticism of the king for delay while his subjects were slaughtered, and the account does ring true.

One other chronicle of the twelfth century adds an important crumb of information about the battle. Florence, also known, perhaps more correctly, as 'John', of Worcester, followed by several slightly later chroniclers, claims that the Norse ships had sailed into the Humber.[14] Symeon adds that Olaf commanded a fleet of 615(!) ships. The Scots too seem to have used ships. These claims have been seized on as indicating that the battle took place not far from the Humber, perhaps in Holderness or somewhere further south along the long road to London. But what evidence did Florence have to support his statement? Did he have some source unknown to us? As for Symeon and the rest, they may well have copied Florence, but, as Alfred Burne points out, 'they found nothing incredible in the statement; they had no difficulty accepting it'.[15]

A final snippet of information from a charter shows that Olaf was still in Dublin in mid-August, having been busy for much of that year fighting a minor war in Limerick. This indicates that *Brunanburh* was fought late in the season, probably in September. Assuming Olaf took the short way across the Irish Sea, as the war-poem certainly implies, where does that leave Constantine and his allies? The implication, surely, is that Constantine began his march south much earlier in the year. Even unopposed it would have taken him the best part of seven weeks to march from Scone, in modern Perthshire, to York, longer still if *Brunanburh* was on the Irish Sea coast. This could explain Athelstan's delay. He was waiting to see what Olaf would do. Olaf's arrival was the cue for the showdown. Until then, the north would have to do the best it could unaided.

Locating the Battle

Finding the lost battlefield of *Brunanburh* has kept antiquarians and historians busy for a long time. Some forty sites have been proposed, ranging from Axminster in Devon to Dunbar near Edinburgh.[16] Some of these are based on little more than wishful thinking and a fancied resemblance of place-names: Bromfield in Somerset, for example, or Brumford in Northumberland. Such a multiplicity of locations is possible only because there is remarkably little to go on. Nowhere today is there a

Battle of *Brunanburh* as imagined by Guy Halsall

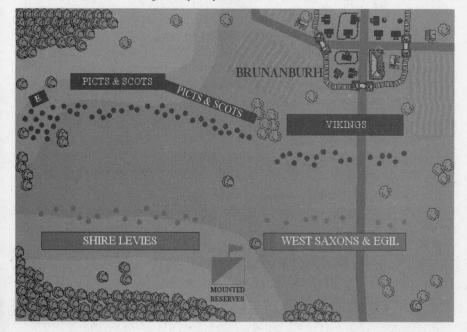

place called *Brunanburh*. Even the early chroniclers refer to the battle under a variety of spellings – sometimes in the same document! Apart from the battle poem's *Brunanburh*, there is the *Brunandune* in the chronicle of Aethelweard, followed by Henry of Huntingdon's *Brunesburh*, Roger of Hovedon's *Brunnanbyrg* or *Bruneberih*, the *Brunnanburch* of the Chronicles of Melrose, and the *Brumford* or *Brunfort* of Ralph Higden of Chester! The chronicler Gaimer had got hold of the name *Bruneswerce*, perhaps a variation of Symeon of Durham's *Brunanwerc*. The sense in each case is something like 'Bruna's fort' or 'Bruna's stronghold', which might be rendered in modern English as 'Brown's town'. 'Dune' as in *Brunandune* means 'open land' and has the same basic meaning as William of Malmesbury's *Brunanfeld* ('Bruna's field') or the Norse word *hethr* as in Vin-heath. *Brunanburh*, then, was evidently open, possibly cultivated land, with some sort of stronghold a little way to the north, possibly situated on a hill.

So where was it? Four candidates stand out. The first in chronological order is Burnswark Hill between Lockerbie and Ecclefechan in Annandale in the old county of Dumfries. This location was put forward with great conviction by George Neilson in 1909.[17] He based his argument on the medieval Scottish chronicler Fordun, who describes the invading fleet landing in the Solway Firth, and on the similarity of the name Burnswark to the *Bruneswerce* of Geoffrey Gaimer. On the basis of the description in the saga, and especially Athelstan's *ruse de guerre* with the tents, Neilson considered that Olaf and the Scots must have camped in a Roman earthwork just north of Burnswark Hill, with Athelstan's army a quarter of a mile to the south. A nearby farm called The Whins might be an echo of Symeon's *Wendun*, while three miles to the south is a place called Brown Moor which could be the saga's Vin-heath. Neilson sited the battle itself on the elevated flat-top of Burnswark Hill – which would certainly have made a dramatic piece of military theatre.

Neilson's theory was criticized in the same journal by Alice Law.[18] She pointed out that his battlefield measures only about 350 by 200 metres – hardly room for up to 20,000 men. The site nevertheless received the weighty support of Sir Charles Oman, the authority on medieval warfare. But Alfred Burne gave it a resounding thumbs-down:

> The imagination boggles at the idea of 40,000 soldiers milling on a polo ground on top of a mountain. It would resemble a monstrous Rugger 'scrum' ... This is to reduce the battle to an affair of boy scouts or schoolchildren on Tom Tiddler's ground.[19]

Nearly thirty years on, W S Angus accepted Neilson's general thesis, but moved the battlefield two miles south-east to Middlebie Hill. Like Neilson, he placed an absolute faith in the truth of Athelstan's trick with the tents, arguing that, 'if the English wished to conceal the weakness of their advanced guard, they would seek a position visible by their enemies but not under close observation'.[20] Angus claimed to have found such a position on the knoll of Middlebie Hill where the enemy would spot the tents but fail to notice Athelstan's main camp beyond the hill in some old earthworks known as the Birrens.

But this sort of rationalizing from topographical features misses the point. If *Egil's Saga* is to be taken at its face value, Athelstan challenged the northerners to battle at a named spot. Is it likely, asked Burne, that he would have named so remote a spot within the kingdom of the Britons of Strathclyde of which he could have had little knowledge? And, if so, would Olaf and Constantine then oblige him by retreating back into their own lands? 'The idea is nonsensical.'[21] In short, the Burnswark site relies on selective evidence from unreliable sources, ignores considerations of military probability and places its reliance on a fictionalized and discredited account. Wherever else it may have been, the battle was not, it seems pretty certain, fought at Burnswark.

Alfred Burne's own favoured site was Brinsworth, near Rotherham in the West Riding of Yorkshire. This site had first been suggested by J H Cockburn in 1930, largely on the grounds of what he considered to be place-name evidence.[22] Cockburn's book on the subject has been described as 'a tissue of implausibles, false etymologies and wrong-headed history, stitched together with all the zeal of a local enthusiast',[23] but others have come to broadly the same conclusion, if by a different route. Like Cockburn, Alfred Burne accepted Florence of Worcester's statement that the invading fleet first sailed into the Humber, and that the battle must therefore have been fought somewhere east of the Pennines and south of the Humber. On the grounds of 'inherent military probability' Burne reasoned that the northerners must have concentrated at Tadcaster where the River Ouse crosses the great north road. If so, it must have been near here that they defeated the northern earls as related in the saga, much as Harald Hardrada did to a similar force of local levies in 1066.

Deducing from a charter reference to his earlier invasion of Scotland that Athelstan would have chosen to advance the same way in 937, Burne has Athelstan concentrating his own force at Derby. The two armies, he reckoned, would make contact somewhere on Ryknild Street, the Roman road that links Derby and Tadcaster. A natural defensive position lies just south of the old Roman town of Templeborough where a bottleneck is formed by the River Rother. On the grounds of its relationship to the description in the saga, as well as the 'village bearing the suggestive name of Brinsworth', Burne placed the battle along an east–west ridge measuring 1,800 metres just west of the Rother between Brinsworth and Catliffe. This, he was confident, satisfied both *Egil's Saga* and military probability. Furthermore, and purely by chance, Burne heard of a local tradition of a big battle that took place in this area long ago, which, he reasoned, could only be *Brunanburh*. Burne dismissed the arguments in favour of Burnswark on the reasonable grounds already made. More brusquely, he dismissed the claims of Bromborough in the Wirral, to which we will return in a moment. The philological evidence in the latter's favour, he claimed, was simply irrelevant. 'Apart from the similarity of name, Bromborough has nothing in common with either Egil's Saga or I.M.P.' (i.e. 'Inherent Military Probability'): Q.E.D. Burne's is still perhaps the best-known account of the battle, owing to the continued popularity of his books. His case is well-argued and persuasive, and his careful selection of the evidence to suit his case is easy to overlook.[24]

Thirty years on, Michael Wood came to broadly the same conclusion as Burne, but as the result of an independent investigation. Like Burne, he drew attention to

> the striking correspondence between the Brinsworth site and the famous description of Vinheath ... with its forts north and south of the field, its gentle slopes north and south, the steep slope to the river, and the narrow gap to the south where the river and the forest come close together.[25]

Only scraps of the forest, now called Tinsley Wood, remain, but Wood showed that at the time of the Domesday Book it had been much larger, measuring about a mile by a mile and a half. He also discovered that the nearby, apparently insignificant, Tinsley Chapel used to receive a royal stipend for a special chantry service. Could this have been a service for the dead of *Brunanburh*? The place where, according to local tradition, a great battle had been fought, was White Hill, near Tinsley. Could this have been the *Weondun* of Symeon of Durham?

There are two main problems with Brinsworth. First, the Old English name for Brinsworth as set out in the Domesday Book is *Brynesford*, which on linguistic grounds cannot be *Brunanburh*. And it is hard to square with the clear statement in the battle poem that Olaf sailed 'shameless and ashamed' back to Dublin from whence he had come. Dublin is a long way from the Humber by sea, even if Olaf was able to transport his boats overland from the Forth to the Clyde. Burne gets around that problem by explaining that there were in fact two Olafs, and that the Anglo-Saxon Chronicle simply made a mistake by merging them into one. The Olaf who actually sailed back to Dublin was, he argued, a different Olaf, the son of Sihtric the One-eyed, the sometime king of York. Confusingly this second Olaf later became king of Dublin in his turn. Perhaps, therefore, the task of this second Olaf was to make a diversionary raid from Ireland on the west coast. But asserting that our best contemporary source simply got it wrong might seem to some observers to be skating on very thin ice.

A case for a more southern location for *Brunanburh* was made by Alfred Smyth.[26] Smyth used the saga to support his own idea that the battle was fought by the Forest of Bromswold between the Nene and the Welland in Northamptonshire. Bromswold is a good match for William of Malmesbury's *Bruneswald*, and Smyth found other similarities to the landscape described in the saga. In his view, the battle must have taken place in the territory of the southern Danelaw in the East Midlands, the centre of activity in Olaf's subsequent invasions in 940 and 943. But, it could be argued, a battlefield so close to the great abbey at Peterborough, where one of the Anglo-Saxon chronicles was compiled, would never have been 'lost'. And while Olaf's band did indeed manage to take advantage of the death of Athelstan to ravage the Midlands, would the mighty coalition of *Brunanburh* have held together so far from home? And would the Saxon king have allowed them to come so far?

The fourth plausible location for the battle is at Bromborough on the Wirral, close by the Mersey between Birkenhead and Ellesmere Port. Bromborough has at least one thing massively in its favour: as A H Smith demonstrated from a close study of thirteenth-century charters, Bromborough was the medieval *Brunburh*, of which *Brunanburh* would be a logical Old English form.[27] Bromborough, scholars agree, could have been *Brunanburh*. But is it *our Brunanburh*? The location is perfect as a landing ground for a fleet from Dublin. As Stephen Harding has demonstrated using place-name evidence and a surviving fragment of a document known as Ingimund's *Saga*, the Wirral had been settled by a party of Norsemen from Ireland early in the tenth century. It had trading links with other Norse settlements around the Irish Sea and political contact with the mighty neighbouring kingdom of Mercia. The problem for *Brunanburh* seekers was that the Wirral seemed to lack place-names and topographical features that tied it to the battle. Another problem is the battle poem's reference to an all-day pursuit of the Vikings which implied a location further from the sea. However the wording is ambiguous, and isn't easy to square with the poem's assertion that the battle also lasted all day. Another objection is that, while Bromborough is a convenient enough location for Olaf, it would have involved a long and roundabout journey for the Scots and Gall-Gaels, whether by land or sea. And there is no other instance in the whole of the Dark Ages of Scots armies operating so far from home.

Is this *Brunanburh*? Bebington Heath is a haven of green between the River Dibben and Storeton Woods (in the distance). 'Bruna's Fort' is probably the modern Poulton Hall, on the site of a Norman castle. (© Stephen Harding.)

New evidence pieced together by Stephen Harding and his colleagues at Nottingham University may answer at least some of these objections. The Wirral has in fact no fewer than three place-names that could derive from 'Bruna' – three 'Brown's towns': Bromborough, Brimstage and the lost village of Brimston. Bruna, whoever he was, must have been a person of consequence locally. Moreover, Harding, with some help from Judith Jesch, Professor of Viking Studies at Nottingham University, and place-name expert Paul Cavill, has come up with a plausible explanation for that puzzling place mentioned in the poem: *Dinges mere*. He argues that the *ding* refers to a Viking assembly or *thing*, which survives in the modern Wirral town of Thingwall. 'Ding' is simply *thing* said in a Celtic Irish accent ('dat ting, the Ding') – which no doubt the Dublin Vikings would by now have acquired. The site of this particular *thing* is believed to be Cross Hill, near the present A551. Thus *Dinges mere* would have meant 'thing-marsh', perhaps the tenth century name for the treacherous tidal marshes of the Dee.[28]

Harding suggests that the Vikings retreated from the battlefield somewhere near Bromborough, across the spine of the Wirral and down to the Dee marshes where their ships were drawn up. He proposes that the battle was fought at Bebington Heath, with the Vikings occupying a slight ridge just above the woods on Storeton Hill. 'Bruna's fort' may have been a precursor of the present-day Poulton Hall, 'home since 1093 of the Lancelyn-Green family'. If so, the battlefield certainly justifies William of Malmesbury's description of Athelstan's strategy as 'a thunderbolt'. Choosing to crush the enemy on his landing-grounds is reminiscent of King Harold's rapid response to news of invasion before Stamford Bridge, and again before Hastings. Perhaps Harold had Athelstan's example in mind.

The Dee estuary near Heswall on the Wirral, probably the site of *Dinges mere* or 'Thing Marsh', the harbour to which Olafs Vikings fled after the battle. (© Stephen Harding.)

Stephen Harding's case for basing the battle in the Wirral made the headlines.

The Harding battlefield, like the Burne one, lies in a heavily built-up area. Bebington is now a suburb of Bromborough, and the M53 motorway bisects its western flank. In the distance lie the belching towers of the Stanlow oil refinery. The only part of the field still open is Brackenwood golf course. As the *Independent*'s reporter put it, 'the English began their pursuit, chasing their quarry up what is now the fairway of the par 11th hole'.

The claim that the lost battlefield of *Brunanburh* had at long last been found received widespread press and TV coverage in December 2004. 'For the cradle of English civilization, go to the Wirral', suggested the *Independent*. This will be happy news to the Wirral's tourist enterprise, which is working up the area's Viking antecedents. However battlefield-seekers tend to be chary of claims made on linguistic evidence alone. Investigators plan to make a geophysical survey of the site, but Professor Harding believes that the thin soils of the area are unlikely to preserve any substantial military remains. The most that can be said is that Bromborough is far and away the most likely site on place-name grounds but that a plausible military explanation that would unite the Vikings, Scots and their allies at the Wirral is still lacking.

Summing up

The location of *Brunanburh* has challenged battlefield enthusiasts for centuries, and much ink has been spilled over it. In his edition of the battle poem published in 1937, Alistair Campbell famously concluded that 'all hope of localizing *Brunanburh* is lost'.[29] His reason for 'this depressing conclusion', as Burne referred to it, was Campbell's dismissal of *Egil's Saga* as a factual source for the battle. If, as Campbell argued, this part of the saga is a romantic fiction – a medieval version of a Barbara Cartland novel – then the materials for identifying the lost battlefield simply don't exist.

If one chooses to follow Florence of Worcester – and many later chroniclers did – then a location somewhere south of the Humber and east of the Pennines is indicated. If one places more reliance on the near-contemporary battle poem, the battle was more likely fought by the Irish Sea, probably at Bromborough. Alfred Smyth presents a closely argued case for a site in the East Midlands, while Kevin Halloran has, I understand, made a detailed case for a site near Burnley which has yet to be published. If one placed a special weight on medieval Scottish sources, there might even be something to be said for Burnswark. They cannot of course all be right, and it is quite possible that none of them are! For my own part, though my heart is in the Tinsley-Brinsworth site championed by Alfred Burne and Michael Wood, Stephen Harding's case for a site on the Wirral looks more convincing – at least for the moment!

Chapter 9
Spears as Tribute: The Battle of Maldon

Background

The surviving 325-line fragment of an Anglo-Saxon poem, composed around 1000 by an unknown person, gives us an exceptionally close glimpse of a Dark Age battle and the people who fought in it. No one knows what the original poem was called, but since 1846 it has been called *The Battle of Maldon*.[1] Vivid, straightforward and realistic, the poem tells of the death of Byrhtnoth and his men in battle against the Viking invaders at Maldon. The poem was plainly intended to inspire its audience with the same heroic spirit. It celebrates the martial qualities of the warrior, with his physical strength and indomitable courage, sense of honour and pride in his ancestry. Byrhtnoth and several of his companions make exemplary speeches, all to the same purpose: that no one shall reproach them for running away; they will go forward and conquer or die. The poet is showing his audience how men ought to behave in battle. Of course, since everyone who was with Byrhtnoth died at Maldon, a modern audience might wonder how the poet was able to record their last moments so faithfully. The speeches attributed to them were, of course, made up by the poet. It has been called a sort of 'medieval journalism'.[2] All the same, it is not at all unlikely that the simple martial virtues extolled by the Maldon poet were indeed shared by Byrhtnoth and his men. The purpose of the poem was to praise the brave Byrhtnoth and set an example of how to behave when facing death on the battlefield.

There are several other contemporary sources for the battle. There is the usual brief passage in the Anglo-Saxon Chronicle,[3] and a longer one in the *Vita Oswaldi* (Life of St Oswald),[4] both of which provide a broader context for the battle and its aftermath. The account in the *Vita Oswaldi*, composed by a monk of Ramsey, Cambridgeshire, around the year 1000, is generalized but not incompatible with the poem, though it omits all details of the battlefield. The twelfth-century *Liber Eliensis* (*Book of Ely*) gives a different account of the battle[5] – or rather battles, since it presents two battles at Maldon separated by four years (see below). The Viking sagas are surprisingly

Statue of ealdorman Byrhtnoth at Ely Cathedral. (© The Battlefields Trust, www.battlefieldstrust.com)

silent, and the Norman chroniclers have little to add to what we already know. It is a measure of how lop-sided our knowledge is even of this exceptionally well-recorded battle that we do not even know for sure who the Viking leader was.

The Battle of Maldon was fought at the start of the time of the notorious Danegelds of Aethelred the Unready. Before 980, England had experienced no Viking raids for a generation. There was still a large Danish-speaking population in parts of eastern and northern England, but they were farmers and traders, not raiders, and had become assimilated under the peaceful rule of Alfred's great-grandson, King Eadgar. Then, four years after Eadgar's death, the raids began. Out of the blue, in 980, seven longships appeared at *Hamtun* (Southampton) and they slew or took prisoner most of the population. The same year Viking marauders harried Thanet in Kent, while another 'pirate host from the north' plundered the town of Chester. In 981 the longboats destroyed Padstow and all down the coast of Devon and Cornwall. Then it was the turn of Dorset, when Portland was ravaged by 'three pirate crews'. After a lull, the raids stepped up. In 988, the Vikings attacked at Watchet. There was time for organized resistance led by a local thegn, Goda, 'but Goda was slain and many with him'.

The chroniclers reported the raids without suggesting a cause. The most likely reason for the growth of 'pirate' activity is events in Denmark. Since the time of Alfred and Athelstan, Denmark had become Christianized under King Harald Bluetooth. As in England, Christianity brought more than a change of gods. The Church created an exalted form of kingship and smiled on the conquests of the likes of Harald Bluetooth so long as that in doing so he also converted the heathen. Hence warriors and missionaries went to war together. The result was that, as Harald's authority extended into larger and larger parts of Scandinavia, so local leaders who preferred the old anarchic ways felt tempted to try their luck overseas. Unlike the men who fought Alfred, these marauders were not in search of land so much as portable wealth, especially money. With enough of it, they could re-establish their fortunes at home, or at least retire wealthy.

Two political factors may have influenced events. First, in 986 Harald Bluetooth was overthrown in favour of his son, Sweyn Forkbeard. Sweyn's ambitions, as things turned out, extended beyond Scandinavia to England. And England was more vulnerable than for many years past, following the untimely death of King Eadgar in 975. The new king, Aethelred, was a youngster who did not enjoy the same easy authority as his father. Worse, he did not improve with age: Aethelred was weak, indecisive and, on occasion, treacherous. To later generations he was to become Aethelred *Unraed*, that is, Aethelred the Unwise. Later still, he was immortalized as Ethelred the Unready, our 'first Bad King'.

This was the background against which the most dangerous raid so far took place. In 991 a large fleet of 93 ships appeared at Folkestone and harried the lands around the town. It moved on to pillage Sandwich, and thence across the Thames estuary and north along the Essex coast to Ipswich, the attackers 'over-running all the countryside' and sacking the town. Who led this expedition, the largest to trouble England's shores for nearly fifty years? The 'A' or Parker Chronicle names one 'Anlaf', that is, Olaf Tryggvason of Norway. This Olaf was a descendant of the Norse King Harald Finehair, and four years after the Battle of Maldon he succeeded in making himself

Aerial view of the Maldon battlefield. (© The Battlefields Trust.)

king of that country. That he was certainly among the raiders of 991 is proven by the text of a treaty made later that year which names him. However, three years later, in 994, Olaf had joined forces with Sweyn Forkbeard in an attack on London. This expedition disposed of 94 ships, around the same number as at Maldon, suggesting that the 991 raid was on a similar scale, and may therefore have been led by Sweyn himself. A third possibility, based on brief but apparently independent accounts in the *Book of Ely* and the chronicle of Florence of Worcester, names the Viking leaders as Justin and Guthmund, son of Stectan. Perhaps, at the time, no one knew who the leaders were.

'And so on to Maldon', writes the Parker chronicler. What attracted the Vikings to Maldon, a small Saxon *burh* situated on a low hill at the landward end of the sheltered Blackwater estuary? The most likely explanation is that Maldon possessed a royal mint, that is, it was one of sixty-odd places which supplied the hammer-struck silver pennies of King Aethelred. Ipswich was another, and so was Watchet, a town that had been comprehensively sacked by Viking pirates three years earlier. There were likely to be a lot of silver pennies in Maldon. Moreover it was a coastal town by broad and sheltered waters, and so vulnerable to attack from the sea.

The Saxon leader at Maldon was Byrhtnoth, son of Byrhthelm (his name is sometimes mercifully Anglicized as Britnoth, though it is now considered 'historically correct' to preserve the original spelling of Dark Age names: it is pronounced 'boorch-noth'). What little is known of him indicates he was a nobleman of advanced age and great authority. He appears on a charter as ealdorman of Essex as early as 956, and so was probably over sixty at the time of the battle; the *Vita Oswaldi* refers to his 'swan-white hair'. Byrhtnoth was also unusually tall, towering over his men in the battle-line, and still strong. He may have been the senior nobleman in England at the time. Given the heroic circumstances of his death, this might explain why Maldon became such a famous battle.

The Site of the Battle

Maldon is one of the few Dark Age battles of whose location we can be reasonably certain. There is no doubt that the Saxon *Maeldun* is the modern town of Maldon at the landward end of the Blackwater estuary in Essex. The ancient town, which lay on the low hill overlooking the estuary, had been fortified as a *burh* at the time of King Alfred. It was important enough to have been attacked at least twice, in 921 and again in 991. On the first occasion, Danish raiders, assisted by 'pirates', 'went to Maldon and surrounded the fortress'. However, they were unable to prevent reinforcements from entering the town, and eventually gave up the siege. As the Danes retired, they were harried by the garrison who 'slew many hundreds'. This was an encouraging model for the defence of the town. Unfortunately, on the second occasion things did not go so well.

The battlefield of 991 was always assumed to be close to the town, but the first to investigate its whereabouts was E A Freeman in his monumental book, *The Norman Conquest*. Freeman believed that the battle took place around a road bridge, which,

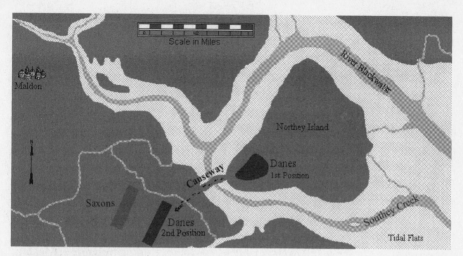

The Battle of Maldon 991

he concluded, must have been at Heybridge just to the north of the Saxon town where the tidal rivers Blackwater and Chelmer unite. In Freeman's view, the Vikings crossed over the Blackwater by this bridge, and so approached the town from the north. The battle would therefore have taken place on the flat land north of the river on what are now suburban housing estates.[6] But, as Burne pointed out in *More Battlefields of England*, this was not one of Freeman's better reconstructions and several factors made his idea wildly improbable. This scenario would result in the Vikings becoming sandwiched between the Saxon army approaching from the north and the garrison of the town, and with no obvious line of retreat. Moreover there is no record of a Saxon bridge there, and any bridge that gets covered over at high tide, would, as Burne put it, 'be a queer one'.[7] Finally the poem explicitly states that Vikings crossed the water from the west yet Freeman makes them move northwards.

Similar considerations apply to another proposed site at Langford, a mile upstream from Maldon where the Rivers Chelmer and Blackwater almost merge. Again, the Vikings would have risked their retreat being cut off and their boats burned if they had strayed so far inland. The main problem with a third possible site, at Osea Island in the middle of the estuary, is the distance of the island from the shore – nearly a mile – rendering it impossible for the shouted exchanges between the Saxon leader, Byrhtnoth, and the Viking herald to be heard. Nor is there any obvious causeway or record of a bridge across the wide channel separating the island from either shore.

This leaves Northey Island, in the estuary a mile and a half east of the town, as by far the most likely location for the Viking base. It was first proposed by E D Laborde in 1925 as the one place where the channel is narrow enough to shout across but where the tides still act. He argued that the word *bricg* in the poem need not mean a bridge, since the word ford (*forda*) is also used. It could apply equally well to a causeway, submerged by the tides but dry at low tide. And there, linking the island to the mainland nearest the town, and facing west, is a perfect candidate, some two hundred yards long and twelve feet wide. As the tide comes in, the water floods towards the causeway from both directions, meeting and joining at just that spot, thus illuminating the passage in the poem referring to 'the loop-currents locking together' that had puzzled historians. The oozy mud of the estuary makes the causeway the only way of reaching the island even at low tide – the Blackwater is aptly named! Hence the Vikings had chosen a secure base for their ships. All they had to do to avoid battle was to sail away on the tide. The actual battle was fought near the south shore, somewhere close to the causeway but on dry ground, most likely between the present-day South House Farm and the estuary.[8]

But coastal land can change a lot over a thousand years. Did the causeway exist in 991? And would the nearby ground have been dry enough to fight a battle on? Evidently so. In 1973, George and Susan Petty took core samples of sediment from the causeway and concluded that it did indeed exist at the time of the Battle of Maldon, except that the causeway was then somewhat narrower and, at about 120 yards, only half the length of the present one. Byrhtnoth would not have had to shout as loud as we

The causeway at Northey Island. (© The Battlefields Trust.)

Low tide on the Blackwater as seen from the causeway. In Saxon times there was less mud and the river was less wide. (© The Battlefields Trust.)

would today![9] The sea level in this area has risen by five or six feet since the battle. Hence the marshes have since encroached much further. In 991 the area between the sea-wall and the estuary would have been dry land. Moreover, just as the sea has risen, so the land in this area has subsided (the higher ground between the town and the estuary today is recent land-fill). At the time of the battle the shore of the estuary was comparatively high and dry, and probably capable of growing crops (we can imagine this August battle being fought amid ripening wheat). The Pettys' findings, which have since been supported by radiocarbon-dated sediment from the estuary, indicate that the Vikings would have crossed from dry land to dry land, and that the marshes were then of very limited extent. Part of the Maldon battlefield probably now lies beneath the mud below the sea-wall.

The Battle

How large were the armies at Maldon? The ship figures carefully recorded by the Anglo-Saxon chronicler during the 990s seem accurate. Longships varied in their carrying capacity, but assuming an average of around thirty fighting men per ship, the fleet of ninety-odd ships indicates an army of nearly 3,000 men. Given that this fleet was only one boat short of the one that burned London and reduced Aethelred's government to its knees, it would be surprising if the number was much fewer.

As for Byrhtnoth's army, much depends on its catchment area. Levies at this time were raised on the basis of one armed man per five hides of land. In the document known as the *Tribal Hidage*, Essex (*East Sexena*) disposes of 7,000 hides, making a theoretical levy of about 1,400 men.[10] If one adds the *burh* levies, which were based on the lengths of walls surrounding the town, plus the hearth-troops of thegns and other noblemen, and assuming some help from surrounding counties, the English would have been able to scrape together a sufficiently large force to challenge the Vikings. It is hard to imagine Byrhtnoth being foolish enough to challenge them to battle with an inferior force. *The Battle of Maldon* and the *Vita Oswaldi* imply roughly equal numbers, though the less reliable *Book of Ely* presents the English as greatly outnumbered.

The surviving fragment of *The Battle of Maldon* begins with Byrhtnoth riding along the lines, 'showing the recruits how to be placed and hold position, their round shields held right firm in fist; to feel no fear'. Later in the poem we learn that the men of Essex had met at the 'moot-place' to decide what to do, and that many there had spoken manfully 'who when there was need would not match their words'. Once his men were in place, the aged ealdorman dismounted and took up his prominent command position 'where he most wanted to be, with his house-troops (*heorthwerod*) he knew wholly loyal'. The English would have lined up on the shore near the causeway to Northey Island where the Vikings were encamped. Assuming an army of 2,000 to 3,000 men lined six deep, their frontage would have stretched for about 500 yards. All accounts suggest that the English fought in a single large mass, though each nobleman was probably among his own household men.

The lane to Northey Island, possible following Byrhtnoth's route to battle. (© The Battlefields Trust.)

The Viking's 'herald' (*Wicinga ar*) hailed the English from across the causeway:

> The brave seamen sent me to you, and told me to say this. Send us silver
> for safety; it would be sensible of you to buy off trouble with tribute rather
> than have us harshly deal out havoc. We needn't be reduced to war if
> you're rich enough. We for gold will give you our guarantee . . . Give us
> treasure for a truce, accept our treaty, and we'll be on our way.

Byrhtnoth gave his famous reply, shaking his spear over his board-shield:

> Can you hear, seamen, what we say on our side? Indeed we have
> something to send you – spears, deadly darts and hard swords; these
> make the war-tax you are welcome to collect! Messenger, make your
> way back, tell your people that here unafraid stands the earl with his
> army who will guard this country well – Aethelred's land, my liege's
> folk and fields . . . It would be humiliating for you to be off with our
> shillings to your ships without a fight, now that you've entered so far
> into our country. You will not so easily earn our money but spear and
> sword will settle it first!

At this point the poem describes the curious tidal effects that have been so useful
in locating the battlefield. With the flood tide two currents locked together over the
causeway. The armies waited for the tide to change in a prolonged stand-off: 'Too long
it seemed till in war they could join weapons'. Neither side 'could damage the other
except in arrow-flight'. Eventually the tide began to ebb and reveal the causeway.
Byrhtnoth thereupon chose three brave champions to hold the 'ford', rather in the
manner of Horatius at the bridge (and also reminiscent of the lone Viking swordsman
at Stamford Bridge). Their names were Wulfstan, Aelfere and Maccus. Wulfstan
killed the first Viking to venture onto the causeway. Then the 'contemptible' Vikings
made Byrhtnoth an offer: let us cross the water and fight us on the land.

Surprisingly perhaps, the 'overconfident' earl agreed: 'There's space for you now',
he called across the cold water, 'Straightway come to grips with us – God himself alone
knows who'll hold sway over this field of struggle.' Was this mere folly on Byrhtnoth's
part? Or was he so anxious to prevent the Vikings from sailing away to pillage another
day that he was willing to relinquish his advantage and gamble on winning a plain fight
within sight of the walls of Maldon?

How long would it take up to 3,000 Vikings to cross a causeway about eight feet
wide? If they filed across two by two it would have been several hours. But evidently
they simply waded through the shallow water, which, according to geological
evidence, was less muddy than now. The Vikings, sang the poet, came on through
the shining wet like 'blood-wolves'. By the time battle was finally joined on the dry
flats beside the estuary, Byrhtnoth's men had been waiting for many hours.

The earl had them form a 'war-wall' (*wihagan* – literally, war-hedge). At this point the poet falls back on an impressionistic description of 'the occasion when fated men must fall in battle'. There was uproar:

> Men sent from their hands hard spears; sharp-pointed, the shafts flew. Bows were busy, board took sword, and wild was the war-urge, warriors falling on both sides the wounded fell. The sturdy men stood their ground.

Byrhtnoth was probably killed early on. He was a prominent target, standing beneath his personal banner and visible from a distance by his great height. According to the *Vita Oswaldi* he 'towered over others; the power of his hand neither Aaron nor Hur [two companions] supported, but manifold piety towards God gave him strength, and he was worthy of it'. The poem presents a blow-by-blow account of Byrhtnoth's last moments. An ordinary Viking soldier, a 'churl', hurled 'a south-made spear' at the tall ealdorman, wounding him above his shield. 'Shoving with his shield until the shaft broke, and banging at the spear till it sprang away', the angry Byrhtnoth hurled his own spear clear through his opponent's throat. A second spear he threw, 'bursting through some man's armour, through the hard rings of mail; in the heart lodged the deadly spear-end. The earl laughed, mighty and brave, giving his Maker thanks for the day's work.' But as he laughed, a second Viking javelin struck him. A young companion, Wulfmaer, Wulfstan's son, drew the weapon and hurled it back. A fight developed around the fallen earl as the Vikings closed in, attempting 'to loot him as he lay of raiment and rings, and [his] richly-worked sword'. Byrhtnoth managed to draw his sword, but a Viking struck and shattered his shoulder. Now defenceless, the earl still found the strength to address his men one last time, appealing to them to stand firm and praying that his soul may speed to heaven, that 'no hell-hound may ever defile it'. Meanwhile earthly hell-hounds closed in, killing Aelfnoth and Wulmaer and finally hacking off Byrhtnoth's head.

The death of the leader normally decided the outcome of a battle. Some of Byrhtnoth's men elected to flee ('they ran from battle who had no wish to be there'). Among the first to take to his heels was Godric, 'the coward son of Odda'. He leapt on Byrhtnoth's own steed, and, with his brothers Godwine and Godwig, 'turned from the war-strife, made for the woods, fled for refuge, saved their wretched lives'. Many others, including perhaps most of the local militia, fled also – 'more people than was in any way proper'. The *Vita Oswaldi* confirms that most of the Saxons fled after Byrhtnoth fell, although it places the earl's death at the end of the battle, just as the English seemed to be winning it.

By contrast, true to their oaths, Byrhtnoth's loyal retainers, his 'hearth-men' fought on: 'they wanted one of two things, to avenge their lord or lay down their lives'. A young Mercian warrior, Aelfwine, son of Aelfric, reminded them of their boasts at the mead-bench, 'heroes in the hall', about what hard fighters they were. 'Now we can discover who really has courage'. For his own part, Aelfwine went on, no one would be able to reproach him for leaving the field now that his lord lay dead. Others voiced similar sentiments. Gadd's son, Offa, had promised Byrhtnoth that the two of them would ride back to Maldon or perish as one in the field of war. They were joined by other named warriors: Aetheric, Leofsanu, Dunnere, Edward the tall, Wistan son of Thurstan, the brothers Oswald and Eadwold, and Ashferth, son of Ecglaf, intriguingly described as a hostage from Northumbria. All of them fought to the death:

> They shattered blanked shields, boldly defended themselves. Shield-rim snapped and chain-mail sang out its gruesome hymn … The seamen came on, raging in war. Weapons transfixed some fated body … War-men fell, on the ground, cut-weary, collapsed lifeless.

The last and most famous words of the battle are given by an older warrior called Byrhtwold, perhaps of Byrhtnoth's kin. 'Full of courage', he addressed his remaining comrades as follows:

> Minds must be the firmer, hearts the bolder, soul's strength the greater, as our resources lessen. Here lies our lord, lethally wounded, good man on the ground. May he grieve for ever who from this war-work would consider withdrawing. I am old in age, away I won't, but myself by my master, by so beloved a man, would finally lie.

True to his word, he went forward fighting to his last breath.

And there the poem fragment ends.

Like the battles in the *Iliad*, the Maldon poet focuses on the speeches and actions of his heroes without telling us much about how the battle was fought. The *Book of Ely* mentions the Vikings forming into a wedge 'and hurling themselves forward like one man'. The casualties on both sides were heavy. 'An incalculable number fell', says the *Vita Oswaldi*, and the Vikings were so heavily mauled that 'they could barely manage to man their boats'. There is no mention anywhere of the town being taken or sacked, so maybe the Vikings were in no state to continue with their raid. The Battle of Maldon is normally considered a Viking victory, since the English fled the field. Perhaps, given the afterglow that settled on the heroic stand of Byrhtnoth and his men, it should be reassessed as a Pyrrhic victory and a moral defeat.

How much of the poem is true? It is, of course, a poem, not a historical record, and uses literary art to heighten the heroism of the defenders of Maldon. Michael Wood suggested that its purpose was not to narrate 'another brutal struggle ending in ignominious defeat' but to elevate the sacrifice to a timeless ritual of service, loyalty and honour.[11] The names of the earl's retainers would have been well-remembered and honoured when the poem was written, within a few years, or at most a few decades, of the battle. And the description of the causeway and its peculiar tides suggests that the poet knew the Blackwater estuary, and perhaps even lived in Maldon. Little details, like the unexplained 'hostage' from Northumbria or Offa's son releasing a beloved hawk, are unlikely to have been invented since they serve no obvious literary purpose.

There is a bare possibility, however, that the Maldon poem has telescoped two separate events. In the *Book of Ely*, there are two battles of Maldon, one preceding the other by four years. In the first, Byrhtnoth pounced on and defeated the Vikings as they were crossing the bridge or causeway. The Vikings swore revenge and descended on Maldon a second time, sending word to the earl that they should hold him a coward if he refused to face them in battle. Byrhtnoth, 'inflamed to a pitch of daring' by this message, arrived at the field with an inadequate force. Even so, he is supposed to have fought with the enemy for an improbable fourteen days and well-nigh put them to flight until one last attack by the Vikings in wedge formation broke through to cut off the earl's head as he fought.[12]

Without taking the details too seriously, is it possible that this account contains a grain of truth? The *Book of Ely* goes on to say that Byrhtnoth's widow had a tapestry made and presented to Ely Abbey. Assuming that the tapestry had a section showing the victory at the bridge and another showing the earl's death in battle, could it be that the poet, perhaps basing his narrative on the tapestry, dovetailed the two events for dramatic purposes? Certainly, when reading *The Battle of Maldon*, the causeway episode seems self-contained, and the link between it and the succeeding battle rather weak. It also offers a solution to Byrhtnoth's inexplicable rashness in accepting the Viking's offer of battle on the grounds that it never happened! Moreever, revenge was a powerful motivation in Dark Age England, as any reader of Richard Fletcher's book *Blood-Feud*, will know.[13]

Maldon Today

The site of the Battle of Maldon is owned by the National Trust, and is a historic battlefield registered by English Heritage. A leaflet about the battlefield with a recommended walk is available from the Tourist Information Centre in Maldon. Access is by way of the riverside footpath from the town or from a private road leading to South House Farm which ends in a small car-park. The National Trust has recently erected a plaque by the lane leading to the Causeway, noting that the battle took place 'on and around this spot'. From there it is only a short walk to the causeway. Try to time a visit so that you can witness the meeting of the waters about an hour-and-a-half before high tide. The battlefield itself, on flat grassland and crop-fields, needs imagination, which isn't helped by the newly built sports and leisure centre between it and the town. The easy circular walk on footpaths and pavements takes about an hour. Maldon Museum in the town has information about

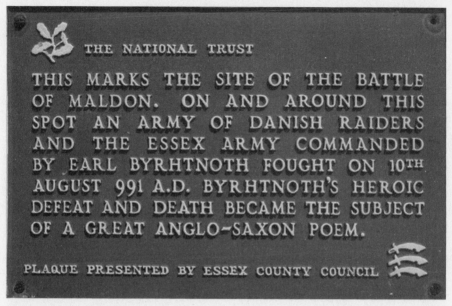

THE NATIONAL TRUST

THIS MARKS THE SITE OF THE BATTLE OF MALDON. ON AND AROUND THIS SPOT AN ARMY OF DANISH RAIDERS AND THE ESSEX ARMY COMMANDED BY EARL BYRHTNOTH FOUGHT ON 10ᵀᴴ AUGUST 991 A.D. BYRHTNOTH'S HEROIC DEFEAT AND DEATH BECAME THE SUBJECT OF A GREAT ANGLO-SAXON POEM.

PLAQUE PRESENTED BY ESSEX COUNTY COUNCIL

Plaque to the battle in the National Trust car-park. Essex County Council's symbol of three Saxon *seax*, an all-purpose blade, is more than usually appropriate here. The *seax* was doubtless put to good use at Maldon. (© The Battlefields Trust.)

the town and its times.[14] Northey Island is normally closed to avoid disturbance to breeding bird colonies; for admission contact the National Trust's warden (normally twenty-four hours' notice needed) or the Tourist Information Centre in Maldon.

After the Battle
Byrhtnoth's headless body was sought out by monks from Ely Abbey, with whom the earl was in some way connected, and given honourable burial there. What may have been his bones were uncovered during building works there in 1769; at any rate they belonged to a headless man estimated to be six feet nine inches tall. The Vikings are said to have carried back the severed head to their homeland as a trophy.

The Vikings continued to raid the English coast and compelled the less Churchillian local rulers of Kent, Hampshire and Wessex to buy peace from them. By the end of the year a treaty was arranged, brokered by Archbishop Sigeric of Canterbury and two ealdormen. The text still survives. The baptism of Olaf, and a series of rules governing trade and the settlement of disputes between Englishmen and Vikings, does little to mollify the payment of 22,000 pounds of gold and silver to the raiders as the price of peace. And all to no avail for, three years later, Olaf Tryggvasson was back as an open enemy, this time accompanied by King Sweyn of Denmark.

This time they were bought off with 16,000 pounds. Aethelred did at least succeed in getting rid of Olaf this time, for the now rich Viking sought a new career in Norway.

He eventually became Norway's king, only to be killed by his erstwhile ally, Sweyn, in 999. Unfortunately, Byrhtnoth's martial offer of 'spears for tribute' did not set the pattern for future dealings with the Vikings. The dismal period of the danegeld had begun when money was used instead of arms. As Rudyard Kipling remembered, giving in to blackmail merely ensures more of the same:

> It is always a temptation for a rich and lazy nation
> To puff and look important and to say: –
> 'Though we know we should defeat you,
> we have not the time to meet you,
> We will therefore pay you cash to go away.'
>
> And that is called paying the Dane-geld;
> But we've proved it again and again,
> That if once you have paid him the Dane-geld
> You never get rid of the Dane.

Chapter 10
Calamity under Aethelred

The years after the Battle of Maldon are some of the most dismal in English history. Alfred had, despite many setbacks, driven the Vikings from Wessex and come to an accommodation with them elsewhere. His grandson, Athelstan, had extended the rule of Alfred's house across England and defeated the greatest Viking invasion ever mounted. By contrast, the long reign of Aethelred, Alfred's great-great-grandson, was marked by continuous failure. He inherited a seemingly strong and rich kingdom, with a proven record of military effectiveness, but it all turned to jelly in his hands. The Anglo-Saxon Chronicle records some of the low points:

993:   Great levies were gathered together, but when they should have joined battle, the leaders were the first to set the example of flight.

998:   Many a time levies were gathered to oppose them, but as soon as battle was about to begin, the word was given to withdraw, and always in the end the [Danish] host had the victory.

1003: Then great levies were assembled, and it was ealdorman Aelfric's duty to lead them, but he was up to his old tricks; as soon as they were close enough for each force to see the other, he pretended to vomit, saying he was ill, thus leaving the men in the lurch.

1006: ... they were on service against the enemy host all the autumn, but with no more success than very often in the past. Despite all this, the host went where it pleased, and the campaign caused all manner of distress to the inhabitants, so that neither the home levies nor the invading host did them any good!

1010: Then they made their way back to the ships with their plunder: and when they were dispersing to the ships, then the levies should have been out, ready in case they should intend to go inland. Then however the levies were on their way home. And when the enemy was in the east, then our levies were mustered in the west; and when they were in the south, then our levies were in the north.[1]

There were isolated successes; some local commanders were far bolder than Aelfric, the terrified ealdorman of Hampshire. But on the whole, the defence of England against the renewed Danish raids was feeble, surprisingly so given its effectiveness under Alfred and Athelstan. What went wrong? To begin with, unlike Alfred and his immediate successors, Aethelred rarely led an army in the field and never against the Vikings until the last year of his long reign. He left the fighting to his subordinates, especially the ealdormen, who were of mixed quality. Aethelred preferred diplomacy to war. He paid off the Danes with ever-increasing piles of treasure, the notorious danegeld. Contemporaries did not criticize him for paying the geld so much as for paying it too late, after the damage had been done. Aethelred attempted, with some success, to divide his enemies, and to play off one side against another. He even formed an alliance with the duke of Normandy, himself of Viking descent, in which the parties agreed not to give shelter to one another's enemies. But none of it was any substitute for meeting and beating the enemy on the battlefield.

Another reason for Aethelred's failure was that the enemy was even more formidable than in the past. The wars of Alfred's time had been against free-booting raiders or loose alliances of Viking bands under a charismatic leader. They were anarchic and tended to lack staying power. But in Aethelred's time, a centralized and aggressive monarchy emerged in Denmark. The picturesquely named Harald Bluetooth, observing that the Christians' God had made his neighbours powerful and rich, became a Christian himself. Harald was ruler of a strongly militarized Scandinavian empire. He and his son and successor, Sweyn Forkbeard, set up at least five military camps in Denmark fortified by moats and stockades, and enclosing thirty-metre-long barracks shaped like ships' hulls. Their location – four were on Jutland, facing the North Sea – suggests that the camps were built as troop assembly points for raids on England. Between them they could house a standing army of around 5,500 warriors. Harald and Sweyn could also call on their Danish subjects for levies of ships and crews. Hence the invasions that brought Aethelred's England to its knees were comparable with Ivar's great army of 867, and far larger than the raiding parties from Ireland or the Western Isles. By the turn of the millennium, Sweyn commanded the most powerful military machine in Northern Europe.

The Battle of Maldon in 991 was only the start of a sixteen-year-long struggle with the raiders, culminating in an all-out campaign of conquest by Sweyn and his son Canute. At first, it must have seemed like a recurrence of the Viking raids of the previous century, with hit-and-run raids on soft targets around the coast. Not that the raids had ever ceased entirely; low-level attacks on coastal settlements had continued even during the supposedly peaceful reign of King Eadgar, Aethelred's much lamented father. It was not until the year 998 that the raiders first wintered in England. Nor were all the raiders from Denmark. Those that attacked the south-western coast probably came from Ireland or south Wales (there was little in Cornwall or Devon to tempt Danish mariners so far). Raiders on the Dorset and Hampshire coast may have operated from the Channel ports in Brittany and Normandy. Kent and East Anglia bore the brunt of the great fleets from Denmark.

Compared with Alfred's day, there were few pitched battles, and most of those went no better than Maldon. Ealdorman Aelfric was blamed for the farcical outcome of an attempt to trap the enemy in the Thames estuary:

> Aelfric, one of those in whom the king had most trust, had the host warned; and the night before the morning on which they were to have joined battle, this same Aelfric fled from the levies, with the result that the host got away.

In 993, the raiders struck north and destroyed Bamburgh. The English caught up with them near the Humber, but once again their leaders let them down. This time three nobles, Fraena, Godwine and Frithugist, were 'named and shamed' for the outcome.

Things went from bad to worse as the new millennium dawned. In 1001, a host from Denmark established a base by the Solent and burned and harried their way east-wards. They were opposed by the men of Hampshire at a place called *Aethelingadene*, possibly present-day Alton. Though small in scale, the battle was noted for a high body count among the nobility; the dead included Aethelweard, the 'king's high-reeve' among five other named leaders. The raiders then turned west towards Devon where they were joined by a turncoat English leader called Pallig. Reinforced by ship's companies landing on the Exe estuary, they penetrated inland as far as Pinhoe, now a suburb of Exeter, where they were opposed by the men of Devon and Somerset led by the shire reeves Kola and Eadsige. One chronicle refers to this army as a 'vast levy', another, perhaps more accurately, as 'such levies as could be mobilised'. Many or few, the force was inadequate. 'As soon as they met the English levies gave ground and the enemy made great slaughter on them.' The Danes went on to burn the manor of Pinhoe and nearby Broadclyst, 'and many other goodly manors of which we do not know the names'. Military resistance having failed, Aethelred was obliged to buy peace.

This time it cost him 24,000 pounds, an enormous sum that could only be levied by special taxation. Later that year, the panic-stricken Aethelred ordered the slaughter on St Brice's Day (13 November) of 'all the Danish people who were in England'. To what extent the order was actually carried out is unknown – the men living in the Danelaw were unlikely to sit back and allow Aethelred's men to slaughter their families. But among the dead was Sweyn's sister Gunnhild, who was living in southern England as a hostage. This injudicious murder added revenge to greed and ambition to Sweyn's motives for helping himself to England.

Sweyn Forkbeard was the most powerful Viking of them all, remembered long afterwards as 'a great man of war, strongest of rulers', the scourge of the northern seas from the Baltic to the shores of England and France. The anonymous writer of an important English source, the *Encomium Emmae Reginae*, saw him in a surprisingly positive light. In Denmark Sweyn was a good and popular ruler, admired by all except his jealous father (whom Sweyn eventually deposed). But, the author added, he was certainly feared and hated by the English, and with good cause. Sweyn's campaign of revenge in 1003 was on an increased scale, probably involving several thousand warriors. A despairing Exeter opened its gates to him, and the host then harried all of Wessex as far as Salisbury before returning to Denmark. The following year, Sweyn turned to East Anglia, the richest and most densely populated part of England. The fleet landed unobserved and made their way upriver to Norwich, which they sacked and then burned to the ground. To avoid similar disasters, the local magnates entered into negotiations for another expensively bought peace. But while these were proceeding, Sweyn secretly struck across country to Thetford, which he also burned.

At this point, an English leader emerged in the person of ealdorman Ulfcytel ('Ulf-kettle' or Ulfkell), known by his Danish enemies as 'Ulfcytel Snilling' or 'Ulfcytel the Valiant'. While Sweyn was inland, Ulfcytel ordered the destruction of the Danish fleet: 'hew their ships to pieces'. Unfortunately, those detailed for the task failed to carry it out. In the mean time, Ulfcytel secretly raised a sizeable force and interposed it between Thetford and the Danish fleet in Norwich. A battle took place near Thetford, traditionally at Wretham Heath north-east of the town where the Norfolk road is crossed by the Roman road known as Peddar's Way. It was fiercely fought with great slaughter on both sides. Many of the chief men of East Anglia were slain there, but, commented the 'E' chronicler, 'if they had been up to full strength the enemy would never have got back to their ships, as they themselves

Thetford Castle, a large Norman motte built towards the end of the eleventh century. Earlier defences at the site were the focus of Viking attacks in the previous century.

admitted'. The 'C' chronicler added that the Danes 'never met with worse hand-play [i.e. battle skill] among the English than Ulfcytel brought to them'.[2] Reading between the lines, it seems that the Danes were left in possession of the battlefield, and did return to their ships. But it was a hard-won victory. Gravely mauled, Sweyn embarked for Denmark.

He returned to England in 1006. Evading a large army levied from all of Wessex and Mercia, Sweyn 'did as he was wont to do, harrying, slaying and burning as he went'. But with the normal campaigning season drawing to a close, the period of the levy expired and the English went home. Now unopposed, Sweyn launched an unexpected mid-winter *chevauchee* through Hampshire and Berkshire, drawing supplies and rations from his well-stocked fortress at Reading. Then, rather than return directly to his ships on the Isle of Wight, Sweyn swept west along the Ridgeway as far as Cuckhamsley Knob (known on modern maps as Scutchamer Knob), at East Hendred, near Wantage. It seems that Aethelred's county levies offered battle at this ancient meeting place on the Ridgeway, but that Sweyn eluded them by going another way. However, the levies of Wiltshire were waiting for him further along the Ridgeway at East Kennet, a few miles west of Marlborough. A battle ensued but the local militia were no match for Sweyn's veterans and were soon put to ignominious rout.[3] Sweyn continued on his way unopposed, mockingly passing beneath the gates of Winchester, 'bringing provisions and treasures from a distance

Scutchamer Knob was a moot place on the Ridgeway, marked by a large earthmound (its present horseshoe-shape is the result of a 'ruthless' excavation in the nineteenth century). Originally marked by an oak stake, Scutchamer Knob would have been visible far and wide on the treeless downs. Here the men of Berkshire planned to intercept Sweyn of Denmark on his westward march through Wessex.

of more than fifty miles inland'. By this time, the Danish host had left its mark on every county in Wessex. Aethelred was forced to make a shameful peace, supplying Sweyn's army from all parts of England, and paying him tribute of another 36,000 pounds raised from his long-suffering subjects.

Aethelred used the time thus expensively bought to build ships, concentrating at Sandwich the largest fleet ever assembled by the English. Aethelred's new strategy was to engage the enemy at sea, before they could land and disappear into the countryside. Unfortunately, the plan fell apart almost at once. A charge of treason had been bought against one of the captains, Wulfnoth, who retaliated by seducing the crews of twenty ships and setting off down the south coast to indulge in some freelance piracy. His accuser followed with eighty ships, but a storm blew them onshore, where many were burned by Wulfnoth's men. Now with too few ships remaining to form a serious threat to the Danes, Aethelred withdrew his fleet to London. When the long-expected Danes did appear off Sandwich on 1 August, they found a deserted anchorage.

The Battle of Ringmere

The fleet that sailed to England from Denmark's military bases in 1009 was the largest yet seen. This time it was commanded not by Sweyn, who was detained in Denmark, but by Thorkell the Tall and his brother Hemming, both experienced and capable commanders, assisted by an earl named in the sources as Eilifr. According to sagas written down much later, there were other great names in their ranks, including Olaf Haraldson, the later king (and unlikely saint) of Norway.[4] This was perhaps an adventure no self-respecting Viking freebooter would want to miss; the Chronicle's unusual name for this army was *folc* – a warrior army of the people. For six months they harried the south-east, avoiding battle, before striking through the Chilterns to Oxford, which they captured and burned. In the spring of 1010, Thorkell and Hemming turned to East Anglia, landing at Ipswich. Learning that, once again, Ulfcytel was preparing to oppose them, the host marched inland towards Thetford. They went, remarks the chronicler, 'straight to where they had heard that Ulfcytel was with his levies'.

The ensuing battle was fought in 1010, either on 5 or 18 May. The Anglo-Saxon chronicler gives the date but not the name of the battle. The Norman chronicler Florence of Worcester names it as Ringmere, and a later Norse saga as *Hringmaraheithr* or Ringmere Heath.[5] Where was it? The site has traditionally been identified with Ringmere Pit, a shallow natural lake on East Wretham Heath, three miles north-east of Thetford. This would place the battle in the same vicinity as the close-fought one of 1004. But since the Danes would have approached Thetford from the south, fighting in a place north of Thetford would have meant abandoning the town to the invaders. This seems most unlikely. Burned and devastated though it was, Thetford was still the key to the conquest of East Anglia. The town lies at the centre of East Anglia, equidistant between the abbeys of Ely, Norwich and Bury, and within striking distance of the towns of Cambridge and points west. It was at the hub of East Anglian communications, controlling the fords of the Icknield Way. The Rivers Thet and the Little Ouse meet there and the horseshoe of rising ground to the north had been fortified since the Iron Age. The Danes had already used this site for their own base, as would the Normans when they built a motte-and-bailey castle on the hill in the heart of the old town. Thetford must have been as important to Thorkell as it was to Ivar, back in Alfred's day. The Battle of Ringmere was surely fought to prevent this vital fortified town from falling once again into Danish hands.

Fortunately there is an alternative site where we might expect it, four miles south of Thetford, at Rymer Point, where no fewer than nine parishes converge. This was an ancient meeting place and so a potential mustering ground for an army. The site occupies a ridge commanding a wide view across the farm fields of the Little Ouse valley and towards Bury from whence the Danes were expected. The name Rymer now survives only in a farmhouse and a barn, but it was formerly a large parish close to the ancient Icknield Way, still an important road in Saxon times. Could the name Rymer, probably made up of the Old English 'rime' meaning border (it lies just inside Suffolk) and 'mere', have been mixed up with Ringmere? The site was probably unenclosed heathland at the time. It was as strong a position as could be found in such a flat, open landscape, with the Black Bourne river guarding one flank.

Of the battle few details are recorded. The thirteenth-century *Knytlinga Saga* attributes the leadership of the Danish army to 'Earl Eirik', a veteran of many battles. 'For ages', wrote Eirik's bard, 'the English were eaten up with hatred of the raven-feeders [i.e. the Danes]'. Yet the East Anglian farmers, 'fretting to defend their fields, stood firm: fiercely the king's men fought them'.[6] Each side fought in two

East Kennet from the Ridgeway towards the Pewsey Downs. Hereabouts, Sweyn defeated the levies of Wiltshire in pitched battle.

divisions, the Danes under Thorkell and Hemming (plus Eirik), the East Anglians alongside the men of Cambridgeshire. Ulfcytel was in overall command of the English forces.

The East Anglian men under one Thurcytel 'Mare's Head' did poorly and soon took flight. The better disciplined Cambridgeshire men held firm, but after a hard-fought battle the Danes prevailed. 'Shrewd Eirik thinned out the English ranks', recalled the bard, 'He destroyed them, reddening Ringmere'. It became a famous Danish victory recalled in several skaldic verses. The *Olafsdrapa* (Olaf's tale) remembered how 'all the race of Ella' stood arrayed there (Ella or Aelle was the last king of Northumbria, but the Danes seem to have regarded him as the king of all England).[7] The same source described the battlefield as 'a bed of death'.[8] *Eirik's Saga* recalled poetically:

> The steerer of the sea-horse fought for the land. Ulfcetel, brave in the rain of battle, got ugly blows where the dark swords shook above the Danish soldiers. The brave warriors, who frequently gave flesh to the raven, marked men with the print of the sword's edge. The bold Eirik often diminished the host of the English and brought about their death. The army reddened Ringmere Heath.[9]

Among the fallen English were Athelstan, described as the king's son-in-law, Oswy, the son-in-law of Byrhtnoth of Maldon, Wulfric son of Leofwine and 'Eadric, Aefic's brother', among 'many other good thanes and a countless number of people'. Thorkell's men helped themselves to horses and roamed far and wide, spreading terror and burning Cambridge, Bedford and Northampton. They returned to their ships with wagon-trains of plunder. The chronicler complains that the levies were never in the right place to resist them, that no shire would help another, and that in the end no one was even willing to raise levies. The overall sense is one of deepening hopelessness.

Thorkell's brilliant campaign was decisive. He showed that exhausted England was no longer capable of defending herself. In 1013, Sweyn returned to England with the plain intention of toppling Aethelred and adding England to his dominions. The *Encomium Emmae* provides a vivid impression of Sweyn's invasion fleet of 200 ships. Each 'towered' ship had its own device, a gilded lion or bull, 'dragons of various kinds' with fire pouring from their nostrils, dolphins and centaurs moulded in electrum, or 'glittering men of gold or silver'. From the mastheads flew windsocks in the shape of birds. The impressive armada landed at Sandwich, 'the most famous of all the ports of the English'. Sweyn seems to have anticipated that at least some of the English magnates were ready to desert Aethelred and accept him as their king, on the grounds that a nightmarish end was better than a nightmare without end. But instead at Sandwich he met stout resistance. Sweyn raised anchor and sailed north to the Humber, where, as he must have known, the men of Lindsey were ready to accept him as king. Sure enough, at Gainsborough by the River Trent, he was met by the leading men of the north and Midlands, many of whom were of Danish ancestry. They supplied him with horses and provisions for his conquest of the south.

It is at this point that we meet Sweyn's famous son, Canute, then in his late teens. (Cnut, or Knut, is the more correct spelling, but both are pronounced 'Can-ute' – let's call him Canute). Sweyn left his boy behind in Lindsey, charged with keeping order in the province and guarding the hostages the Danes had seized as surety. Meanwhile Sweyn's army proceeded south along Watling Street in a show of 'shock and awe', sweeping aside any lingering resistance by overwhelming force. Only London held out, stiffened by Thorkell, who had fallen out with Sweyn and changed sides. Part of Sweyn's force was 'drowned in the Thames, because they did not bother to look for any bridge' (cock-ups were not confined to the English). Even so, London was forced to capitulate, and Aethelred fled to Normandy. Thereupon 'the whole nation accepted Sweyn as their undisputed king'.

Edmund Ironside

At this point, having conquered all England in a far shorter time than it would take William the Conqueror, Sweyn suddenly died, apparently of natural causes. Rumour insisted he had been slain in his sleep by the ghost of St Edmund, the East Anglian king martyred by Ivar. More likely Sweyn knew he was dying and, according to the *Encomium Emmae*, he made a lengthy deathbed speech, reminding Canute of the rules of wise governance and Christian practice, and bequeathing the royal sceptre to him. The crews of the Danish fleet at Gainsborough at once gave Canute their allegiance, but the English had other ideas. Their magnates sent a delegation to Aethelred in Normandy saying, in effect, that they were prepared to have him back so long as he swore to be a better king and rule more justly than before. Two months after the death of Sweyn, the English were once more in the field, with, for a change, their king at their head. Canute decided to withdraw, abandoning his English allies to the vengeance of Aethelred's men. But before embarking for Denmark, Canute cut off the noses, ears and hands of his hostages and left them bleeding on the beach at Sandwich. Our remembrance of the benign rule of good King Canute is definitely the product of hindsight.

As a younger son, Canute lacked a kingdom: Denmark and Norway went to his elder brother Harald, with whom he seems to have remained on good terms. Instead, Canute set his sights on England. He returned in summer 1015 with 160 ships, a smaller force than his father had commanded, but still large enough to offer a serious challenge to the now ailing Aethelred. Landing briefly at Sandwich, Canute sailed on to Poole Harbour to establish a base for operations in his chosen theatre of operations in Wessex. The basic plan was to ravage and ravage again until the magnates accepted him as king. The real military strategists of the ensuing war were Thorkell the Tall, now back on the Danish side, and one Eirik, who later became ruler of Norway under Canute's suzerainty. The *Encomium Emmae* credits these two as the king-makers, and they were certainly richly rewarded for their efforts.[10] Whether Canute's brother Harald was also present at the siege of London, as the encomiast claims, is more doubtful.

By now the political cross-currents were complicated. Aethelred was clearly not long for the world. His ealdormen, long used to fending for themselves, had their own agendas, and they were becoming used to making difficult choices. Survival under these circumstances demanded great cunning. In the shifting cat's cradle of alliances in 1015–16, men did what seemed to be in their best interests. To some, Canute may not have seemed a much worse prospect than Aethelred. In Lindsey, for example, Aethelred had burned manors and executed leading men for their support of Sweyn in 1014. The most powerful ealdorman in England was Eadric Streona of Mercia, who turned self-serving into a political art. Though low-born he was silver-tongued and plausible, a consummate politician. His power base lay in the area known as the Magasaetan, in present-day Shropshire.

Another independent player was Aethelred's son, Edmund, later surnamed Ironside. In contrast to his father, Edmund was a fighter, a man of iron resolution and ferocious energy. In 1015, he identified his interests with the northern half of England and rebelled against his father. The Danish-dominated part of central England known as the Five Boroughs repudiated Aethelred and accepted Edmund as their lord. Both Eadric and Edmund led what amounted to private armies.

In the emergency created by Canute's arrival, Edmund and Eadric buried their considerable differences and joined forces. However, the two did not get on, and Eadric soon decided it would be more politic to abandon Edmund and go over to Canute. In the process he persuaded the English crews of forty ships to follow him. Edmund retaliated by ravaging the lands of Eadric and his chief men in the West Midlands, the one area to have largely escaped the raids of the past twenty years. Even so, by winter 1015, Canute seemed to be on the verge of success, in firm possession of the north, and with the vast resources of Eadric's Mercia at his disposal.

Early in 1016, Canute rejoined his fleet at Poole Harbour and prepared for the culminating blow of his plan of conquest, an attack on London. At this point Aethelred died. In the opinion of the historian Sir Charles Oman, dying was the greatest service he ever did for his country.[11] More charitably, the chronicler noted that 'he ended his days after a life of much hardship and many difficulties'. By this time, Edmund had returned to London and 'all the councillors that were in London chose him as king'. But a rival assembly meeting at Southampton swore fealty to Canute. And Canute took advantage of the westerly winds of May to sail upriver and establish siege lines around the city. According to the Anglo-Saxon Chronicle:

> They dug a great channel on the south bank and dragged their ships to the west side of the bridge, and then afterwards built earthworks outside the city so that no one could get in or out, and attacked the city repeatedly, but they withstood them valiantly.

The political struggle had now simplified into a straight fight between Canute and Edmund Ironside.

Somehow – and no chronicler explains how – Edmund managed to reverse the decision at Southampton and win over the men of Wessex. There could not have been much love for Canute in war-ravaged Wessex, and once Edmund showed himself to be a bold and determined leader, men gathered to his banner. The first battle in that year of battles, 1016, was *aet Peonnum*, that is, at Penselwood, near Gillingham in Dorset. Edmund, having escaped from London, raised his banner at the same place as Alfred had in 878. His strategy was evidently to draw Canute away from London and so relieve the city. The Battle of Penselwood took place in late May or early June, near the place where King Cenwalh of Wessex had defeated the Britons in 658. All we know about the battle is that it was indecisive.[12] Canute may not have been present, for this battle is missing from the saga praising his deeds.

The second battle of that year, fought 'after midsummer', was at *Scearstan*, the modern village of Sherston near Malmesbury. Canute's skald, Ottar, claims that this time the Danes were led by Canute in person. This is more likely than the version in the *Encomium Emmae* which mistakenly sited the battle on the Kentish coast and had Thorkell fighting the battle with forty ship's companies against a vastly superior English army. In fact the sides were evenly matched. With Canute were a host of men from the Midlands under Eadric Streona and another English magnate called Aelfmaer Darling. Sherston was remembered as 'one of the most famous battles of the time', in which 'there was great slaughter on both sides'. The village lies by the River Avon a mile west of the Fosse Way, that great Dark Age highway from Wessex to the Midlands. Its location suggests that Canute might have joined forces with Eadric's Mercians at Cirencester and encountered Edmund's army coming up from Bath. The exact site of battle is unknown, but it may have taken place where the Fosse Way passes the village near Ladywood Farm. The battle is remembered locally in the legend of John Rattlebone, a local hero who died of wounds sustained in the battle. Sherston's Rattlebone Inn is named in his honour.

Sherston was another drawn battle. The Anglo-Saxon Chronicle makes the interesting comment that it was not the leaders but the armies themselves that broke off the fight. The *Knytlinga Saga* embellishes this bare record with detail that may not be reliable but which broadly agrees with the Chronicle. King Edmund is said to have charged on horseback straight into the heart of the Danish army to within striking distance of Canute's distinctive white banner. Edmund's blow was parried by Canute, but the force of it sliced through his shield and into the neck of his horse. The Danes counter-attacked and drove Edmund back, but not before 'he had killed a good many Danes without suffering much in the way of wounds himself'. Unfortunately, while this was going on, word had got around that Edmund had been killed. His men began to break ranks and flee. Riding after them, Edmund shouted at them to turn back, 'but no one showed any sign of hearing him'.[13]

The saga attributes victory to Canute: 'the crow's sleep was unsettled by Sweyn's son at Sherston'. Another praise poem of Canute by his skald Ottar the Black also

The sign of the Rattlebone Inn, obviously based on the Bayeux Tapestry, remembers a legend of the Battle of Sherstone.

claims victory: 'Bold son of Sweyn, you led an attack at Sherstone ... There, I know, you took the Frisians' lives, breaker of the peace of shields.'[14] But the truth seems to be that both armies decided to call it off. Subsequent events suggest that Canute was badly mauled and, for the first time since his landing, he lost the initiative.

Edmund succeeded in assembling shire levies for the third time for the relief of London. They marched east, according to the 'C' chronicle 'keeping north of the Thames all the time, and coming out through the wooded slopes by Clayhill', in Tottenham. Catching the Danes off guard, he broke through their lines and relieved the garrison, driving the enemy back to their ships. Two days after entering London, Edmund forded the river at Brentford to assault the Danes in their camp on the south bank. But although they are said to have 'fought against the

The Fosse Way near Sherstone. The battle may have been a contact battle with both armies meeting along the old Roman road in this area.

host and put it to flight', the English suffered unnecessary casualties when a portion of the army, having gone ahead in search of booty, somehow managed to drown in the river. In the saga version of events, Brentford was presented as a Danish victory. 'You showed no friendship', wrote Canute's skald, Ottar, 'when you shattered Brentford with its habitations. Edmund's noble kinsmen met with deadly wounds. The Danish force shot down the men with spears, but you pursued the flying host.'[15]

The battle at Brentford seems to have been another costly affair, for Edmund was forced to return to Wessex once more to raise yet another army while the Danes reoccupied their entrenchments. Once more London was invested and 'attacked fiercely by land and water'. But, says the chronicler, 'God delivered us'. After so long a siege, Canute was running out of supplies. He was finally forced to abandon his lines and withdraw to his ship-base in the Orwell estuary. From there, Canute moved into the Medway, probably to refit his fleet before another assault on London. But Edmund, responding with his customary speed, 'called up all the people of England', and, crossing the Thames at Brentford, moved into Kent, and caught up with a detachment of Danes at Otford. Like King Alfred at *Ethandun*, a small victory snowballed into a rout of the whole Danish force in Kent, and they were driven back to Canute's ship-camp on the Isle of Sheppey. Edmund 'slew as many of them as he could overtake', but for the moment Sheppey could not be taken. Eadric Streona, seeing the way the wind was blowing, changed sides again, joining Edmund at Aylesford. In need of Eadric's men, Edmund took him back into favour. But 'no greater error of judgment was ever made than this', commented the chronicler, with the advantage of hindsight.

The Battle of *Assingdun*

Edmund Ironside was winning the war. He had broken Canute's siege of London, the most elaborate military operation of the age, and won over most of the English magnates. Canute had been reduced from an acclaimed king-in-waiting to a mere Viking war-lord in command of nothing but a fleet, and facing the prospect of humiliating defeat by the forces closing in on him.

To supply the remains of his army, Canute needed to raid. In October, having moved north to one of the river estuaries on the Essex coast, he led a punitive expedition towards East Mercia, 'destroying and burning everything in his path as was [his] custom'. For the fifth time that year, Edmund called out the county levies. According to the Chronicle, 'all the people of England' flocked to his banner. But from those named in the forthcoming battle, it seems that most of this army was in fact drawn from East Anglia and the East Midlands, with some assistance from Hampshire. Eadric's contingent was made up of men from the *Magesaetan*, Eadric's heartland in Shropshire. Though not quite living up to its billing as a national army and, as it turned out, gravely divided, Edmund's army must have been a large one, perhaps numbering upwards of 5,000 men. He almost certainly outnumbered Canute's mainly Danish force.

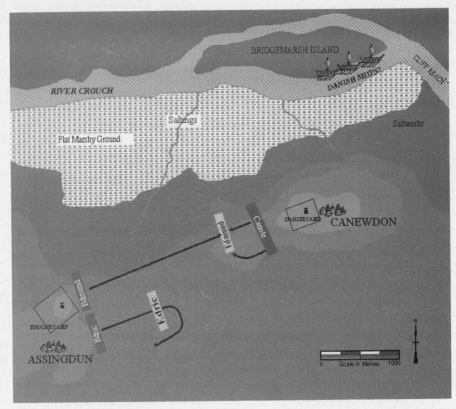

Battle of *Assingdun* 1016 (conjectural)

Locating the forthcoming battle of *Assingdun* depends on the wording of the Anglo-Saxon Chronicle at this point. According to the 'D' Chronicle, Edmund 'followed them up', overtaking Canute 'in Essex at the hill called *Assingdun*'. The 'F' chronicle clarifies a little by adding that Edmund had actively pursued Canute rather than simply encountered him. What is not clear is whether Edmund intercepted Canute as the latter returned from his foray, or whether Edmund followed him and pounced before Canute ever reached his goal. Two other sources offer clues. The *Encomium Emmae*, which dates from around 1041, within living memory of the battle, remembered that Edmund had challenged the Danes to stand and fight, but that Canute retorted that he would fight only on ground favourable to himself, and so 'continued to retreat'. According to Florence of Worcester, writing more than a century afterwards, the Danes did in fact fall back all the way to the Essex coast where the ships were moored.[16]

The battle that decided the destiny of England was fought on St Luke's Day, 18 October 1016. The name of the battle was *Assingdun* or 'the hill at *Assingdun*'. The *Encomium Emmae* explains that this meant 'the hill of ash trees', which is more likely than Florence's guess of 'hill of asses'. Before looking at the contending locations for the battle, let us review the battle itself. As usual, information is sparse, and most of it is problematical. Florence implies that both armies were camped on hills within sight of one another. Edmund began his advance at dawn the next day (the *Encomium Emmae* says it began at the hour after Matins, that is, at nine o'clock in the morning). Canute's force approached the battlefield more slowly. The armies clashed on level ground between the hills, though, by implication, nearer to Canute's hill than Edmund's.

The combat was fierce and protracted. The most detailed account is in the *Encomium Emmae*, and it does at least give a sense of a Dark Age battle as recalled by a near contemporary. Here is this rarely quoted source in full:

> [King Edmund, as usual, led from the front. He] advanced into the midst of the enemy, cutting down the Danes on all sides, and by this example, rendering his noble followers more inclined to fight. Therefore a very severe infantry battle was joined, since the Danes, although the less numerous side, did not contemplate withdrawal, and chose death rather than the danger attending flight. And so they resisted manfully, and protracted the battle, which had begun at 9 o'clock in the morning, until the evening, submitting themselves, though ill-content to do so, to the strokes of the swords, and pressing upon the foe with a better will with the points of their own swords. Armed men fell on both sides, but more on the side which had superiority in numbers [i.e. the English]. But when evening was falling and night time was at hand, longing for victory overcame the inconveniences of darkness, for since a graver consideration was pressing, they did not shrink from the darkness, and disdained to give way before the night, only burning to overcome the foe. And if the shining moon had not shown which the enemy was, every man would have cut down his comrade, thinking he was an adversary resisting him, and no man would have survived on either side, unless he had been saved by flight. Meanwhile the English began to be weary, and gradually to contemplate flight, as they observed the Danes to be of one mind either to conquer, or to perish all together to a man. For then they seemed to them more numerous, and to be the stronger in so protracted a struggle. For they deemed them stronger by a well-founded suspicion, because, being made mindful of their position by the goading of weapons, and distressed by the fall of their comrades, they seemed to rage rather than fight. Accordingly the English, turning their backs, fled without delay on all sides, ever falling before their foes, and adding glory to the honour of Canute and to his victory, while Edmund, the fugitive prince, was disgraced. The latter, although he withdrew defeated, giving way to the stronger side, was not, however, yet entirely without hope, and betook himself to safe positions, in order that ultimately he might assemble a more powerful force, and try again if by any chance any measure of good fortune could turn in his favour. The Danes, on the other hand,

did not pursue the fugitives far, for they were unfamiliar with the locality, and were held back by the darkness of night. The English, being familiar with the locality, quickly escaped from the hands of their enemies, whom they left to seize the spoil, as they themselves withdrew to places of dishonourable refuge.

The Danes passed the rest of the night on the battlefield 'among the bodies of the dead'. The following day they buried the bodies of their fallen comrades, but, after stripping the English dead of anything of value, 'left their bodies to the birds and the beasts'. This was probably the usual custom.

The battle, then, seems to have been desperately fought and went on long after dark. One reason why evenly matched battles went on for so long seems to have been fear of turning your back on the enemy: as the encomiast puts it, they 'chose death rather than the danger attending flight'. In the end the superior military stamina and morale of the Danes turned the tide. Not knowing the lie of the land, Canute had more to lose than the English from flight. Moreover, according to the encomiast, he had received a sign that the Danes would be victorious. Canute had a 'magic' banner 'of wonderfully strange nature'. At normal times it was of unadorned white silk, but at time of war a raven miraculously appeared which grew manic in the hour of victory 'opening its beak, flapping its wings and restive on its feet' but looked droopy and subdued after a defeat. Before the Battle of *Assingdun*, the raven was looking chirpy. It was a good omen.

However, as all accounts agree, there was a more prosaic reason why the English were defeated. According to the Chronicle,

> ... ealdorman Eadric did as he had so often before: he and the *Magesaete* were the first to set the example of flight, and thus he betrayed his royal lord and the whole nation.[17]

The *Encomium* has him telling his comrades from the West Midlands: 'Let us flee and snatch our lives from imminent death ... for I know the hardihood of the Danes.' Acordingly he concealed his banner and withdrew from the battle, leading a large proportion of his men. Some said he did so in fear, but others believed he had made a secret arrangement with Canute and so betrayed Edmund out of treachery. This gave the later Norman chroniclers their cue. Henry of Huntingdon has Eadric crying out: 'Flet Engles! Ded is Edmund!' just as it looked as though the Danes might be wavering. This is not very likely for once battle commenced Eadric would have had great difficulty making himself heard. More probably the ploy was prearranged and Eadric's men were never fully engaged. The shifty Mercian evidently waited until Edmund's division was committed before giving the order to leave the field. The supposition is that Eadric had little to expect from Edmund once victory had been gained and the Danes expelled. While a victory for Canute might also be awkward for him, he could plausibly present himself as Canute's covert ally, having surrendered to Edmund only in order to undermine him. His best hope, perhaps, was the death of both leaders, leaving Eadric as king-maker.

Eadric's desertion must have ruined Edmund's battle plan and made him vulnerable to a flank attack by the unengaged body of Danes. Like King Harold's brave housecarls at Hastings, Edmund's men stood their ground, and the casualties were heavy. Among the dead were the valiant earl Ulfcytel of East Anglia, the rather less valiant Aelfric of Hampshire, the bishop of Dorchester, the abbot of Ramsey, ealdorman Godwine (Edmund's leading man in Lindsey) and Aethelweard, son of ealdorman Aethelsige – 'all the flower of England', in fact.[18] It is possible that Edmund himself was gravely wounded, for he was evidently unable to take to the field again afterwards.

Ottar, Canute's skald, praised his master's prowess at '*Assatun*':

> Mighty scylding, you fought a battle
> Beneath the shield at Assatun.
> The blood-crane got morsels brown [i.e. with blood]
> Prince, you won renown enough
> With your great sword,
> North of Danaskogar ['Dane's Wood']
> But to your men
> It seemed a slaughter indeed.[19]

Unlike the other battles of 1016, *Assingdun* proved decisive. Canute had destroyed or neutralized the leaders of Saxon England, and ensured that he would become king. However, in a deal brokered by Eadric and reminiscent of the treaty between Alfred and Guthrum, Canute agreed to a division of England that gave Wessex to Edmund, and England beyond the Thames (but including London) to Canute. The terms were surprisingly generous to Edmund. The two kings swore a compact of friendship, and fixed a sum of money as payment to Canute's men. Perhaps Canute knew that Edmund's days were numbered. At any rate, King Edmund did indeed 'pass away' shortly afterwards, on St Andrew's Day, 30 November 1016. Medieval chroniclers, both in England and Iceland, believed that he had been assassinated, perhaps inevitably with Eadric's connivance,[20] but the wording of the Anglo-Saxon Chronicle makes that seem unlikely. More probably he was taken ill on campaign, or died from wounds received at *Assingdun*. King Edmund Ironside's year of glory and tragedy in 1016 is reminiscent of that of King Harold in 1066 (as was his impulsive nature). He deserved to win, but there are few happy endings in Dark Age history.

The Site of *Assingdun*

Where was *Assingdun*? The place ought to be easy enough to pin down. We know it was fought on a hill in Essex – and Essex is not a notably hilly place. The trouble – a familiar one by now – is there are two possible *Assingduns*, both with strong claims.

It all began in the sixteenth century, when Camden favoured Ashingdon, near Southend, whilst Holinshed proposed Ashdon, on the border with Cambridgeshire between Saffron Walden and Haverhill. Ashingdon's claim was championed by the Victorian historian E A Freeman in his immensely influential tome, *The History of the Norman Conquest*, and later by Alfred Burne in *More Battlefields of England*.[21] Apart from the correspondence of the place-names, the location turns on Florence of Worcester's description of the battlefield. Freeman visited the site in 1866, and 'went over the ground, Florence in hand. We found the place exactly answered his description.' This is not quite true. Florence speaks of one hill, but at Ashingdon there are two, one at the northern end of the modern village and the other three miles to the east at Canewdon, connected by a broad ridge of clay. To the north lie flat crop fields which in the Middle Ages were studded with the lagoons of salt-works. This is, in fact, a much more dramatic location than the one Florence describes, inviting the proposition that Canute was encamped at Canewdon (perhaps 'Canute's dun') at one end of the ridge, and Edmund at Ashingdon at the other. In Freeman's (and Burne's) reconstruction the two armies clashed on the ridge in between. A deep-water anchorage at Burnham Roads on the River Crouch lies only a short distance from Canewdon. Thus the site conforms to Florence's statement that Canute regained contact with his fleet before the battle. Nineteenth-century antiquarians thought that a series of low mounds by the north bank of the River Crouch were battle graves. They have since been excavated and found to be salt-works (salterns) of Roman to medieval date. None of the earthworks detected around the two churchyards can be securely dated to the time of the battle.

The counter-claims of Ashdon, in the north-east corner of Essex far from the sea, were argued largely from place-name evidence by Henry Swete in 1893.[22] In 1925, a well-known Essex archaeologist, Miller Christy, weighed the claims of the rival locations and came down in favour of Ashdon.[23] The matter was reopened by Cyril Hart in 1968,[24] and most recently by Warwick Rodwell in 1993.[25] Supporters of Ashdon claim that Canute was more likely to have chosen the River Blackwater or the Stour than the River Crouch. The Stour in particular offered the best natural harbour, at Harwich, from which there was a faster and more direct route into the Midlands than from the River Crouch, especially if Canute's first objective was Cambridge. Naval activity on the Crouch would be observable from north Kent, where Edmund's forces were last seen, and was dangerously close to London, now in Saxon hands. And a base on the Crouch would have required a sixty-mile route across Essex that offered no rich pickings to Canute, no wealthy monasteries, large boroughs or economic centres – indeed nothing much to 'destroy and burn' except for a succession of modest villages and farms. Military probability would therefore favour an estuary in the north of the county.

Ashdon, at roughly fifty miles from London and the coast at Harwich, is in the right area if we assume that Edmund marched from London and intercepted Canute *before* he reached the East Midlands. Etymologists also insist that Ashdon's medieval name of *Essendun* or *Assendun* is a better match for the Chronicle's *Assingdun* than

Canewdon church, perhaps built on the remains of Canute's camp, overlooking the marshes of the River Crouch.

Ashingdon (which is more likely to come from 'Assa's Dun'). And, unlike Ashingdon, it has associated Danish place-names such as 'Dane's Croft' and the field called 'Long Dane'. Finally, Ashdon has a plausible candidate for the 'Dane's Wood' mentioned by the saga in Hale's Wood, a now fragmented ancient wood south of the village. There are no ancient woods to the south of Ashingdon and Canewdon, and that area seems to have been poorly wooded as long ago as the eleventh century. One might add that ash

Images of Edmund Ironside and Canute on the road signs at Ashingdon and Canewdon.

trees grow better on the chalky soils of Ashdon than they do on salty air and soggy London clay of Ashingdon.

Clinching evidence would be the identification of the minster church that Canute had built on the battlefield. Work began within a month or so of the battle, and was completed by 1020 when Canute himself attended its consecration. The 'F' chronicle notes that it was 'built of stone and lime for the souls of those men who had been slain there'. The church, which one chronicle calls a 'minster', was endowed with lands and placed in the care of a senior member of the clergy. William of Malmesbury added that Canute had built churches on several of his old battlefields, although *Assingdun*'s is the only documented one.

This church, which would certainly pin down the location of the battlefield and perhaps mark its very centre, is something of a mystery. Records never mention it again, and it evidently never became a parish church. Rodwell examined the claims of four medieval churches at Ashingdon, Canewdon, Ashdon and Hadstock, and found that none were a good match for Canute's minster church. Only Hadstock has surviving Saxon masonry. Ashingdon's hill-top church proudly proclaims its origin as Canute's church – and has even appealed to Denmark for restoration funds – but its proportions make that most unlikely. Moreover Ashingdon was a poor parish, as the Domesday Book confirms. Canute's endowments and gifts would surely have created a relatively wealthy parish – somewhere like Ashdon, for example.

Ashingdon churchyard looking towards the hill-top church at Canewdon. In the scenario, the armies clashed along the ridge linking the two churches.

The location of Canute's church still eludes us. As a place of special character which never became a centre of parish worship, it probably fell into disuse after the Reformation and was pulled down (perhaps along with Canute's other battlefield churches). However a possible site has been suggested at 'Old Church Field' which lies a few hundred yards to the west of the rectory at Ashdon. This place-name occurs on a document from 1522 and lies on land adjacent to the glebe land of Ashdon church but not part of it. It seems therefore to be part of what was once a self-contained ecclesiastical estate. Was this the long-lost minster church of *Assingdun*? Only archaeological investigation will provide an answer. But, as Rodwell pointedly asks, if it is not here, then where is it?[26]

Ashdon would therefore seem to have a stronger claim than Ashingdon, both on the grounds of military probability and on documentary evidence. Ashdon supporters must ignore Florence of Worcester's claim that Canute regained contact with his ships before fighting the battle, but, it is suggested, writing so long afterwards, Florence is not a reliable source. From the point of view of the battlefield walker the balance of probability in favour of Ashdon is unfortunate. The ridge between Ashingdon and Canewdon offers a splendid physical background on which the battle can be refought in the mind's eye. This is not so of Ashdon, which stands in a gently rolling landscape of villages and farm fields with few features to anchor the battle. It is, in effect, a location without a battlefield.

Gazetteer of Dark Age Battles 410–1065

Unless otherwise indicated, all quotations are from the Anglo-Saxon Chronicle.

c.429: 'The Alleluia Battle'
Probably near Mold, Clwyd. Britons under St Germanus defeat 'the Saxons'.

c.437: *Guoloph*
Probably Wallop, near Andover, Hants, possibly at the hill-fort of Danebury. Fought between the adherents of Vortigern and Ambrosius, rival British rulers. Outcome unknown.

455. *Aegelesthrep*
Probably Aylesford, Kent. 'Hengest and Horsa fought against king Vortigern . . . and his brother Horsa was slain. And after that Hengest succeeded to the kingdom [of Kent] and Aesc, his son.'

456 or 457. *Crecganford*
Crayford, Kent. 'Hengest and Aesc fought against the Britons . . . and there slew four companies; and the Britons then forsook Kent and fled to London in great terror.'

465. *Wippedesfleot*
Possibly Ebbsfleet, Kent. 'Hengest and Aesc fought against the Welsh [i.e. British] near *Wippedesfleot* and one of their thanes, whose name was Wipped, was slain there.'

473. Unknown
'In this year Hengest and Aesc fought against the Welsh and captured innumerable spoils, and the Welsh fled from the English like fire.'

477. *Cymenesora* (Cymen's Shore)
The Owers, south of Selsey Bill, West Sussex; battlefield now under the sea. Aelle and his sons Cymen, Wlencing and Cissa 'slew many Welsh and drove some to flight into the wood called Andredesleag (the Sussex Weald)'.

485. *Mearcraedesburna* (Mercred's stream)
Unknown, possibly by the River Cuckmere. 'Aelle fought against the Welsh near the bank of *Mearcraedesburna*.' Outcome unknown.

491. *Andredescester*
The Roman Saxon Shore fortress of Anderida, later called Pevensey Castle, East Sussex. 'Aelle and Cissa besieged *Anderedescester* and slew all the inhabitants; there was not even one Briton left there.'

495. 1st Battle of *Cerdicesora* (Cerdic's Shore)
Unknown, probably by the Solent or Southampton Water. 'Cerdic and Cynric his son came to Britain with five ships (landing) at *Cerdicesora*, and the same day they fought against the Welsh.' Outcome unknown.

*c.*496. *Mons Badonicus* (Badon Hill)
The most likely sites are Liddington Hill, near Swindon, Wilts, or Little Solsbury Hill, near Bath. A different tradition places it on Dumbarton Rock. Britons, probably led by Ambrosius Aurelianus (but remembered in later times as Arthur), defeated the Saxons, probably led by Aesc and Aelle.

501. *Portesmutha* (Portsmouth)
Portsmouth, Hants, at or near the harbour. 'Port and his two sons, Bieda and Maegla, came with two ships to Britain at the place called *Portesmutha* and slew a young Briton, a very noble man.'

508. *Natanleag*
Probably Netley, near Hamble, Hants. 'Cerdic and Cynric slew a Welsh king, whose name was Natanleod, and five thousand men with him.'

514. 2nd Battle of *Cerdicesora*
'The West Saxons Stuf and Wihtgar came to Britain with three ships, landing at the place called *Cerdicesora* and fought the Britons and put them to flight.'

519. *Cerdicesford* (Cerdic's Ford)
Possibly Charford, Hants. 'Cerdic and Cynric fought against the Britons at a place now called *Cerdicesford*.' Outcome unknown.

527. *Cerdicesleag* (Cerdic's Wood)
Unknown location. 'Cerdic and Cynric fought against the Britons at the place which is called *Cerdicesleag*.'

530. *Wihtgaraesburh*
Isle of Wight, possibly at Carisbrooke, near Newport. 'Cerdic and Cynric obtained possession of the Isle of Wight and slew a few men at *Wihtgaraesburh*.'

*c.*537. *Camlann*
Possibly Birdoswald (Camboglanna) on River Irthing by Hadrian's Wall. Traditionally at Camelford, Cornwall. 'The strife . . . in which Arthur and Medraut fell.'

552. *Searoburh*
Old Sarum, near Salisbury, Wilts. 'Cynric fought against the Britons . . . and put the Britons to flight.'

556. *Beranburh*
Barbury Castle, near Swindon, Wilts. 'Cynric and Ceawlin fought against the Britons at *Beranburh*.' Outcome unknown.

568. *Wibbandun*
Possibly Whitmoor Common, Worplesdon, Surrey. 'Ceawlin and Cutha fought against Aethelberht [king of Kent] and drove him into Kent; and they slew two princes, Oslac and Cnebba, at *Wibbandun*.'

571. *Biedcanford*
Possibly Bedford. 'Cutha fought against the Britons . . . and captured four villages; and in the same year he passed away.'

573. *Arfderydd* (Arthuret)
Near Lockerbie, Dumfries, possibly by the Roman fort of Netherby. Rival British faction-fight between the sons of Eliffer and Gwenddolau son of Ceido. Gwenddolau was killed 'and Merlin went mad'.

577. *Argoed Llwyfain*
Site unknown. Urien of Rheged and his son Owen defeated 'a fourfold army' of Angles led by *Ffamddwn* ('firebrand', probably local chief called Theodoric) and Ulph.

577. *Deorham*
Dyrham, Glos. Decisive battle in which West Saxons moved into the Severn valley. 'Cuthwine and Ceawlin fought against the Britons and slew three kings, Coinmail, Farinmail and Condiddan ... and they captured three cities, Gloucester, Cirencester and Bath.'

584. *Fethanleag*
Probably Stoke Lyne, Oxon. 'Ceawlin and Cutha fought against the Britons ... and Cutha was slain; and Ceawlin captured many villages and countless booty, and departed in anger to his own [country].'

592. *Wodnesbeorh*
Adam's Grave on Pewsey Downs near Alton Priors, Wilts. 'In this year there was great slaughter at *Wodnesbeorh* and Ceawlin was driven out.' The victor was Ceol, possibly Ceawlin's nephew, aided by the native British.

*c.***593.** *Catraeth*
Catterick, North Yorks. Britons of Din Eidyn and Gododdin and their Welsh allies were defeated by 'the Saxons'. Celebrated in the epic poem, *The Gododdin*.

603. *Degsastan*
Probably Dawston in Lidderdale, Borders. Aethelfrith of Northumbria decisively defeated an alliance of Britons, Scots and Irish led by Aedan of Dal Riata.

614. *Beandun*
Probably Bindon, near Axmouth, Devon. 'Cynegils and Cwichelm [of Wessex] fought and slew two thousand and sixty-five Welsh.'

616. *Caerlegion* (Chester)
Aethelfrith defeated the Welsh under Selyf ap Cynan and 'slew a countless host' including 200 priests.

617. River Idle
Near Bawtry, South Yorks. Raedwald, king of East Anglia defeated and killed Aethelfrith of Northumbria.

628. Cirencester
'Cynegils and Cwichelm fought against Penda [king of Mercia] ... and they came to an agreement.'

633. *Heathfelth*
Hatfield, South Yorks, or more probably Cuckney, Notts. Penda and Caedwallon, king of Gwynedd, defeated and killed Edwin of Northumbria and his eldest son.

634. *Hefnfelth* or *Denisesburna*
'Heavenfield' by Hadrian's Wall was probably the mustering point. The battle took place by Rowley Burn, south of Hexham, Northumberland. Oswald, king of Northumbria defeated and killed Caedwallon.

637. *Mag Rath*
Unknown site in Co. Down. The high-king Domnall son of Aed defeated Domnall Brecc of Dal Riata. As a result the Dal Riatan Scots lost control of their Irish homeland.

641 (5 August). *Maserfelth* or *Maes Cogwy*
Probably Oswestry, Salop. King Oswald defeated and killed by Penda.

642. *Strathcarron*
By the River Carron, Stirling. Owain of Strathclyde defeated and killed Domnall Brecc. 'I saw an array, they came from Kintyre, and splendidly they bore themselves around the conflagration ... I saw great sturdy men, they came with dawn. And the head of Dyfnwal Frych [Domnall Brecc], ravens gnawed it.'

652. *Bradenforda*
Bradford-on-Avon, Wilts. 'In this year Cenwalh [of Wessex] fought at *Bradenforda*', probably against the Welsh.

655 (15 November). *Winwead* or *Maes Gai*
Probably Whin Moor near Leeds or River Went near Wragby, West Yorks. Oswy, king of Northumbria, decisively defeated Penda and his allies Aethelhere of East Anglia and Cadfael of Gwynedd.

658. *Peonnan*
Penselwood, Somerset. 'Cenwalh [king of Wessex] fought at *Peonnan* against the Welsh and drove them in flight as far as the Parret.'

661. *Posentesburh*
Probably Posbury, Devon. 'At Easter, Cenwalh fought at *Posentesburh*; and Wulfhere, son of Penda ravaged as far as Ashdown.'

665. *Wirtgernesburh*
Probably Bradford-on-Avon, Wilts. West Saxons defeat Welsh in alliance with men of Mercia. This may be the same battle as a 2nd Battle of Mons Badonicus fought between the Saxons and Welsh the same year.

*c.*671. 'The Two Rivers'
Unknown location but possibly on the River Tay. Ecgfrith, king of Northumbria, 'slew an enormous number of [Pictish] people . . . and reduced them to servitude'.

675. *Biedanheafod* ('Beda's Head')
Unknown, possibly near Marlborough, Wilts. 'Wulfhere, son of Penda, and Aescwine [of Wessex] fought at *Biedanheafod*, and the same year Wulfhere passed away.'

679. River Trent
Unknown, possibly near Marton, Lincs. Aethelred, king of Mercia decisively defeated Ecgfrith and slew his brother Aelfwine.

685 (20 May). Dunnichen or *Nechtanesmere*
On or near Dunnichen Hill, Angus. Bridei, king of the Picts defeated and killed Ecgfrith of Northumbria and a great part of his army. The beginning of the end of Northumbrian hegemony, according to Bede.

710. *Haefe* and *Caere*
'In this year ealdorman Beorhtfrith fought against the Picts between *Haefe* [River Avon?] and *Caere* [probably River Carron].'
   The same year, Ine, king of Wessex and his kinsman, Nunna, fought against Geraint, king of the Britons of Cornwall, at an unknown location.

711. *Manaw*
Plain of the Forth, possibly near Clackmannan. The Northumbrians slaughtered the Picts 'in the Plain of Manaw'.

715. 2nd Battle of *Wodnesburh*
Adam's Grave (Alton Priors, Wilts). Ine of Wessex and Ceolred of Mercia fought at Adam's Grave. Outcome unknown.

725. Unknown
'Ine fought against the South Saxons and there slew Ealdberht.'

733. *Sumurtun*
Somerton, Somerset. 'In this year Aethelbald [king of Mercia] captured Somerton: and all circle of the sun was become like a black shield.'

752. *Beorgfeord*
Possibly Burford, Oxon. 'Cuthred [of Wesex] fought [and probably won] against Aethelbald at *Beorgfeord.*'

776. *Ottanford*
Otford, Kent. Mercians fought Kentishmen 'and strange adders were seen in Sussex'. Outcome unrecorded.

779. *Bensington*
Benson, Oxon. 'In this year Cynewulf [of Wessex] and Offa contended around Benson, and Offa took the village.'

786. *Merantun*
Unknown, possibly Martin, Hants, or Marden, Wilts. Assassination of Cynewulf, king of Wessex by his kinsman Cyneheard, followed by the slaughter of their respective retinues.

802. *Cynemaeresford*
Kempsford, Glos. 'Ealdorman Aethelmund rode from the Hwicce over [the Thames] at *Cynemaeresford* and was met by ealdorman Weohstan with the men of Wiltshire. There was a great battle, and both the ealdormen were slain there, and the men of Wiltshire won the victory.'

*c.*820. *Cherrenhul*
Near Abingdon, Oxon. Ecgbert, king of Wessex, defeated Ceolwulf, king of Mercia.

825. *Gafalford*
Galford Down, near Lydford, Devon. 'In this year there was a battle at *Gafalford* between the Britons [of Cornwall] and the men of Devon.'

825. *Ellandun*
Ellingdon, now Wroughton, Wilts. Ecgbert, king of Wessex, decisively defeated Beornwulf, king of Mercia, 'and great slaughter was made there'.

836. *Carrum*
Carhampton, Somerset. 'Ecgbert fought against 25 ship's companies at *Carrum*; and great slaughter was made, and the Danes had possession of the place of slaughter.'

838. *Hengestdun*
Hingston Down near Callington, Cornwall. Ecgbert made an expedition against 'a great pirate host' united with the Britons of Cornwall, 'fought against them . . . and there put to flight both Britons and Danes'.

839. Unknown
Unnamed battle in which the Vikings slaughtered the men of Fortriu (i.e. central lowlands of Scotland) 'beyond counting', including several members of the royal house of Fergus. The battle left the way clear for Kenneth mac Alpin to unite the kingdoms of Picts and Scots.

840. *Hamwic*
Southampton, Hants. 'Ealdorman Wulfheard fought at *Hamwic* against 33 ship's companies and made great slaughter there and won the victory.'

840. *Port*
Portland, Dorset. 'Ealdorman Aethelhelm fought against the Danes at *Port* with the men of Dorset, and the ealdorman was slain, and the Danes had possession of the place of slaughter.'

843. 2nd Battle of *Carrum*
Carhampton, Somerset. 'King Aethelwulf fought at Carrum against 35 ship's companies, and the Danes had possession of the place of slaughter.'

848. River Parret
'Ealdorman Eanwulf with the men of Somerset and bishop Ealhstan and ealdorman Osric with the men of Dorset fought against a Danish host at the mouth of the Parret (*Padride*), and made great slaughter there and won the victory.'

850. *Wicgeanbeorg*
Possibly Wigborough, Somerset. 'Ealdorman Ceorl with the men of Devon fought against the heathen . . . and made great slaughter and won the victory.'

851. *Aclea*
Possibly Ockley, Surrey, or East Oakley, near Basingstoke, Hants. Aethelwulf and his son Aethelbald with the West Saxon levies fought and defeated the Danes 'with the greatest slaughter of a heathen host that we have ever heard tell of'.

851. *Sandwic*
Sandwich, Kent. 'Athelstan and ealdorman Ealhhere fought in ships and destroyed a great [Danish] host at *Sandwic*, and captured nine ships and drove off the rest.'

853. *Tenet* (Thanet)
Isle of Thanet, Kent. 'Ealhhere with the Kentishmen and Huda with the men of Surrey fought in Thanet against a heathen host, and at first were victorious, and there many men were slain and drowned on either side, and the ealdormen both dead.'

860. *Wintanceaster* (Winchester)
Outside the walls of Winchester, Hants. 'A great pirate host landed and stormed Winchester. And against the host fought ealdorman Osric with the men of Hampshire and ealdorman Aethelwulf with the men of Berkshire, and [they] put the host to flight . . .'

867 (21 March). York
The Danes led by Ivar and Halfdan besieged the city of York in November 866 and stormed the walls on 21 March the following year. 'And some of them got inside; and immense slaughter was made of the Northumbrians there, some inside, some outside, and both the kings [of Northumbria] were slain, and the remnant made peace with the host.'

869 (20 November). Unknown site
Possibly Hoxne, Suffolk, more probably Hellesdun, Bradford St Clare, Suffolk. Ivar and the Danes defeated and killed Edmund, last king of East Anglia.

870–1. *Alt Cluith* (Dumbarton)
The Danish host under Olaf and Ivar attacked the Britons on Dumbarton Rock, and stormed and sacked the town after a four-month siege.

870 (31 December). *Englafeld*
Englefield, near Reading, Berks. Ealdorman Aethelwulf and the men of Berkshire fought against the Danes, killed one of their leaders and won the victory.

871 (4 January). *Readingum* (Reading)
Probably King's Meadow, by the Thames. 'King Aethelred and Alfred his brother led great levies there and fought against the host . . . and ealdorman Aethelwulf was slain, and the Danes had possession of the place of slaughter.'

871 (8 January). *Aescesdun* (Ashdown)
Probably on the Berkshire Downs between Lowbury Hill and Starveall Farm. Aethelred and Alfred fought the Danish host, and killed their king, Bagsecg, and five jarls. 'Both their hosts were put to flight, and there were many thousands slain; and the fighting went on till nightfall.'

871. *Basengum* (Basing)
Probably at the site of Basing House, Old Basing. 'And a fortnight later king Aethelred and Alfred fought against the host camped at Basing, and there the Danes won the victory.'

871. *Meretun* or *Maeredun*
Possibly Martin, Hants, or Marten, Wilts. 'And two months later Aethelred and Alfred fought against the host at *Maeredun*, and . . . for a long time were victorious; and there was great slaughter on either side, but the Danes had possession of the place of slaughter.'

871. Wilton
Probably at the site of Wilton House, near Salisbury. 'King Alfred fought with a small force against the entire host . . . and for a long time drove them off, and the Danes had possession of the place of slaughter.'

875. Dollar
The Danes under Halfdan defeated and massacred the Picts and Scots, possibly led by King Constantine I, possibly at Dollar, near Clackmannan. 'It was on that occasion that the earth burst open under the men of Scotland' (Irish Annals).

877. Strangford Lough
Naval battle in which Halfdan, in a bid for the kingship of Dublin, was defeated and slain by a larger fleet led by Bardr Eysteinsson of Dublin.

878. *Cynwit*
Countisbury, near Lynton, or Cannington Park, near Cambwick, both in Devon. The men of Devon fought Jarl Ubbe, slew 800 of his men and captured the Raven banner.

878 (11 May). *Ethandun*
Edington, Wilts. The decisive battle in which King Alfred, with the men of Somerset, Wiltshire and Hampshire, fought the Danes, put them to flight and pursued them 'up to the fortification'.

885. Stourmouth
At the mouth of the Stour estuary. 'Alfred sent a naval force into East Anglia and as soon as they came to the mouth of the Stour they met sixteen ships of pirates, and fought against them, and captured all the ships, and slew all the crews . . . on their way home they met a great fleet of pirates, and fought against them . . . and the Danes were victorious.'

893. *Fearnhamm* (Farnham)
Farnham, Surrey. Alfred's levies intercepted the Danes under Haesten, 'fought against them and recovered the plunder; and they fled'.

893. *Bleamfleote* (Benfleet)
South Benfleet, Essex, in the vicinity of Hadleigh Castle Country Park. The English put the Danes under Haesten to flight, 'stormed their fort and seized everything inside it, both property and

women and also children, and conveyed them all up to London: and all the ships they either broke up or burned, or brought up to London or Rochester'. Human bones and charred timbers were found near South Benfleet railway station in the nineteenth century.

893. *Buttingtun*
Probably Buttington-on-Severn, near Welshpool, Powys. A large force from the west under ealdormen Aethelred, Aethelhelm and Aethelnoth and the king's thanes besieged the Danes in their fortress by the river. Eventually, having eaten most of their horses, 'they sallied forth against the men encamped on the east side of the river and fought against them, and the Christians had the victory'. 'These things done at Buttington are still proclaimed by old men' (*Chron. Aethelweard*). Probable grave-pits found near the church in 1838.

896. Uncertain
Sheltered water on south coast, possibly Poole Harbour. After blockading the harbour with nine ships, the English seized two of the six Danish ships and slew their crew. At low tide the crews fought a battle in which sixty-two English and their Frisian allies were killed and 120 Danes. Four of the Danish ships escaped, but two were later captured and their crews hanged.

904. The *Holm*
Probably near Holme, Cambs. A holm is a large flood-meadow. 'In (this) year was fought that battle at the *Holm*' between the Kentishmen allied to King Edward the Elder and East Anglian Danes allied to his rebellious cousin Aethelwold. The Danes suffered greater losses, including their king, Eohric, but drove the Kentishmen from the field.

910 (6 August). *Teotanhaele* (Tettenhall)
Tettenhall, Staffs. Mercians and West Saxons led by King Edward the Elder fought against the (Danish) host under Halfdan and Eowils near Tettanhall, and were victorious.

914. 1st Battle of Corbridge (*Corebricg*)
Corbridge, Northumberland. Ragnall (or Raegnald), Danish king of York, defeated the Bernicians and their Scottish allies.

916. *Brecenanmere*
Probably Langorse Lake, near Brecon, Powys. Aethelflaed, 'Lady of the Mercians', led an army into Wales and stormed *Brecenanmere*, capturing the Welsh king's wife 'and 33 other persons'.

917. *Ircingafeld* (Archenfield)
Archenfield, Herefords. The men of Herefordshire and Gloucestershire fought a Danish raiding party and slew one of their leaders, Hraold, 'and a great part of his host'. The rest were driven into an enclosure where they surrendered hostages and promised to depart.

917. *Deoraby* (Derby)
Derby. 'In this year before Lammas (August), Aethelflaed won the borough called Derby with God's help ... four of her thanes who were very dear to her were slain there within the gates.'

918. 2nd Battle of Corbridge
Bernicians and the Scots led by King Constantine II and his 'great steward' (*mormaer*) fought four divisions of Norsemen, slaying two of their leaders, Ottar and Crowfoot. At dusk, Ragnall turned the tables by ambushing the pusuing Scots. Both sides claimed victory.

918. *Temesanford* (Tempsford)
Near Wednesfield (*Uodnesfelda campo*), three miles east of Tempsford, Beds. 'In this summer a great force ... marched to Tempsford and besieged the fortress: they attacked it until they took it by storm, and slew the [Danish] king, and jarl Toglos, and his son, jarl Manna, and his brother, and all the garrison who put up a resistance.'

921. *Maeldun* (Maldon)

Maldon, Essex. A great host of Danes, 'to avenge the reverses they had suffered, went to Maldon, surrounded the fortress and attacked it until reinforcements came from without to their relief ... the garrison sallied out in pursuit of the Danes ... and slew many hundreds of them, both pirates and others'.

937. *Brunanburh*

Possibly Bromborough in the Wirral or near Brinsworth in South Yorkshire. The great battle between Saxon England under Athelstan and the Celtic north and west led by Olaf of Dublin and Constantine, king of Scots. 'With the help of Christ [Athelstan and his brother Edmund] had the victory and there slew five kings and eight jarls.'

943. *Tameworthig* (Tamworth)

Tamworth, Staffs. 'In this year Anlaf [Olaf] stormed Tamworth and there was great slaughter on both sides: the Danes had the victory and carried great booty away with them.'

948. Castleford

Castleford, Yorks. The (Viking) host of York under Eric Bloodaxe 'overtook king [Eadred's] rearguard at Castleford and there was great slaughter'.

950. Nant Carno

Near Carno, mid-Wales, south-east of Llanbrynmair. Sons of Hywel Dda clashed with the sons of Idwal over the inheritance of Gwynedd. Idwal's sons won, and went on 'to lay waste to Dyfed, twice'.

954. Stainmoor

'A stony waste' in the Pennines, possibly at Rey Cross, ten miles west of Barnard's Castle, Co. Durham. Eric Bloodaxe, the last Viking ruler of York, was 'betrayed' by earl Oswulf of Bernicia and slain by Northumbrian forces along with other Viking leaders.

954. Gwrgystu or Conwy Hirfawr

Llanrwst in the Vale of Conwy, Gwynedd. 'A great slaughter' between the sons of Hywel and sons of Idwal. Outcome not recorded, but afterwards 'Ceredigion was ravaged by the sons of Idwal'.

991 (10 or 11 August). Maldon

By Northey Island near Maldon, Essex. A force of Danes probably led by Olaf Tryggvason defeated the men of East Anglia led by ealdorman Byrhtnoth in a famous battle.

999. Rochester

Rochester, Kent. 'In this year the [Danish] host came up the Medway to Rochester. They were opposed by the Kentish levies and a sharp encounter took place: but alas! All too quickly they turned and fled because they did not get the support they should have had.'

1001. *Aethelingadene*

Probably Alton, Hants, or between West and East Dean, West Sussex. Small encounter battle in which the Danes were opposed by the men of Hampshire led by the king's high-reeves, Leofric and Aethelweard. 'The Danish casualties were heavier but they had possession of the place of slaughter.'

1001. *Peonho* (Pinhoe)

Pinhoe, near Exeter, Devon. The Danes, aided by the English traitor Pallig, pillaged their way to Pinhow were they were opposed by the high-reeves Kola and Eadsige 'with such levies as could be mobilized'. The Danes put them to flight, and burnt down the manor of Pinhoe 'and other goodly manors'.

1004. Thetford

Probably Wretham Heath, north of Thetford. The Danish raiders led by Sweyn were opposed by ealdorman Ulfcytel and the men of East Anglia. The Danes drove them from the field but 'they never met with worse hand-play among the English than Ulfcytel brought to them'.

1006. Kennet

East Kennet, on the downs near Marlborough, Wilts. 'The levies were mustered there . . . and they joined battle, but the Danes soon put that force to flight.'

1010 (18 May). Ringmere

Probably Rymer, south of Thetford. The men of Cambridgeshire and East Anglia under Ulfcytel fought the Danes led by Thorkell the Tall. After a fierce struggle, in which 'countless numbers' died, the Danes won, 'got horses for themselves and . . . harried and burnt that land'.

1014 (Good Friday, 23 April). Clontarf

Between the Rivers Tolka and Liffey opposite the island of Clontarf near Dublin. Epic battle between the forces of Brian Boru, high-king of Ireland and Sihtric 'Silky-beard', king of Dublin, limiting, if not ending, Danish power in Ireland. Pyrrhic victory for Brian Boru, who lost his life, as did his enemy Sigurd the Stout of Orkney. Perhaps the best documented battle of the Dark Ages.

1016. *aet Peonnum*

Penselwood, near Gillingham, Dorset. Indecisive battle in which men of Wessex led by Edmund Ironside fought the Danes.

1016. *Scearstan*

Sherston, near Malmesbury, Wilts. Edmund Ironside fought the Danes under Canute 'after mid-summer' 'and there was great slaughter on both sides, and it was not [the leaders] but the armies themselves who broke off the fight'.

1016. Brentford

Brentford, west London. 'The king [Edmund] crossed the river at Brentford, and fought against the [Danish] host and put it to flight; and a great number of the English were drowned through their own negligence . . .'

1016. *Ottanford*

Otford, Kent. 'King Edmund called up all the people of England . . . and went into Kent, and the host fled before him with their horses into Sheppey, and the king slew as many of them as he could overtake.'

1016 (18 October). *Assandun* or *Assingdun*

Probably Ashdon or Ashingdon, both in Essex. Decisive battle in which Canute defeated the men of Wessex and Mercia under Edmund Ironside and ealdorman Eadric Streona. 'Canute was victorious and won all England by his victory.' Among the dead: three ealdormen, an abbot 'and all the flower of England'.

1018. *aet Carrun*

Carham-on-Tweed, near Wark, Northumberland. Decisive victory of the Scots under King Malcolm II and Owen, king of Strathclyde, over the men of Northumbria under their earl, Eadulf Cudel. As a result Lothian was ceded permanently to Scotland and the border established on the Tweed.

1022. Abergwili

Abergwili, near Carmarthen. 'In this year an Irishman claimed to be Rhain ap Maredudd [the local king]. He was accepted by the men of the south, and he led then against [Llywelyn ap Seissyl of]

Gwynedd. And the men of Gwynedd defeated him at Abergwili with great slaughter on both sides. And he was never seen again. And then the men of Gwynedd ravaged the whole land.' (*Chron. Ystrad Fflur*). The battle is described in some detail in the *Brut y Twysogion*.

1039. Rhyd y Groes

Rhyd y Groes, near Forden, six miles south-east of Welshpool. Gruffydd ap Llywelyn ambushed and defeated the English, killing Edwin, brother of Leofric, earl of Mercia, 'and very many other good men'.

1052. *Portloca*

Porlock, Somerset. Earl Harold fought 'the men of Devonshire and Somerset gathered to oppose him, and he put them to flight and slew there more than thirty good thanes besides other men'.

1054 (27 July). *Dunsinan*

Probably Dinsinane Hill near Perth, Tayside. 'In this year earl Siward [of Northumbria] invaded Scotland with a great host both by land and sea, and fought against the Scots. He put to flight their king Macbeth, and slew the noblest in the land, carrying off much plunder ... but his son Osbern and numbers of his housecarls as well as those of the king [Edward the Confessor] were slain there on the Festival of Seven Sleepers.'

1055. Hereford

Probably at Glasbury-on-Wye near Hereford. Aelfgar, the exiled earl of East Anglia, supported by the Welsh under Gruffydd ap Llywelyn, fought against earl Ralph the timid and put him to flight, 'and many were slain in that rout' (Anglo-Saxon Chronicle). 'And Gruffydd pursued them to within the walls of Hereford, and there he massacred them and destroyed the walls and burnt the town. And with vast spoil he returned home eminently worthy.' The defeat was attributed to the ineptness of the English mounted troops, fighting 'contrary to their custom' (*Chron. Ystrad Fflur*).

Notes

Chapter 1: Introduction
1. Eddius, *Life of Wilfrid*, in Webb (1965: 152).
2. All quotations unless otherwise sourced are from the Everyman edn. of the Anglo-Saxon Chronicle, tr. Garmonsway (1953).
3. *Annals of Ulster*, AD 490–500.
4. *Annales Cambriae*, www.kessler.web.co.uk. *Chronicle of Ystrad Fflur*, www.webexcel.nidirect.co.uk
5. Books on Dark Age arms and armour include Pollington (1996), Siddorn (2003) and Underwood (1999).
6. 'bows were busy' (*Bogan waeron bysige*). *Battle of Maldon*, Griffiths (2000: 27).
7. 'make a war-hedge' (*wyrcan thone wihagen*). Ibid. 27.
8. Vegetius, *De re militaris*. For discussion of this source, see Ferrill (1983: 127–33).
9. See, for example, Tom Cain, online correspondence, Society Medieval History, http://scholar.chem.nyu.edu
10. Strickland (2001).
11. Smyth (1984: 142).
12. Bede 4. 22.
13. Fletcher (2001).
14. Strickland (2001).
15. English Heritage, *Battlefield Register*.
16. The Gazetteer for Scotland, *Scottish Battle Register*, www.geo.ed.ac.uk

Chapter 2: The Saxon Conquest of England
1. *Historia Brittonum*. Cited in Morris (1993).
2. Bede 1. 15.
3. Rayner (2001: 2–5).
4. Bede 1. 15.
5. Geraint poem quoted in Morris (1993: 104–5). The poem calls the place *Llongborth*, meaning 'ship-port'.
6. *Chron. Ystrad Fflur*: '577: In this year the battle of Dyrham was lost'.
7. Burne (1952: 16–21).
8. Smurthwaite (1984: 33).
9. Stenton (1971: 29).

Chapter 3: Arthur and Mount Badon
1. Gildas, *De excidio et conquestu Britanniae* (On the Ruin and Conquest of Britain).
2. Wood (1981b: 44).

3. Full translation: 'From that time now our countrymen won, then the enemies, so that in this people the Lord could make trial (as He does) of this latter-day Israel to see whether it loves him or not. This lasted right up to the year of the siege of Mount Badon, pretty well the last defeat of the hated ones, and certainly not the least. This was the year of my birth; as I know, one month of the forty-fourth year since then has already passed.'

4. Wood (1999a: 31–8).

5. Morris (1993). His uncited source seems to be *Historia Brittonum*: 'On Hengest's death his son Octha came down from the north of Britain to the kingdom of the Kentishmen. Then in those days Arthur fought against them with the kings of the Britons, but he was the commander (*dux*) in the battles.'

6. Burne (1950: 1–10).

7. On dating the battle from Gildas, see Wood (1999a: 31–8), and summary on *Battle of Mons Badonicus* online on Wikipedia.org

8. *Chron. Ystrad Fflur*: '570. In this year Gildas, wisest of Britons, died.'

9. Bede 1. 16: 'Under [the leadership of Ambrosius] the Britons took up arms, challenged their conquerors to battle, and with God's help inflicted a defeat on them. Thenceforward victory swung first to one side and then to the other, until the battle of Badon Hill, when the Britons made a considerable slaughter of the invaders. *This took place about forty-four years after their arrival in Britain ...*'

10. Howlett (1998).

11. Myres (1986).

12. Burkitt and Burkitt (1990).

13. For excavations at Liddington Hill, see Hirst and Rahtz (1996).

14. Myres (1986: 159–60).

15. Burne (1952: 8–10).

16. Rayner (2002: 40–1).

17. See online *Guide to Arthurian Archaeology*: www.arthuriana.co.uk

18. See Goodrich (1989)

19. Tennyson, *Idylls of the King, The Passing of Arthur*:

> On the waste sand by the waste sea they closed.
> Nor ever yet had Arthur fought a fight
> Like this last, dim, weird battle of the west.
> ... So all day long the noise of battle roll'd
> Among the mountains by the winter sea
> Until King Arthur's Table, man by man,
> Had fall'n in Lyonesse about their lord,
> King Arthur.

20. Malory, *Le Morte d'Arthur*, book 21, ch. 3: 'And then King Arthur drew him with his host down by the seaside westwards toward Salisbury; and there was a day assigned betwixt King Arthur and Sir Mordred, that they should meet upon a down beside Salisbury, and not far from the seaside ... Thus they fought all the long day, and never stinted till the noble knights were laid to the cold earth; and ever they fought still till it was near night, and by that time was there an hundred thousand laid dead upon the down.'

21. *Chron. Ystrad Fflur*: '550. In this year Derfei Gadern, who fought at Camlann, and Teilo went to the Lord.'

22. Crawford (1949). Crawford was a pioneer of the use of aerial photographs in archaeology, as well as retaining the imagination of an antiquarian in a scientific age.

23. For example, Carroll (1996).

24. Ibid. Summary at: www.legendofkingarthur.com/camlann
25. Morris (1993: 118-23) records many early Welsh Arthurian traditions of doubtful historical reliability.
26. For celebrations at Camelford see www.tintagelweb.co.uk/Battle
27. *Chron. Ystrad Fflur*: '573. In this year the battle of Arfderydd between the sons of Eliffer and Gweddolau son of Ceido; in which battle Gwenddoleu fell; Myrddin went mad. And this was the third futile battle of the island of Britain.'
28. Goodrich (1989).

Chapter 4: The Battles of Northern England

1. Praise poems by Taliesin quoted in Morris (1993: 232–3).
2. From Nennius, *Historia Brittonum*: 'Urien blockaded [Theodoric] for three days and three nights on the island of Metcaud. But he was butchered during this undertaking on the instigation of Morcant, from jealousy, because his military skill surpassed that of all other kings.'
3. For quotations from *The Gododdin*, I used Short (1994). A full translation is available online at www.missgien.net
4. The identification of Catterick with *Catraeth* is generally accepted. The name has survived 2,000 years from the Roman Cataracta through the Old English Cetreht or Cetrehttun and the Domesday Book's Catrice to the medieval Kateric, now spelt Catterick. It probably comes from the Latin word for waterfall, though it may also incorporate the British *catu-* meaning 'war'.
5. The elegy for Cadwallon is a Welsh poem, *Moliant Cadwallawn* (In praise of Cadwallon), preserved in the Panton collection in the Welsh National Library as MSS 55. Its date is uncertain.
6. The date of the Battle of *Catraeth* is much disputed. Around 600 was the usual best guess, but Koch (1997) made a closely argued case for *c*.570. See also 'Gododdin Revisited', the review of the book by Tim Clarkson (1999) in *The Heroic Age*, 1.
7. For detailed archaeological excavations see Wilson (2002) and summary at www.english-heritage.org.uk
8. Smyth (1984).
9. Morris (1993: 237).
10. Bede 1. 34.
11. Aedan's military potential discussed in Evans (1997: 31).
12. For site of *Degsastan*, see Bannermann (1974).
13. Mael Umai is killed in the battle as related in Adomnan's *Life of St Columba*, but died a decade later in 612 in *Annals of Innisfallen*.
14. Halsall (undated, but *c*.1985).
15. Maund (2000: 29–30).
16. *Chron. Ystrad Fflur*: '615. In this year was the Massacre of the Saints of Bangor Iscoed and Selyf ap Cynan Garwyn was defeated by Aethelfrith at Chester'. *Annals of Ulster* have 'Chester where the saints were slain.'
17. Bede 2. 2.
18. Bede 2 12.
19. Bede 2. 16.
20. *Moliant Cadwallawn* (see n. 5 above).
21. Bede 2. 20.
22. For legends surrounding Edwinstowe and environs, see www.nottshistory.org.uk
23. Wood (1999b: 216).
24. Bede 3. 2.
25. Zeigler (2001).
26. Bede 3. 1.
27. Adomnan, *Life of St Columba*.

28. Bede 3. 2.
29. *Annales Cambriae*: *Catscaul*. *Annals of Ulster*: *Cantscaul*.
30. Bede 3. 11.
31. *Annales Cambriae*: 'The battle of *Cogfry* in which Oswald king of the Northmen and Eawa [Eoba] king of the Mercians fell'. Bede and the *Chronicle of Ystrad Fflur* call the battle *Maserfelth*. Having dismissed the battle in a few lines, Bede devotes most of book 3, chs. 9 to 12, to describing the miracles wrought at Oswald's cross and tomb.
32. Bede 3. 14.
33. Bede 3. 24.
34. *Historia Brittonum*, 64–5. *Iudeu* was probably a hill fortress on the way to, if not actually on, Stirling Rock.
35. Ibid.
36. *Chron. Ystrad Fflur*: '655. At the end of the year was the slaughter of the field of Gai and Oswy killed the king of the Britons, and Penda with them, save only Catamail Catguommed.'
37. Churchill (0000: book 1, ch. 5).
38. Edmund Bogg's 1893 article is reproduced online at www.oldtykes.co.uk as 'Elmet's Battles of the so called Dark Ages'. See also 'The Battle of Winwaedfield' by Arthur Bantoft, published in *Journal of Barwick-in-Elmet Historical Society*, reproduced online at www.winwaed.com
39. Walker (1948).
40. Bede 3. 24.

Chapter 5: Dunnichen: Destiny in the North

1. Stephan, *Vita Sancti Wilfridi*, 19.
2. Nennius, *Historia Brittonum*, 57.
3. The ties of kinship between Ecgfrith and Bridei are discussed, together with a reconstructed family tree, in Fraser (2002: 22–3).
4. Bede 4. 26.
5. Source is a Gaelic poem preserved in the *Life of Adomnan*, quoted in Fraser (2002: 22).
6. Gaelic poem, *Iniu feras Bruide cath*, quoted and discussed in Fraser (2002: 21–2).
7. *Annals of Tigernach*: 'The Orcades were annihilated (*deletae sunt*) by Bridei'.
8. Bede, *Life of St Cuthbert*, 24, 27.
9. Symeon, *Historia Dunelmensis Ecclesiae*: 'Ecgfrith . . . was slain with the greater part of his warriors he had brought with him to lay waste the land of the Picts . . . at *Nechtanesmere*, which is the lake of Nechtan (*quod est stagnum Nechtani*)'.
10. 'Bellum Ecgfridi'. Adomnan's *Life of St Columba*.
11. *Annals of Ulster*: 'Bellum Duin Nechtain'. *Annals of Tigernach*: 'Cath Duin Nechtain'.
12. *Historia Brittonum*, 57. Ecgfrith 'is the one who made war against his *fratruelis*, who was the Pictish king Birdei . . . and he fell there with all the strength of his army and the Picts with their king emerged as victors, and the Saxon thugs never grew thence to exact tribute from the Picts. From that time the battle is called *Gueith Lin Garan*.'
13. Cruickshank (1999b).
14. Fraser (2002).
15. Ibid. 45, 70–3.
16. Anonymous *Life of St Cuthbert* in: *Two Lives of St Cuthbert*, ed. Bertram Colgrave (1940).
17. Bede 4. 26.
18. Wainright (1948).
19. Alcock (1996).
20. Fraser (2002: 65–88).
21. Cruickshank (2000).
22. Bede, *Life of St Cuthbert*, 27.

23. Halsall (1984).
24. Anonymous *Life of St Cuthbert*.
25. Bede 4. 26.
26. Cruickshank (1999a)
27. Fraser (2002: esp. app. 6).
28. Anderson (1973).
29. Bede 4. 26.
30. Cruickshank (1999a), Fraser (2002: 104–5).
31. Julia Fox Parsons, 'The First Battle for Scottish Independence: The Battle of Dunnichen, AD 685', MA thesis, State University of East Tennessee, 2002.
32. Cruickshank (1999a).

Chapter 6: Ecgbert and the Coming of the Vikings
1. 'And Ecgbert succeeded to the kingdom of Wessex: and the same day ealdorman Aethelmund rode from the Hwicce over [the Thames] at Kempsford, and there was met by ealdorman Weohstan with the men of Wiltshire. There was a great battle, and both the ealdormen were slain there, and the men of Wiltshire won the victory.'
2. Burne (1952: 28–9).
3. Spicer (2001).
4. Henry of Huntingdon, *Historia Anglorum*.
5. Burne (1952: 31).
6. Halsall (1985b)
7. In Higden's *Polychronicon*, cited by Halsall (1985b).
8. Halsall (1985b).
9. Grundy (1918).
10. Burne (1952: 32–3).
11. Spicer (2001).
12. *Scottish Chronicle*, cited in Smyth (1984). The 'men of Fortriu' were slaughtered 'beyond counting' in a battle against the 'gentiles' or heathen Vikings. Among the dead was 'Uven' (Owen), last of the independent Pictish kings, and his brother, Bran.
13. Smyth (1984: 151–2).
14. Ibid.
15. Asser, 9, in Keynes and Lapidge (1983: 69).
16. Asser, 5, in Keynes and Lapidge (1983: 68).
17. Keynes and Lapidge (1983).
18. *Passio de Sancti Eadmundi*, in Smyth (1995: 21–2).
19. Discussed in Smyth (1979: 189–94).
20. Cited in Whitelock (1969)
21. Smyth (1977).
22. Whitelock (1969).
23. Gaimar, cited in Whitelock (1969).
24. Smyth (1995: 28–9).
25. King Alfred, prose preface to Gregory's *Pastoral Care*, in Keynes and Lapidge (1983: 124–5).
26. *Annals of Ulster*, 871. 'Amalib [Olaf] and Imar [Ivar] returned to Ath Cliath [Dublin] from Alba with two hundred ships bringing away with them in captivity to Ireland a great prey of Angles and Britons and Picts.'

Chapter 7: The Battles of King Alfred
1. From the preface to Gregory's *Pastoral Care*, Keynes and Lapidge (1983: 125). 'To the track' is a hunting metaphor.

2. Asser, 35.
3. Geffrei Gaimar, *L'Estoire des Englais*, cited in Smyth (1995: 34).
4. Asser, 37–8.
5. Smyth (1995: 186–8).
6. Underwood (1999: 131–5).
7. Asser, 39
8. Traditional site of Ashdown summarized in Grinsell (1937). For a more accessible summary of Uffington legends, see www.berkshirehistory.com/legends/alfred
9. Burne (1950: 17-18). Burne's site for Ashdown is less closely argued than for most of his other Dark Age battles.
10. Asser, 42.
11. Asser, 55.
12. Grundy (1918).
13. The Anglo-Saxon Chronicles all use similar wording.
14. Asser, 56.
15. Smyth (1995: 94–6).
16. Burne (1952: 39).
17. Channel 4, *Weapons that Made Britain*, 31 July 2004.
18. Smyth (1995: 95). Edington was Alfred's 'finest hour', not only for his victory but for his diplomacy in its aftermath, culminating in Guthrum's baptism.
19. 'The Footpaths of Edington', booklet published by Edington Parish Council.

Chapter 8: *Brunanburh*: The Greatest Battle
1. On the confusion of Olafs at *Brunanburh* I have followed Smyth (1984: 201–5).
2. From the battle poem, 'better workmen were in the conflict of banners, the clash of spears, the meeting of heroes'.
3. Quotations from *Egil's Saga* are from the Penguin edn. (Scudder and Oskardottir, 2004).
4. William of Malmesbury, *Gesta Regum Anglorum*, in Whitelock (1979).
5. The *Brunanburh* poem is contained in the Winchester ('A') manuscript of the Anglo-Saxon Chronicle against the year 937.
6. Cited in Wood (1981a: 212–13).
7. Cited in Wood (1999b: 203–4), from prophetic poem *Armes Prydein* (Great Prophesy) in the *Book of Taliesin*.
8. McDougall (2004), who concludes that 'Setting off to find Brunanburh equipped only with a copy of Egil's Saga offers prospects of little more than a pleasant walk and a good read.'
9. Scudder and Oskardottir (2004: 218).
10. William of Malmesbury, in Whitelock (1979).
11. Symeon of Durham, *Historia ecclesiae dunelmensis*, in Whitelock (1979).
12. William of Malmesbury, in Whitelock (1979).
13. Wood (1999b).
14. Florence (John) of Worcester, *Chronicle*, in Whitelock (1979).
15. Burne (1952: 45).
16. Hill (2004: 135–60) looks at over twenty competing sites.
17. Neilson (1909).
18. Law (1909)
19. Burne (1952: 53).
20. Angus (1937).
21. Burne (1952: 53).
22. Cockburn (1931).
23. Wood (1999b: 205).

24. Burne (1952: 44–60).
25. Wood (1999b).
26. Smyth (1979).
27. Smith (1937: 56–9).
28. Harding (2004: 22–3).
29. Campbell (1938).

Chapter 9: Spears as Tribute: The Battle of Maldon

1. Quotations from *The Battle of Maldon* are from the text and translation edited by Griffiths (2000). The key modern source on the battle is Scragg (1991).
2. Irving (1961).
3. The most detailed of the Anglo-Saxon Chronicles is the 'Parker Chronicle' ('A'), which runs as follows: 'In this year came Anlaf [Olaf Tryggvason] with ninety-three ships to Folkestone ... and so on to Maldon. Ealdorman Byrhtnoth came to meet them with his levies and fought them, but they slew the ealdorman there and had possession of the place of slaughter.'
4. *Vita Sancti Oswald*, cited in Griffiths (2000: 7-8).
5. Griffiths (2000).
6. Freeman (1877).
7. Burne (1952: 61-9).
8. Laborde (1925).
9. Petty and Petty (1976).
10. *Tribal Hideage*, discussed in Stenton (1971: 295-7).
11. Wood (1981b: 180-4).
12. *Book of Ely*, cited in Griffiths (2000: 8-10).
13. Fletcher (2001).
14. English Heritage (2003). Maldon is one of six battlefield walks set out in booklet form.

Chapter 10: Calamity under Aethelred

1. The events of Aethelred's reign are recounted in most detail in the Laud or Peterborough ('E') Chronicle. Instead of being a mere list of dates and events, it offers a commentary on the Danish invasions. Obviously written in hindsight, the chronicler strikes a pessimistic note in line with other writings of the time, most notably Bishop Wulfstan's 'Sermon of the Wolf'. Whoever he was, our chronicler was literate, well-informed and with a nice line in irony.
2. 1004: 'The next morning when [the Danes] planned to retire to their ships, Ulfcytel came up with his force and there was a fierce encounter and great slaughter on each side. There were slain the chief men of East Anglia, but if they had been up to full strength the enemy would never have got back to their ships, as they themselves admitted' ('E' Chronicle). The battle cannot be located exactly but is believed to have taken place on East Wretham Heath, four miles north-east of Thetford on the road to Norwich.
3. 1006: 'They went to Wallingford and burned it to the ground and proceded along the Berkshire Downs to Cuckhamsley Knob, and there awaited the great things that had been threatened, for it had often been said that if they ever got as far as Cuckhamsley Knob, they would never again reach the sea; but they went back by another route. Then levies were mustered there at East Kennet, and there they joined battle; but the Danes soon put that force to flight, and bore their plunder to the sea.' The village of East Kennet lies on the Ridgeway close to the point where it crosses the Kennet and near a crossroads formed by a Roman road from Marlborough to Bath. The battle probably took place close to the present village.
4. The sources for Ringmere are the Anglo-Saxon Chronicle and several Scandinavian praise poems, notably the *Olafsdrapa* or Olaf's Saga and Snorri Sturlusson's *Heimskringla*, both of which refer to 'Hringmera Heath in Ulfkell's land'.

5. Florence of Worcester says it was fought on 5 May, a date confirmed by the twelfth-century Ely Calendar. However, the Chronicle, being much closer in time to the battle, has priority.
6. Palsson and Edwards (1986).
7. *Olafsdrapa*: 'All the race of Ella stood arrayed at Hringmaraheldr (Ringmere Heath)/Men fell in battle when Harold's heir stirred up strife', in Whitelock (1979).
8. Ibid.
9. *Eiriksdrapa*, in Whitelock (1979).
10. Campbell (1949: 35–6).
11. Oman (1885): the starting point of modern Dark Age and medieval battlefield studies.
12. The exact site of the Battle of Penselwood is conjectural. The area is rich in archaeological remains, but none can be linked to the battle.
13. The main sources for the Battle of Sherstone are the Chronicle and *Knutsdrapa*, the praise poem of Canute by Ottar the Black, quoted in Whitelock (1979). The most recent assessment of Canute is Rumble (1994).
14. *Knutsdrapa*, in Whitelock (1979).
15. Ibid.
16. Movements of the armies before *Assingdun* are discussed in Rodwell (1993: 131–9).
17. The wording is the same in the 'E' and 'F' chronicles.
18. The dead of *Assingdun* and their significance are discussed by Higham (1997: 66–8).
19. *Knutsdrapa*, in Whitelock (1979).
20. The Norman chroniclers offered several lurid versions of the murder of Edmund Ironside. William of Malmesbury had heard he was murdered by a 'sharp basulard' as he sat down to relieve himself. Another version has him being hit by an arrow driven by a secret mechanism within a wooden statue. Gaimar combines both versions by having the unfortunate king shot in the nether parts 'as far as the lugs' by an assassin hiding in the latrine.
21. Burne (1952: 75–8).
22. Swete (1893), and, more accessibly, via www.meetingpoint.org
23. Christy (1925).
24. Hart (1968).
25. Rodwell (1993).

References

Alcock, Leslie (1982) *Arthur's Britain: History and Archaeology AD 367–634*. London: Penguin Books.

Alcock, Leslie (1996) 'The Site of the Battle of Dunnichen', *Scottish Historical Review*, 75, 130–42.

Anderson, Marjorie (1973) *Kings and Kingship in Early Scotland*. Edinburgh: Rowman & Littlefield.

Angus, W H (1937) 'The Battlefield of Brunanburh', *Antiquity*, 11, 283–93.

Arnold, C J (1984) *Archaeology of the Early Anglo-Saxon Kingdoms*. London: Routledge.

Bannerman, John (1974) *Studies in the History of Dalriada*. Edinburgh: Scottish Academic Press.

Brooks, Richard (2005) *Cassell's Battlefields of Britain and Ireland*. London: Weidenfeld & Nicolson (the most comprehensive compendium of British battlefields to date).

Burkitt, Tim, and Burkitt, Annette (1990) 'The Frontier Zone and the Siege of Mount Badon: A Review of the Evidence for their Location', *Somerset Archaeology and Natural History*, 134, 81–93.

Burne, Alfred H (1950) *The Battlefields of England*. London: Methuen.

Burne, Alfred H (1952) *More Battlefields of England*. London: Methuen.

Campbell, A, ed. (1938) *The Battle of Brunanburh*. Edinburgh: Heinemann.

Campbell, A, ed. (1949) *Encomium Emmae Reginae*. London: Camden series, 73.

Campbell, James, ed. (1982) *The Anglo-Saxons*. Oxford: Phaidon.

Christie, M (1925) 'The Battle of Assandun: Where was it Fought?', *Journal British Archaeological Association*, 31, 168–80.

Churchill, Winston (1956–8) *History of the English Speaking People*. London: Cassell.

Carroll, D F (1996) *Arturius: A Quest for Camelot*. Cottingham, E. Yorks.

Cockburn, J H (1931) *The Battle of Brunanburh and its Period Elucidated by Place-Names*. Sheffield: W C Leng & Co.

Colgrave, Bertram, ed. (1940) *Two Lives of St Cuthbert* Cambridge: Cambridge University Press.

Cooper, J, ed. (1993) *The Battle of Maldon: Fact and Fiction*.London: Hambledon.

Crawford, O G S (1949) *Topography of Roman Scotland North of the Antonine Wall*. Cambridge: Cambridge University Press.

Cruickshank, Graham (1999a) *The Battle of Dunnichen*. Forfar: Pinkfoot Press.

Cruickshank (1999b) 'The Battle of Dunnichen: Whose Name is it Anyway?', *Scottish Local History Journal*, 46, 21–6.

Cruickshank, Graham (2000) 'The Battle of Dunnichen and the Aberlemno Battle-Scene', in E J Cowan and R A McDonald (eds), *Alba: Celtic Scotland in the Middle Ages* (East Linton: Tuckwell Press), 69–87.

Duncan, A A M (1975) *Scotland: The Making of the Kingdom*. The Edinburgh History of Scotland. Edinburgh: Oliver & Boyd.

Ekwall, Eilert (1960) *The Concise Oxford Dictionary of English Place-Names*, 4th edn. Oxford: Clarendon Press.

Ellis, H R, ed. (1962) *The Sword in Anglo-Saxon England*. Oxford: Clarendon Press.

English Heritage (2003) *Battlefield Hikes*, vol. 1. London: English Heritage.

Evans, Stephen S (1997) *The Lords of Battle: Image and Reality of the Comitatus in Dark-Age Britain*. Woodbridge: Boydell Press.

Ferrill, A (1983) *The Fall of the Roman Empire: The Military Explanation.* London: Thames & Hudson.

Fletcher, Richard (2001) *Bloodfeud: Murder and Revenge in Anglo-Saxon England.* London: Allen Lane.

Fraser, James E (2002) *The Battle of Dunnichen, 685.* Stroud: Tempus.

Freeman, E A (1877) *History of the Norman Conquest of England.* London.

Garmonsway, G N, tr. (1954) *The Anglo-Saxon Chronicle.* Everyman Edition. London: Dent.

Goodrich, Norma (1989) *King Arthur.* London: HarperCollins.

Griffiths, Bill (2000) *The Battle of Maldon: Text and Translation*, rev. edn. Hockwold-cum-Wilton, Norfolk: Anglo-Saxon Books.

Grinsell, L V (1937) *White Horse Hill and Surrounding Country.* [n. pl.]: St Catherines Press.

Grundy, G B (1918) 'The Ancient Highways of Wiltshire, Berkshire and Hampshire and the Saxon Battlefields of Wiltshire', *Archaeological Journal*, 75.

Hackett, Martin (undated) 'The Battle of Buttington, AD 894', *Wargames Illustrated*, 75.

Halsall, Guy (undated) 'The Battle of Degsastan, AD 603', *Miniature Wargames*, 3.

Halsall, Guy (1984) 'The Woeful Disaster of Nechtansmere', *Miniature Wargames* (Dec.), 14–17.

Halsall, Guy (1985a) 'A Conflict of Banners–: The Battle of Brunanburh, 937 AD', *Miniature Wargames* (Aug.), 11–13; (Sept.), 36–41.

Halsall, Guy (1985b) 'The Battle of Ellendun, AD 825', *Miniature Wargames* (Feb.), 38–42.

Halsall, Guy (1986) 'Stern, Sudden, Thunder-Motion–: The Battle of Clontarf, 23rd April 1014', *Miniature Wargames* (Jan.), 36–40.

Halsall, Guy (2003) *Warfare and Society in the Barbarian West, 450–900.* London: Routledge Warfare and History Series.

Harding, S (2000) *Ingimund's Saga: Norwegian Wirral.* Birkenhead: Countryvise.

Harding, S (2004) 'Viking Wirral and the Battle of Brunanburh', *Battlefield*, 10(2), 22–23.

Harrison, Mark (1993) *Anglo-Saxon Thegn AD 449–1066.* Oxford: Osprey Publishing.

Hart, Cyril (1968) 'The Site of Assandun', *History Studies*, 1, 1–12.

Heath, Ian (1985) *The Vikings.* Oxford: Osprey Publishing.

Hennessy, W M, ed. and tr. (1887) *Annals of Ulster.* Dublin.

Higham, N J (1997) *The Death of Anglo-Saxon England.* Stroud: Sutton Publishing.

Higham, N J (2001) *Edward the Elder: 899–924.* London: Taylor & Francis.

Hill, David (1981) *An Atlas of Anglo-Saxon England.* Oxford: Basil Blackwell.

Hill, Paul (2004) *The Age of Athelstan: Britain's Forgotten History.* Stroud: Tempus.

Hirst, S, and Rahtz, P (1996) 'Liddington Castle and the Battle of Badon: Excavation and Research, 1976', *Archaeological Journal*, 153, 1–59, esp. pp. 8–19.

Hollister, Warren C (1962) *Anglo-Saxon Military Institutions.* Oxford: Clarendon Press.

Howlett, D R (1998) *Cambro-Latin Compositions, their Competence and Craftsmanship.* Dublin: Four Courts Press.

Irving, E B (1961) 'The Heroic Style in the Battle of Maldon', *Studies in Philology*, 58, 456–67.

Keynes, Simon, and Lapidge, Michael, eds (1983) *Alfred the Great: Asser's Life of King Alfred and Other Contemporary Sources.* Harmondsworth: Penguin Books.

Koch, J T (1997) *The Gododdin of Aneirin: Text and Context from Dark Age North Britain.* Cardiff: University of Wales Press.

Laborde, E D (1925) 'The Site of the Battle of Maldon', *English Historical Review*, 40, 161–73.

Lavelle, Ryan (2003) *Fortifications in Wessex c.800–1066.* Oxford: Osprey Publishing.

Law, Alice (1909) *Scottish Historical Review.*

McDougall, Ian (2004) 'Discretion and Deceit: A Re-Examination of a Military Stratagem in Egil's Saga', at: www.deremilitari.org/RESOURCES/ARTICLES

Magnusson, Magnus, and Palsson, Hermann, eds (1966) *King Harald's Saga.* London: Penguin Books.

Marren, Peter (1990) *Grampian Battlefields: The Historic Battles of North-East Scotland from AD 84 to 1745.* Edinburgh: Mercat Press.

Marren, Peter (2004) *1066: The Battles of York, Stamford Bridge and Hastings.* Barnsley: Pen & Sword.

Maund, Kari (2000) *The Welsh Kings: The Medieval Rulers of Wales.* Stroud: Tempus.

Morris, John, ed. (1980) *Nennius: British History and the Welsh Annals.* London and Chichester: Phillimore.

Morris, John (1993) *The Age of Arthur: A History of the British Isles from 350 to 650.* London: Phoenix Press.

Muter, John E (1999) 'Battles on British Soil, 55 BC–1797', at: www.geocities.com/

Myres, J N L (1986) *The English Settlements*. Oxford History of England. Oxford: Clarendon Press.

Neilson, G (1909) *Scottish Historical Review*.

Nicolle, David (1984) *Arthur and the Anglo-Saxon Wars*. Oxford: Osprey Publishing.

Oman, Sir Charles (1885) *The Art of War in the Middle Ages: AD 378–1515*. London.

Palsson, H, and Edwards, P, trs. (1986) *Knytlinga Saga: The History of the Kings of Denmark*. Odense: Odense University Press.

Petty, George R and Susan (1976) 'Geology and the Battle of Maldon', *Speculum*, 51, 435–46.

Pollington, Stephen (1996) *The English Warrior from Earliest Times to 1066*. Hockwold-cum-Wilton, Norfolk: Anglo-Saxon Books.

Prestwich, J O (1968) 'King Aethelhere and the Battle of Winwaed', *English Historical Review*, 83, 89–94.

Rayner, Michael (2001) 'Wales: A Register?', *Battlefield*, 6(3), 2–5.

Rayner, Michael (2002) 'The Battle of Maldon, AD 991', *Battlefield*, 8(2), 2–7.

Rayner, Michael (2004) *English Battlefields: 500 Battlefields that Shaped English History*. Stroud: Tempus.

Rodwell, Warwick (1993) 'The Battle of Assandun and its Memorial Church: A Reappraisal', in J Cooper (ed.), *The Battle of Maldon: Fact and Fiction* (London: Hambledon Press), 127–58.

Rumble, A, ed. (1994) *The Reign of Canute, King of England, Denmark and Norway*. Leicester: Leicester University Press.

Scragg, Donald, ed. (1991) *The Battle of Maldon, AD 991*. Oxford: Oxford University Press.

Scudder, B, and Oskarsdottir, S, eds (2004) *Egil's Saga*, tr. Bernard Scudder, ed. and with an introduction and notes by Svanhildur Oskardottir. London: Penguin Books.

Shirley-Price, Leo, ed. and tr. (1968) Bede, *History of the English Church and People*. London: Penguin.

Short, Steve, ed. (1994) *The Gododdin*. Felinfach: Llanerch Publishers.

Siddorn, J Kim (2003) *Viking Weapons and Warfare*. Stroud: Tempus.

Smith, A H (1937) 'The Site of the Battle of Brunanburh', *London Medieval Studies*, 1, 56–9.

Smurthwaite, David (1984) *The Ordnance Survey Complete Guide to the Battlefields of Britain*. Exeter: Webb & Bower.

Smyth, Alfred P. (1977) *Scandinavian Kings in the British Isles 850–880*. Oxford; Oxford University Press.

Smyth, Alfred P. (1979) *Scandinavian York and Dublin: The History and Archaeology of Two Related Viking Kingdoms*. Dublin: publ?.

Smyth, Alfred P (1984) *Warlords and Holy Men: Scotland AD 80–1000*. The New History of Scotland. London: Edward Arnold.

Smyth, Alfred P (1995) *King Alfred the Great*. Oxford: Oxford University Press.

Spicer, Tony (2001) 'The Battle of Ellandun and Lydiard Tregoze', *Battlefield*, 7(1), 29–32.

Stafford, P (1989) *Unification and Conquest: A Political and Social History of England in the Tenth and Eleventh Centuries*. London: Edward Arnold.

Stenton, Frank (1971) *Anglo-Saxon England*, 3rd edn. Oxford History of England. Oxford: Oxford University Press.

Strickland, Matthew, ed. (1992) *Anglo-Norman Warfare*. Woodbridge: Boydell Press.

Strickland, Matthew (2001) 'Killing or Clemency? Ransom, Chivalry and Changing Attitudes to Defeated Opponents in Britain and Northern France, 7–12th Centuries', at: www.deremilitari.org/RESOURCES/ARTICLES

Swete, H B (1893) 'On the Identification of Assandune with Ashdon', *Transactions Essex Archaeological Society*, 4, 5–10.

Underwood, Richard (1999) *Anglo-Saxon Weapons and Warfare*. Stroud: Tempus.

Wainwright, F T (1948) 'Nechtanesmere', *Antiquity*, 86, 82–97.

Walker, Ian W (2000) *Mercia and the Making of England*. Stroud: Sutton Publishing.

Walker, J W (1948) 'The Battle of Winwaed and the Sutton Hoo Ship-Burial', *Yorkshire Archaeological Journal*, 37.

Webb, J F (1965) *Lives of the Saints: The Voyage of St Brendon, Bede: The Life of St Cuthbert, Eddius: The Life of St Wilfred*. London: Penguin Books.

Whitelock, Dorothy (1954) *The Beginnings of English Society*, 2nd edn. London: Penguin Books.

Whitelock, Dorothy (1969) 'Fact and Fiction in the Legend of St Edmund', *Proc. Suffolk Institute of Archaeology*, 31, 217–33.

Whitelock, Dorothy (1977) *The Importance of the Battle of Edington, AD 878*. Printed lecture at the annual meeting of the Friends of Edington Priory Church, 7 August. Printed by Holloway Brothers, Westbury.

Whitelock, Dorothy, ed. (1979) *English Historical Documents, 500–1042*, 2nd edn. London: Eyre & Spottiswood.

Wilson, P (2002) *Cataractonium: Roman Catterick and its Hinterland 1958–1997*. York: Council for British Archaeology, Research Reports, 128, 129.

Wood, M. (1981a) 'Brunanburh Revisited', *Saga-Book of the Viking Society*, 20, 212–13.

Wood, Michael (1981b) *In Search of the Dark Ages*. London: British Broadcasting Corporation.

Wood, Michael (1999a) 'King Arthur: Lost Again?', in *In Search of England: Journeys into the English Past* (Harmondsworth: Penguin), 23–42.

Wood, Michael (1999b) 'Tinsley Wood', in *In Search of England: Journeys into the English Past* (Harmondsworth: Penguin), 203–21.

Woolf, Alex (1998) 'Pictish Matriliny Reconsidered', *Innes Review*, 49, 147–67.

Ziegler, Michelle (2001) 'Oswald and the Irish', *The Heroic Age*, 4; at: www.mun.ca/mst/heroicage/issues

Index